THEATER
IN THE
AMERICAS

A Series from
Southern
Illinois
University
Press
SCOTT
MAGELSSEN
Series Editor

MEMORY, TRANSITIONAL JUSTICE, AND THEATRE

in Postdictatorship Argentina

NOE MONTEZ

Southern Illinois University Press

CARBONDALE

Southern Illinois University Press
www.siupress.com

Cover illustration: publicity photo for Lola Arias's *Mi vida después* (cropped). PHOTO BY LORENA FERNÁNDEZ. COURTESY OF LOLA ARIAS.

Library of Congress Cataloging-in-Publication Data
Names: Montez, Noe Wesley, author.
Title: Memory, transitional justice, and theatre in postdictatorship
Argentina / Noe Montez.
Description: Carbondale : Southern Illinois University Press, 2017. | Series:
Theater in the Americas | Includes bibliographical references and index.
Identifiers: LCCN 2017015367 | ISBN 9780809336296 (paperback) |
ISBN 9780809336302 (e-book)
Subjects: LCSH: Theater—Argentina—History—20th century. | Theater—
Argentina—History—21st century. | Argentine drama—20th century—
History and criticism. | Argentine drama—21st century—History and
criticism. | Theater and society—Argentina—History—20th century. |
Theater and society—Argentina—History—21st century. | BISAC:
PERFORMING ARTS / Theater / History & Criticism. | PERFORMING ARTS /
Theater / Direction & Production.
Classification: LCC PN2451 .M59 2017 | DDC 792.0982/09049—dc21
LC record available at https://lccn.loc.gov/2017015367

To Mom and Dad. Thank you.

Contents

Illustrations

Acknowledgments

WHEN I BEGAN THIS project as a graduate student nearly a decade ago, I did not realize the extent of the ways the book would develop and how many people would play a significant role in shaping it. Scott Magelssen and Kristine Priddy of Southern Illinois University Press helped this manuscript take final shape and shepherded the book through production. I am grateful to them, copy editor Joyce Bond, indexer Andrew Ascherl, the entire Southern Illinois University team, and my anonymous readers for their diligence, generous criticism, and thoughtful strategies for strengthening my analysis and argumentation.

Much of this book was developed at Tufts University, where I received a subvention from the College of Arts and Science. Additional institutional support came from the Center for Humanities at Tufts and the Faculty Research Awards Committee, which funded research visits, conference attendance, travel to Buenos Aires, and equipment to conduct and record interviews with the artists I encountered. Colleagues in my home department of Drama and Dance, as well as a robust community of scholars in the American Studies, Latino Studies, and Latin American Studies programs, provided helpful and incisive commentary. Natalya Baldyga, Barbara Wallace Grossman, Kareem Khubchandani, Heather Nathans, Monica White Ndounou, and Laurence Senelick welcomed me into the department warmly and provided mentorship and guidance so that I could write this book without being overburdened by other distractions of faculty life. Each has read or listened to me talk about portions of the book, enriching it with their advice and intellect.

My graduate students also played a key role in the book's development, and I am particularly grateful to the students enrolled in my Latin

American Politics and Performance seminars in 2012 and 2016, where students read, challenged, and honed portions of the text. Many other colleagues at Tufts have also been generous with their knowledge and counsel. I am grateful in particular to Nina Gerassi-Navarro, David Guss, Eulogio Guzmán, Deb Pacini Hernandez, Lisa Lowe, Helen Marrow, Stephen Pennington, Cristina Sharpe, Peter Winn, Adriana Zavala, and my cohort at the Center for Humanities at Tufts where I was a faculty fellow in 2015–16.

Before working at Tufts, I was warmly mentored as a student at Indiana University and Grinnell College. I received critical dissertation input from Rakesh H. Solomon, Ronald Wainscott, Catherine Larson, and John Holmes McDowell. Additionally, I'm grateful to Peter Guardino, Daniel James, and Rachel James for introducing me to the coursework that ultimately shaped this project. I also thank Amy Cook and Roger Herzel for their personal support and involvement in my success. Ellen Mease, Christopher Connelly, Lesley Delmenico, and Erik Simpson all served as early inspirations who demonstrated deep compassion and taught me how to sharpen the skills that will serve me for the rest of my career.

I also recognize the support and friendship of the large community of Latin Americanists engaged in theatre and performance studies. Although I wish I could acknowledge each individual's specific instance of mentorship and guidance, I would like all of you to know how much I appreciated the cups of coffee, theatre outings, and academic counsel, as well as the shared scripts and contact information. Jean Graham-Jones, Paola Hernández, Jimmy Noriega, Ana Elena Puga, Analola Santana, Brenda Werth, Anna White-Nockleby, Patricia Ybarra, and Katie Zien, I appreciate your openness and generosity. Moreover, several ideas in this text emerged from conference panels and interactions at annual meetings for the American Society for Theatre Research, the Association for Theatre in Higher Education, and the Mid-America Theatre Conference. I thank Leo Cabranes-Grant, Sara Freeman, Brian Herrera, Patricia Herrera, Jorge Huerta, Andrew Kirchner, Tiffany Ana Lopez, Leticia Robles, Jon Rossini, and Rob Shimko for perceptive observations and thoughtful questions over the years.

This project would not exist without the assistance of so many benevolent Buenos Aires–based actors, designers, directors, and playwrights who met with me over café and medialunas, and subsequently responded to my e-mails, phone calls, and Skype conversations with forthrightness and insight into their rehearsal and production processes. Thank you to

Patricio Abadi, Ana Alvarado, Lola Arias, Marcelo Bertuccio, Maruja Bustamante, Luis Cano, Julio Cardoso, Fabián Díaz, Javier Daulte, Matías Feldman, Lisandro Fiks, Carlos Furman, Héctor Levy-Daniel, Federico León, Marcelo Mangone, Paula Daiana Marrón, Mariana Mazover, Alejandra Pía Nicolosi, Mariano Pensotti, Mariana Eva Perez, Lucila Piffer, Damiana Poggi, Cecilia Propato, Diego Quiroz, Christophe Raynaud de Lage, Fernando Rubio, Juan José Santillán, Magdalena Viggiani, Emilio García Wehbi, and Patricia Zangaro. I am also grateful to the librarians and staff at the Archivo General de la Nación, Biblioteca Nacionál, Archivo de las Abuelas de la Plaza de Mayo, and especially the Centro Documentación de Teatro y Danza at the Teatro San Martín for providing access to their archives.

On a personal note, David Ogura, Tom Oldham, Tom Robson, Gabriel Rosenberg, Geoff Swenson, and Lauren Wright offered kind gestures and friendship that kept me energized and supported during long stretches of writing. My parents, Noe and Irene Montez, created a warm and loving space that always facilitated learning. My grandparents spent long hours watching over my siblings and me and doing the yeoman's work of teaching us how to read and write before we reached kindergarten. My brothers, Angel and Chris, created a space of imagination and argumentation. Finally, I thank Alison LaRosa Montez, who read large portions of the book, asked insightful and sometimes frustrating questions, and challenged me to write with greater clarity. She has shared in so much of the joy that I have experienced in creating this project, and she continues to expand my world to see what is possible in the present and what I might envision in the future.

Memory, Transitional Justice, and Theatre
in Postdictatorship Argentina

Introduction:
Shaping Memory and Performance in Postdictatorship Argentina

THEATRE AND THE MODERN Argentine national identity have always been intertwined. Presently, Buenos Aires stands as an underappreciated hotbed of theatrical activity. Several hundred productions are staged on any given night across dozens of theatres, bars, and other public and private spaces during a typical week in the Argentine capital.[1] Moreover, the city's production models facilitate one-act plays to encourage active theatregoers to traverse the renowned Avenida Corrientes in addition to the Palermo, Boedo, and San Telmo neighborhoods to see multiple productions on any given weekend. The sheer scope of the city's theatrical output is all the more impressive, as theatre historian Jean Graham-Jones notes, given the elimination of virtually all corporate funding as well as significant reductions in state support of the theatre following Argentina's 2001 economic collapse.[2] Theatre artists have often commented on contested sociopolitical issues in Argentina and challenged dominant political narratives, but working alongside human rights groups, political organizations, and entities promoting specific policies is fraught with peril.

In 2000, director Daniel Fanego, playwright Patricia Zangaro, and actress Valentina Bassi received an invitation to collaborate with the Grandmothers of the Plaza de Mayo, a human rights organization, in developing a short play that would reach an audience of university-age students. The Grandmothers provided Fanego and his collaborators with a wealth of dramaturgical material to achieve two goals. First, the Grandmothers sought to call attention to the Argentine dictatorship's practice during the Process of National Reorganization (1976–83) of kidnapping newborn children of political opponents who were "disappeared" (*desaparecidos*) and giving the infants to political supporters. Second, they wanted to raise awareness

1

among an audience in their early twenties of the importance of knowing one's biological lineage and heredity as part of the ongoing process of postdictatorship transitional justice. In working toward these ambitions, the Grandmothers of the Plaza de Mayo hoped that the production would serve the organization's primary objective—finding the children of the disappeared so that they could be reunited with their biological families. To monitor the play's development, members of the organization regularly attended rehearsals and invited similarly aligned groups to sit in as well.

Although both Zangaro and Fanego insist that their rehearsals were open to all interested parties and that such a public process did not alter their creative ambitions, ten years after the play, *A propósito de la duda*, opened, the director recalled in an interview with the Buenos Aires newspaper *Tiempo Argentino* an instance when members of the human rights organization H.I.J.O.S. (Sons and Daughters for Identity and Justice against Forgetting and Silence) attended rehearsals. At one point during scene work, the director referred to the protagonist's adoptive father and mother as the boy's parents. Almost immediately, a human rights activist sitting in the rehearsal space began to shout at the director, arguing that the characters should not be thought of as parental on any level and should be referred to only as appropriators.[3] While Fanego communicated the anecdote as an instance in which he had to learn the proper vocabulary of the Grandmothers and their supporters to stage the play effectively, it also reinforces how the Grandmothers used their support of the production as a way of ensuring that the play delivered the organization's preferred message precisely.

Memory, Transitional Justice, and Theatre in Postdictatorship Argentina sets out to explore memory narratives and their effects on the nation's postdictatorship transitional justice policies by considering how Buenos Aires's popular and highly attended theatres have constructed particular modes of political engagement and activism. In the decades since Argentina's Process of National Reorganization ended, countless performances have renewed public awareness of the dictatorship's violence and advocated for approaches memorializing Argentina's estimated thirty thousand *desaparecidos*.

To achieve these goals, I provide a detailed overview of Argentine history and transitional justice policies in the thirty-four years following the dictatorship and the Process of National Reorganization (hereafter known as the Process), then address the evolution of national memory narratives, as well as their theoretical and practical limitations and the difficulties of creating competing discourses. Finally, I discuss the ways this project draws on, challenges, and expands current scholarship on Buenos Aires's contemporary theatre artists and memory studies and how both disciplines inform knowledge on memory narratives and transitional justice policy. *A propósito de la duda* proved to be an astounding success, launching the *Teatroxlaidentidad* festival, which is addressed at greater length in this book's second chapter, and Daniel Fanego's rehearsal experience illustrates how political advocacy shaped the theatre in Argentina's postdictatorship and vice versa.

Theatre wields the power to communicate meaning. Director Eugenio Barba notes that dramatic performance endows performers with "the possibility of changing ourselves and thereby of changing society."[4] During the Process and the decades that followed, performance artists and theatre makers have used national and international stages to present material that has contested the transitional justice policies of presidential administrations and empowered human rights activists to advance memory narratives that lead to a more meaningful commemoration and remembrance of the nation's thirty thousand disappeared. Amid the authoritarianism of Argentina's dictatorship, several politically charged performances questioned the government's intrusion into public life. However, theatre scholars and Argentine historians place most focus on the *Teatro Abierto*, in which theatre artists, responding to censorship and the perceived erasure of a national theatre curriculum, staged a two-month festival. During this event, more than two hundred playwrights, actors, directors, and designers produced a cycle of one-act plays that were championed by human rights activists and seen as a challenge to official and unofficial forms of dictatorial suppression. This theatrical movement has been written about extensively and is among the most examined events in twentieth-century Argentine performance.[5]

The theatre again arose as a form of resistance to President Carlos Menem and his transitional justice practices in the early 1990s. Menem reinvigorated the debate over memory politics by overturning prison sentences for dictatorship leaders Jorge Rafael Videla, Emilio Massera, and Leopoldo Galtieri, as well as numerous other soldiers, political officials, and police officers awaiting trial for crimes connected to political violence. Theatre artists countered these measures by staging and producing plays that criticized governmental efforts to close the book on Argentina's Process. Many young theatre artists whose names now populate Buenos Aires's major commercial theatres devoted their time and energies to critiquing the national state of affairs. These playwrights and directors, many of whom are discussed in chapter 1, appropriated postmodernist techniques to create intertextual and self-referential theatre about the process of producing memory. These texts and performances implicated spectators from Buenos Aires, Argentina, and around the globe in passively accepting the Menem administration's justification for impunity policies and called attention to public inaction during the worst years of Argentina's state-enacted violence.

In both of these cases, the theatre creates what oral historian Tina Campt has coined "memory narratives"—selective reconstructions of history in which individuals configure their memories to strategically produce a narrative of the past.[6] Rather than making meaning only of one's personal biography, however, the theatre expands on these notions of memory narratives by producing an interpretation of history intended for mass cultural consumption. International relations scholars Brandon Hamber and Richard A. Wilson note that the past can remain "a site of struggle" so long as competing dialogues remain within the public consciousness.[7] Moreover, performative memory narratives such as those produced by the theatre can work to yield changes in transitional justice policies by galvanizing human rights supporters and other activists to oppose state-sponsored discourses for remembering the past.

Conversely, in moments when social actors and the state are aligned in their strategies and goals for remembering and commemorating historical events, it is possible to produce memory narratives that grant legitimacy to transitional justice policies. Within the past decade, theatre artists have created plays and performances for international and national audiences that acknowledge the significant strides that Néstor and Cristina Kirchner's presidential administrations have made in redressing the ramifications of dictatorship. Their presidencies have been marked by renewed legal pursuits of those accused with committing violence on behalf of the state, symbolic gestures of commemoration, and initiation of conversations designed to encourage Argentines to think about creating their own personal archives so as to prevent disappearances such as those that occurred during the Process. Additionally, the presidential duo has devised strategies for publicly honoring the soldiers who participated in the Malvinas (Falkland) Islands War, separating their valor from the war's connection to the dictatorship. Since these actions, theatre artists have produced and staged plays that reinscribe governmental action. The Argentine theatre has produced a number of works that call attention to the need to self-archive and to commemorate, ranging from documentary performances to realistic dramas, many of which are covered in chapter 3.

The Ebbs and Flows of Transitional Justice and Memory Narratives

Societies across the globe confront the political, legal, and ethical predicaments and impasses associated with dictatorial violence and human rights violations following the end of government-enacted trauma. Often this challenge is an emerging democracy's first major test as precariously formed governments must balance demands for justice with constraints that vary given the circumstances of an authoritarian regime's departure. This practice of responding to human rights violations and state-sanctioned violence through governmental action is known as transitional justice. As international relations scholar Francesca Lessa describes it, transitional justice is a multifaceted practice enacted through a combination of legislative action, judicial measures, and cultural production responding to outrage and calls for accountability after a period of repressive violence or other restraints on human rights.[8]

There is no consensus on the best practices for enacting transitional justice, and approaches that have found great success in one country may fail in another. If there is an agreement to be reached, say legal scholars Laurel Fletcher and Harvey Weinstein, it is that sophisticated and pliable strategies fulfilling the needs and obligations of numerous constituencies are essential for a nation to find success in redressing past atrocities.[9] These approaches can include trials, amnesties, or reparations. Because contemporary societies are complex and multilayered, there is an increased awareness that strategies must be "contextually and culturally appropriate and give heed to local heritage and cultural traditions."[10] In Argentina's postdictatorship, several government-enacted transitional justice mechanisms have been employed and are worth discussing while also noting cultural producers' work to create memory narratives that challenge or reinforce these political maneuvers.

Argentina's dictatorship came to an end in a rapid disintegration following defeat in the Malvinas War with Great Britain. The reverberation of failure brought attention to the nation's economic woes, and more important, journalist Marina Walker notes, the citizenry blamed its military leaders for this moment of public embarrassment.[11] When military restructurings occurred in the aftermath of Argentina's surrender to the British, the armed forces began to pave the way for a transition to a democratically elected government, albeit one that it hoped would prevent future inquiry into the military's behavior. However, the dictatorship's diminished power led to increased social activism from the Mothers of the Plaza de Mayo (a human rights group made up of mothers whose children disappeared during the Process), trade unions, and other political organizations, mobilizing the public in such a way that the dictatorship could not assure its own impunity prior to the 1983 presidential election. Instead, presidential candidate Raul Alfonsín, who had criticized the military throughout the Process, ran for office on a platform of human rights activism and handed Argentina's long-dominant Peronist party its first defeat in a democratic election.

Alfonsín swept into Argentina's presidency as a twelve-point victor. On being sworn in on December 10, 1983, the newly elected leader developed a transitional justice strategy reliant on assuring the public of a commitment to justice through circumventing military tribunals. The president relied on the national judiciary and established independent commissions to examine the extent of state-enacted violence. In one of his first acts, Alfonsín decreed that the nine leaders of the military dictatorship—including coup orchestrators Jorge Videla and Emilio Massera, as well as former dictatorial leaders Roberto Viola and Leopoldo Galtieri—would stand trial for homicide, unlawful deprivation of freedom, and torture. To this day, these proceedings are the only example of large-scale judicial action staged by a democratic government against a dictatorial government of the same country in South America's history. The trial, which began in 1985 after significant delay, saw the imprisonment of several military leaders who had governed Argentina during the Process and the courts-martial of other affiliated officers.

Additionally, Alfonsín established the National Commission on the Disappearance of Persons (CONADEP), charged with investigating military crimes enacted during the previous regime, offering justice to thousands of Argentines who had been tortured and disappeared, in addition to countless others who felt physical, mental, and emotional trauma following this horrific period. CONADEP was given six months to gather information about the extent of the Process's cruelty and release a report on its findings. After preparing files for 7,380 cases comprising thousands of testimonies from relatives of the disappeared, people released from detention centers, and members of the military who had taken part in criminal acts, CONADEP concluded that more than three hundred secret detention centers had existed in Argentina under military administration.[12] Additionally, the report provided evidence that uncovered mass burial sites where the dictatorship disposed of the remains of the disappeared. The commission presented its findings publicly in a book-length publication titled *Nunca Más*, a bestseller that has been in print since its first production. While the report is historically important as the first major step in Argentina's efforts at transitional justice, public affairs scholar Priscilla Hayner argues that CONADEP's work was limited by its focus solely on the dictatorial past, its position as a temporary body with a fixed end date, and its connections to the state.[13]

The quick and efficient manner by which Alfonsín ordered a truth commission to investigate the full extent of military wrongdoings, and initiated prosecutions based on those findings, instilled hope in human rights activists that all perpetrators of political violence would face punishment for their crimes. However, political tensions between Alfonsín's fledgling democracy and the prodictatorship military meant that the president needed to speedily resolve the post-Process transitional justice phase. The trial of dictatorial leaders created significant military and political unrest among those who believed that state-enacted violence was necessary as a response to the perceived threat of leftist guerrillas. In April 1985, just eighteen months into his presidency, Alfonsín appeared on national television to denounce efforts to stage a coup born out of protest of the president's transitional justice policies.

Moreover, continued threats of subversion forced Argentina's leader to make a series of concessions to the military to preserve democracy. On December 24, 1986, the Argentine parliament passed the Full Stop Law, which set a sixty-day limit for bringing accusations against the military. Facing continued pressure from the armed forces, the president signed the Due Obedience Law, exempting all military subordinates who had followed the orders of their superior officers from charges of murder, theft, assault, and other illegal deprivation of liberties. Alfonsín's passage of these two laws effectively ended the initial prosecutory phase of Argentina's transitional justice measures. Alfonsín shifted postdictatorship transitional justice policies away from a position of justice and punishment and toward a state of amnesty and forgetting.

Even with these judicial constraints, government and military tensions remained. One instance of martial resistance occurred in April 1987 following a summons that requested Army Major Ernesto Barreiro to appear in court over accusations of torture. Lieutenant Colonel Aldo Rico, leader of Argentina's Special Forces, the *Carapintadas* (Painted Faces), took over the Campo de Mayo Infantry School outside Buenos Aires as a demonstration of solidarity with Barreiro. Although the rebellion was quashed, Rico attempted another uprising in January 1988, and a third disturbance was staged in December of that year when Colonel Mohamed Alí Seineldín took control of a military base in the hope of securing a pardon for the dictatorship's leaders. Conversely, the Mothers of the Plaza de Mayo continued to demonstrate near the presidential palace to demand further accountability regarding the whereabouts of their disappeared children, and Inés Gonzáles-Bombal details extensive media efforts to expose to the Argentine public the military's violence and the dictatorship's abuse of power through reports releasing details about detention centers and mass grave discoveries.[14]

The Buenos Aires theatre also played a role in questioning the nation's recent turn toward impunity policies after the state had promised to find and sentence the perpetrators of torture. South American literature scholar Brenda Werth reads Laura Yusem's 1986 production of Griselda Gambaro's play *Antígona Furiosa*, which reimagines the Antigone myth as a commentary on justice, law, and testimony in postdictatorship Argentina, as one of many examples of an artistic production whose critical success influenced transitional justice discourses.[15] Alfonsín faced significant opposition from advocates on his political left and right promoting memory narratives designed to challenge the president's transitional justice policies. Ultimately, the government's equivocation failed to reconcile the differences between military and civil society, and that in combination with a failing economy, public unrest, and diminished relationships with trade unions led Alfonsín to resign from office six months before the end of his second term.

This book explores the relationship between memory narratives and transitional justice practices in the years since Alfonsín's resignation and how the theatre has continued to reflect shifts in attitudes toward Argentina's postdictatorship policies and actions. Although the opening anecdote notes a specific instance in which a theatrical production arose with funding and support from a specific human rights organization, in most instances, artists are functioning as independent agents seeking to participate in the public discourse surrounding Argentina's response to the dictatorship and the ongoing efforts of Presidents Carlos Menem, Néstor Kirchner, Cristina Fernández de Kirchner, and Mauricio Macri to enact transitional justice measures.

The book also considers the theatre's recent preoccupation with the soldiers who fought in the Malvinas War. These combatants, who served

Argentina during one of the most publicly celebrated wars in the nation's history and then later returned home as national pariahs, live in a liminal state at the fringes of postdictatorship transitional justice, where their memories and legacies have been used as a justification for everything from acquiescing to military pressures under the Alfonsín administration to encouraging Argentine citizens to link their memories of courageous soldiers to the memory of heroic *desaparecidos*. The latter was proposed in 2012 when Cristina Fernández de Kirchner declared that the Argentine government has a moral and patriotic obligation to remember the Malvinas soldiers while simultaneously trying to separate their legacies from the dictatorship that initiated war.[16] If at times the text reads as though the theatre responds to government-enacted memory narratives rather than advancing its own agenda, it is only because of a concerted effort on my part to provide historical contextualization to a readership that I presume may be unfamiliar with recent Argentine history and the nation's current political landscape.

Memory and the Shaping of Narratives

Argentina's evolving memory narratives and their intertwining with national transitional justice policies make the country ripe to join post-Shoah Europe, postapartheid South Africa, post-Pinochet Chile, and numerous other nations that have become case studies for the "memory boom" in the humanities.[17] Memory studies have grown significantly as a field of academic inquiry, particularly for researchers engaged in addressing the collective experiences of those traumatized by state violence throughout the world.[18] Scholarly reflection has surfaced to investigate events that trigger memory, practices for disseminating memory narratives among a nation's citizenry, and transgenerational diffusions of memory. In theatre and performance studies, several historians and theorists have explored the intersections of trauma, memory, transitional justice, and performance drawing from case studies across the globe. Rebecca Rovit's *The Jewish Kulturbund Theatre Company in Nazi Berlin*, Vivian Patraka's *Spectacular Suffering*, and Freddie Rokem's *Performing History* explore the ways the Holocaust has been represented and the significance of those representations based on varied temporal and geographic contexts. All three of these monographs explore plays and performances staged across numerous countries and how performance constructs collective identity. Megan Lewis's *Performing Whitely in the Postcolony* and Catherine Cole's *Performing South Africa's*

Truth Commission explore South African performances of reconciliation on a global stage, focusing on the years following apartheid.

Similarly, numerous texts exploring collective memory in South America were published in the early twenty-first century.[19] In theatre and performance studies, Francine A'Ness's "Resisting Amnesia" and Katherine Nigh's "Performing Trauma" both look to Peruvian productions that create spaces for audiences to collectively work through trauma. Catherine Boyle writes about narratives of transition following the Pinochet regime in her essay "Text, Time, Process and History in Contemporary Chilean Theatre." In all these writings, a clear definition of memory is elusive, but a growing consensus emerges suggesting that memory draws on societal and cultural ways of knowing the past while also being connected to the present and filtered through an individual's experiences. Consequently, memory's meaning can always be contested and reconstructed in what Spanish literature scholar Michael Lazzara calls the "relation to present circumstances and future expectations."[20]

Social groups and institutions manipulate and manufacture memory. Following Maurice Halbwachs's pioneering writings on collective memory, the academic community has also come to understand the psychological process as something that is not just individually experienced but also collectively felt.[21] This does not mean that collective memory is shared by society as a whole, but rather that personal remembrances are given meaning through affiliation with groups or contexts that assign significance to the past based on current circumstances and aspirations. These collective memories are then disseminated through "vehicles for memory, such as books, monuments, museums, films, and history books."[22] These convergences of lived experiences and mediatized discourse are curated, constructed, and constantly changing in response to current considerations of past events. This designation also reaffirms that not all past experiences automatically become memories. Argentine sociologist Elizabeth Jelin writes that memories emerge because individuals engage with them and endow them with contexts that intensify meaning.[23] Memory is choosing what, among a multitude of possibilities, is kept in mind, privileging some things and obscuring others. It is selective and subjective.

In postdictatorship Argentina, the amnesties and pardons enacted by the Alfonsín and Menem administrations indicate that the government constructed a transitional justice strategy for resolving the Process's horrors that fundamentally diminished survivors' lived experiences and personal recollections. Where human rights activists and postdictatorship survivors viewed the traumas of the dictatorship as a still extant memory that must be redressed, political realities led the first two postdictatorship administrations to create a memory narrative of closure and forgetting. Resistant counternarratives surfaced to make meaning of past experiences, creating ideological interpretations of the dictatorship that varied in legitimacy and appeal. These challenges of transitional justice practices also emerged because of the concerted efforts of invested groups or institutions, including Process survivors, human rights organizations, Argentina's military, and cultural producers such as film, television, and the theatre, that generated meaning through representations of the past. Jelin refers to these entities as "memory entrepreneurs," moral figures who organize efforts on behalf of a cause.[24] These competing entities have sustained varied narratives about the dictatorship to advance political goals and mobilize like-minded activists on their behalf.

In the years since the dictatorship's conclusion, national memory narratives have fluctuated among demands for justice and information about the disappeared, reconciliatory equivocations that attempt to frame the military dictatorship as unwilling respondents to subversive guerrilla organizations, and calls to forget the past and embrace a new direction for the nation. As Argentina transitions into the postdictatorship generation, transitional justice policies under the Kirchner administrations appear to have unified around a discourse of redress and the restoration of practices that will rectify the pardons and impunities of the years prior. Nevertheless, social actors and political organizations continue to promote memory narratives that challenge the nation's current transitional justice policies under President Mauricio Macri's administration.

Theatrical performance can be a tool that memory entrepreneurs use to create narratives that modify and redefine an individual's understanding of historical trauma. Performance creates fictive worlds in which narratives can be reified or contested, depending on the goals of a production team. This is not to suggest that the memory narratives depicted in performances completely assimilate into a person's way of thinking. The cognitive process mediates the impact of these performances. For example, a dramatic performance portraying the dictatorship represents one possible strategy for understanding historical trauma, alongside multiple other narratives that an individual stores in his or her lived experience and historical understanding. Andreas Huyssen's *Present Pasts* suggests that memory is "called upon to provide a bulwark against obsolescence and disappearance [and] to counter our deep anxiety about the speed of change and the ever-shrinking horizons of time and space."[25] Huyssen is particularly interested in practices of cultural memory that enable spectators to slow down and reflect in order to develop new faculties for negotiating space and memory in daily life. The theatre, with its emphasis on liveness and interior reflection, can provide a model for this labor. As performances build deeper ties and connections among memory narratives, the performer and the listener become dually invested in the traumatic event.

Memory Narratives and Scholarship on Contemporary Theatre and Performance

Theatre scholars have long written about Buenos Aires's extraordinary output of theatrical production and the theatre's engagement with memory politics and human rights. Perhaps no other country in South America produces theatre that is written about as extensively as the performances staged for audiences of Buenos Aires residents, or *porteños*. In this book, I position myself as part of a community of researchers informed by and indebted to the work of Jean Graham-Jones. Her *Exorcising History: Argentine Theatre under Dictatorship* provides a historical contextualization and general overview of the ways Buenos Aires's artistic production was influenced by the militarism and authoritarianism of the Process. Like Graham-Jones's work, this book is a local study, limited to the Buenos Aires theatre at a particular moment in its history and thus separated from less focused and more broadly conceived texts on Latin American theatre and performance.

I recognize that I am writing for a predominantly English-speaking audience who cannot access the numerous Argentine plays that are often unpublished or available only in Spanish. Additionally, I am mindful that geographic distance prevents readers from seeing many of the productions that I cite as case studies. Therefore, I have primarily selected performances that either have toured internationally or are available in Buenos Aires's major theatrical video archive, the Teatro San Martín's Center for Documentation of Theatre and Dance, so that they might be accessible to my core readership of American scholars in theatre and performance studies. Unfortunately, this selection process means that the book inevitably excludes some major authors of the 1990s and early twenty-first century who continue to play a major role in the city's massive theatre scene.

Nevertheless, *Memory, Transitional Justice, and Theatre in Postdictatorship Argentina* fills an important gap in studies of Latin American performance over the past twenty years. Although research on Argentine theatre's response to the dictatorship is vast—including scholarship written by Graham-Jones, Ana Elena Puga, and Diana Taylor—much of this work tends to focus on performances staged during and immediately after the dictatorship, typically ranging from the 1970s to the mid-1980s. Additionally, these books draw on artists who had already established careers in theatre prior to the dictatorship or who lived through Argentina's Process as adults. By drawing instead on the works of playwrights who began their careers in the 1990s or later, I trace the artistic lineage of Argentine playwriting practices and explore the ways the dictatorial past continues to inform and shape the theatrical creation of artists who have come of age and built their careers in a time of transitional justice.

Within the past decade, a number of additional monographs have contributed to academic discourse on the contemporary Argentine theatre, including Paola Hernández's *El teatro de Argentina y Chile*, Phillipa Page's *Politics and Performance in Post-dictatorship Argentine Film and Theatre*, Cecilia Sosa's *Queering Acts of Mourning in the Aftermath of Argentina's Dictatorship*, and Brenda Werth's *Theatre, Performance, and Memory Politics in Argentina*. Each of these texts presents important insights into contemporary Argentine films, novels, political spectacles, and other performances, but they are largely written from the perspective of scholars in Spanish language and literature. My training as a theatre historian and background as a director and dramaturg led me to explore the initial theatrical production in addition to the play script to present the clearest possible understanding of the ways theatrical production affected the transitional justice debate through specific choices in directing, design, and performance, in addition to the text. Moreover, I am mindful of how venue communicates semiotic meaning.

This book begins with an exploration of postmodern and deconstructive resistances to memory narratives in chapter 1, "Resisting the Menem Administration's Narratives of Reconciliation and Forgetting." This chapter comprises four plays that call attention to the limits of a government's ability to enforce discourses of forgetting and impunity, while nevertheless challenging transitional justice advocates who would argue that they hold a specifically enlightened understanding of Argentina's dictatorial past. The works in this chapter are often nonlinear, ludic, multitextual, and draw from the influence of the European avant-garde to present theatrical strategies for understanding how collective memory was fiercely contested by numerous entities under Carlos Menem's presidency.

From there, the book investigates and acknowledges one of the Argentine theatre's most fruitful collaborations with human rights activists in chapter 2, "*Teatroxlaidentidad*: The Right to Memory and Identity." This chapter showcases a Buenos Aires theatre festival's partnership with the Grandmothers of the Plaza de Mayo to produce a multiyear play cycle that served the theatre by being a space where emerging artists could develop their artistic skills on behalf of an important political cause. Simultaneously, the acclaimed human rights organization employed theatre makers to create a memory narrative of remembrance informed by the language of biological identity and traditional family structures.

Chapter 3, "Reparation, Commemoration, and Memory Construction in the Postdictatorship Generation" directs its attention to theatrical productions staged under the administrations of Néstor Kirchner (2003–7) and his wife, Cristina Fernández de Kirchner (2007–15). The tandem presidencies marked a major shift in Argentina's transitional justice practices, as they not only reversed several of the policies set in place by previous national leaders but also actively encouraged Argentines to begin their own process of self-documenting and establishing personal archives. The performances in this chapter draw on personal artifacts, documentary materials, and multimedia to explore the limits of curating one's own identity and how creating specific memory narratives about the present cannot predict the ways those collections might be maintained for the greatest possible efficacy or interpreted in the future.

Chapter 4, "Performing Public Memorialization of the Malvinas War," calls attention to a series of productions staged alongside national commemorations of the Malvinas War's thirtieth anniversary. This chapter focuses on productions ranging from critiques of the government's treatment of veterans to celebratory performances designed to memorialize the soldiers using the same language and aesthetic techniques that artists use to commemorate the disappeared. The book concludes with "The Next Stages of Theatrical Production, Postdictatorship Memory, and Transitional Justice," which addresses memory politics under President Mauricio Macri, contemporary figures in Argentine theatre, and new intersections of postdictatorship political activism and performance.

Several of the playwrights discussed in this book (for example, Lola Arias, Javier Daulte, Federico León, and Patricia Zangaro) have begun to

receive scholarly attention in the past decade; other playwrights and theatre artists featured in this study (for example, Mariana Mazover, Patricio
Abadi, Damiana Poggi, and Virginia Jáuregui) are receiving attention from
non-Argentine academics for the first time. All these artists have earned
considerable critical attention, including, but not limited to, prizes from
the Argentine theatre and literary community. Several of the theatrical
pieces covered rank among the most critically acclaimed productions in
Buenos Aires over the past twenty years, but a significant number of the
plays remain unpublished and without translation.

Unless otherwise noted, all translations are my own and are among the
first in English. Additionally, I have attended or acquired access to video
recordings of the first major productions in Buenos Aires of many of these
plays, and I engage in thick description of these performances in my critical
analysis when appropriate. Ultimately, I strove for works representing a
diverse range of genres and styles, including realism, documentary performance, and object theatre, to provide a strong understanding of the
Argentine theatre's depth and breadth. The chapters are organized roughly
chronologically to facilitate a description of the theatre's development as a
space where postdictatorship memory narratives are formed. These productions illustrate and foreground shifting discourses on the dictatorship
and transitional justice policies throughout the nineties and into the start
of the twenty-first century.

Transitional justice, memory narratives, and cultural production are
inextricably linked in postdictatorship Argentina. The theatre continues to
draw millions of spectators annually, playing a major role in constructing
political conversations that authenticate or subvert transitional justice policies. Major plays and productions generate stories about momentous events
in national history, contributing to collective memory and providing contexts for traumatic events that profoundly affect spectators' lives. This book
emphasizes the dynamic relationship between the theatrical production
of memory narratives and transitional justice to study their interactions
at critical moments in Argentina's postdictatorship. The dramatic works
explored in this book represent a diversity of styles and forms, but the
works are united in their desire to address resistance, complicity, impunity,
absolution, and accountability in the aftermath of political violence and
human rights violations. Rather than address these concerns with moral
handwringing about the nation's failures and injustices, the performances
and productions comment on political changes occurring throughout the

Menem and Kirchner presidencies and the ways these administrations have referenced the dictatorship and its historical legacy to serve diverse and divisive political agendas.

Argentina strives to be acknowledged as a global and regional protagonist in legal and extralegal efforts toward accountability following its dictatorship, illustrating the notion that transitional justice and memory are what political theorist Jon Elster refers to as multigenerational processes, continuously changing and progressing in time.[26] Although the nation's efforts toward accountability and fairness have faced setbacks at times, human rights activists have created a constructive environment for the cultural production of memory narratives that advocate and educate those who wish to engage with the nation's dictatorial past. Argentina's efforts at transitional justice have acquired increased urgency at a time when the nation must grapple with the recent deaths and contested legacies of Néstor Kirchner, Jorge Videla, and Raul Alfonsín, among other key figures from the dictatorship and its aftermath. Additionally, Argentine courts continue to sentence former military officers charged with crimes committed during the Process to life sentences under house arrest or in prison, although it is questionable how much this activity will continue under Mauricio Macri's presidency.

These constantly changing developments remind interested parties in Argentina and beyond that the quest for better transitional justice policies and richer conversations about postdictatorship collective memories is far from finished. The following chapters demonstrate that theatre can provide a forum for shaping public discourse in postdictatorship Argentina. Theatre makers are using the stage to call for changes in transitional justice policies and advocate for human rights efforts in an extralegal setting. In this book, which directs a significant amount of attention to the work of a generation of playwrights and artists who have not received major attention, I hope to provide an understanding of how ongoing political engagement can lead toward a more hopeful future by exploring instances where transitional justice policies have changed as a result of transformative memory narratives brought about by performative actions, particularly the utilization of theatre. My intention is that the framework I provide in this book will be helpful to readers in understanding that neither transitional justice policies nor memory narratives remain static, but that they continually evolve, and theatrical performances can intervene in the process of creating social and political change.

1

Resisting the Menem Administration's Narratives of Reconciliation and Forgetting

MIDWAY THROUGH HIS PLAY *Los murmullos* (2002), dramatist Luis Cano rises from his seat and makes his way onto the playing space, carrying a copy of the script in hand. He stops the performance and questions how he or any author writing in Argentina's postdictatorship can adequately dramatize the struggle for memory and commemoration under political administrations that would encourage citizens to forget the past. On impulse, Cano begins to crumple the pages from his script and cram them into his mouth, before the play's antagonist interrupts him. The performer brings the author further into the performance space, then physically assaults Cano and submerges his head in a water bucket, replicating an act of torture performed in Argentina's detention camps. Although Cano and many of the other young playwrights addressed in this chapter explore the instability of truth claims and personal memory, this particular scene emphasizes the stakes of such performances. The plays function as a form of resistance to government-supported narratives of impunity in an effort to prevent authoritarian violence from returning.

After Alfonsín's passage of the Full Stop and Due Obedience Laws, politicians sympathetic to the military called on their countrymen and women to leave the horrors of the Process behind them and build a stronger, more unified Argentina. This reconciliation narrative met with resistance from human rights organizations and the nation's political left, but Alfonsín could not maintain an antagonistic relationship with his armed forces indefinitely. Additionally, public discourse shifted from postdictatorship and human rights concerns to the nation's growing economic crisis. Argentina suffered from massive hyperinflation throughout the 1980s, straining the president's relationship with trade unions whose support was necessary

17

to pursuing a meaningful domestic agenda. The combination of popular unrest, economic disarray, and continued military rebellion that threatened the Argentine democracy led the nation into a tailspin that could be alleviated only by Alfonsín resigning from the presidency six months ahead of schedule in hopes that newly elected president Carlos Menem could begin leading a national recovery.

Although human rights activists hoped for a change in the rhetoric of military appeasement from the former political captive turned Argentine president, Menem's inaugural address clearly highlighted his past in a plea for the nation to move forward with reconciliatory practices as part of the Argentine government's continued transitional justice strategy:

> From the deepest corner of my jail, during the most painful moments of my torture, and from the saddest side of my imprisonment, I asked the Lord to allow me to dream about a moment like this. I asked Him to make me open my arms to my opponents, and not to close my fists to my enemies.[1]

Within three months of his inauguration, Menem advanced amnesty measures well beyond what the previous administration had envisioned, pardoning hundreds of officers who had been tried and convicted of human rights violations, along with several hundred guerrilla activists and military figures who had attempted open rebellion against Alfonsín. The pardoned leaders were released with little fear of public reprisal. Menem stated, "I know there will be discontent, as there is in all things in life, but I am also convinced that there are millions of Argentines who will applaud these measures."[2]

In exchange, the armed forces maintained a tacitly agreed-upon code of silence about military operations conducted during the dictatorship. This pact relied on what sociologist Leigh Payne refers to as the "vital lies" of omission, which military leaders insisted on as a necessary measure to evade public scrutiny.[3] Nevertheless, Menem's pardons ignited protests, which drew tens of thousands of demonstrators to the Buenos Aires streets, and public opinion polls revealed that over 70 percent of Argentines opposed reprieve for the dictatorship's leaders.[4] Although the president's acts of clemency were met with significant resistance, he successfully created an amnesty policy that turned military and legislative attention away from debating transitional justice and toward his neoliberalist privatization strategies for solving Argentina's economic crisis.

By the end of Menem's first term, conversations about the Process, impunity, and transitional justice had largely disappeared from mass media and popular culture. Argentina's economy underwent a period of rapid growth in the early 1990s, Menem rose in popularity, and the human rights activists attempting to reinvigorate memory narratives about the dictatorship became increasingly marginalized. However, as the president began his campaign for a second term in 1994, numerous developments brought the Process back into the national conversation. Several notable anniversaries rekindled collective memory among Argentines. The tenth anniversary of *Nunca Más*'s publication led to the release of a new 1994 edition that sold hundreds of thousands of copies. The twentieth anniversary of the coup that had sparked the dictatorship in 1976 spawned new waves of conversation about commemoration and memory, including the publication of several histories and documentary films. Public support for reconsidering the past's reverberations was made particularly visible in March 1996, when 150,000 Argentines participated in public demonstrations marking the twentieth anniversary. Political parties of all stripes, unions, neighborhood associations, and theatre artists stood alongside human rights organizations in numbers that far exceeded previous commemorations.

Additionally, the formation of H.I.J.O.S. (Sons and Daughters for Identity and Justice against Forgetting and Silence) in 1995 brought an aggressive and youthful spirit of political activism to the quest for human rights and a restoration of punitive and judicially oriented transitional justice policies. The organization's most renowned method of protest—the theatrical *escraches*—publicly exposed former repressors and political sympathizers who believed that they had achieved immunity from prosecutions for actions committed in the midst of the Process. These spectacle-driven demonstrations, which typically drew hundreds of supporters and involved music, banners, puppets, placards, and dances, named the perpetrators of atrocities and revealed personal information about these individuals to the culprits' neighbors. In doing so, the *escraches* facilitated alternative memory narratives about the dictatorship that shifted public conversation from complacent acceptance of reconciliation strategies to questioning whether Menem's policies were truly moving Argentina into a state of forgiveness and forgetting.[5]

The most dramatic development was Adolfo Scilingo's televised and printed confession about his involvement in politically sanctioned death flights. In November 1994, Scilingo, a retired naval captain, grew disenchanted over perceived inequities in naval and governmental promotions.

In an act of retribution, the officer approached acclaimed political columnist Horacio Verbitsky on a Buenos Aires subway platform and informed the journalist of his work at ESMA, Argentina's notorious Naval Mechanics School, where the dictatorship enacted thousands of insidious tortures. Scilingo and Verbitsky met several times, engaging in a series of conversations that included new revelations about the dictatorship's use of violence.[6] In a recorded conversation, the former military officer described his involvement in "death flights" during the dictatorship, in which Scilingo and other military officers loaded drugged, but living political captives into airplanes and flew thirteen thousand feet over the Río de la Plata, where soldiers threw out the incapacitated bodies. Verbitsky compiled the recorded interviews in his 1995 book, *El Vuelo* (*The Flight*), and by year's end, Scilingo had appeared on numerous Argentine television shows and radio stations, becoming a media sensation—the first military official to admit to deliberate acts of violence—and a confessor of human rights violations during the dictatorship. Verbitsky's book became a best seller, redirecting the nation's attention toward the unhealed traumas of the Process and the ongoing efforts of human rights activists and transitional justice workers who sought continued prosecutions for political violence.

In December 1995, Scilingo was joined in public confession by Naval Sergeant Victor Ibanez and Police Sergeant Julio "El Turco" Simón, who publicly admitted their participation in murders, torture, kidnapping, and other atrocities in first-person accounts delivered on Argentine television and print media. Within twenty-four months, six other officers admitted culpability for disappearances.[7] Each man's motive for confession differed, but all believed themselves immune from prosecution under the Due Obedience Law and other political reprieves passed during the Alfonsín and Menem administrations, an assumption that would later prove erroneous when a Spanish court convicted Scilingo of Process-related kidnapping and sentenced him to a lengthy prison sentence.

These mediatized confessions opened new models of presenting memory narratives about the Process's atrocities by giving voice to the perpetrators of violence rather than solely relying on the testimonies of political survivors or the disappeared's families. The large number of Argentines who had ignored ongoing discussion of the dictatorship's aftermath following the return to democracy received a reminder that although presidential speeches and military pardons could create reconciliation policies, these actions could not wholly shape postdictatorship memory narratives.

Consequently, the Menem administration saw its near authoritative control over postdictatorship memory discourse diminish, and public opinion began to cede to the influence of human rights organizations, public protesters, and political activists who could engage with citizens through mass-media disseminations of popular culture. As official memory narratives destabilized, the theatre became a site where artists and spectators could explore the precariousness of state-sanctioned memory politics and consider the ways that commemorative discourses might be manipulated to resist policies of impunity and forgetting. The theatre was in a particularly fortuitous position to address the relationship between politically driven memory politics and public resistance, given the changes transpiring in Buenos Aires performances through an emerging generation of playwrights, directors, and actors.

Buenos Aires Theatre: From Inertia to Aesthetic Diversity

Jean Graham-Jones's scholarship about Buenos Aires theatre during the dictatorship notes that in the years immediately following Argentina's return to democracy, playwrights and directors struggled to find an aesthetic and thematic identity beyond psychologically based dramas of opposition to authoritarian oppression.[8] Although several important theatre makers, including Ricardo Bartís, Griselda Gambaro, Ricardo Monti, and Eduardo Pavlovsky, continued their active and productive careers as playwrights, directors, and political critics after the Process concluded, Argentine theatre scholar Osvaldo Pellettieri observes that the nation's theatre artists struggled to develop a new artistic language or approach to making performance that addressed Argentina's economic crisis, the public's state of social unease, or the ongoing debate over transitional justice policies focused on reconciliation rather than retribution. Consequently, Buenos Aires's historically vibrant theatres began to lose their audiences in the 1980s, while the nation's state-sponsored and commercial theatres became increasingly reliant on foreign productions, during what Pellettieri considers a moment of national theatrical pessimism.[9]

Although scholars and artists agree that theatre in Buenos Aires largely failed to find new dramatic modes of discourse, it would be imprudent to suggest that the city's stages lacked artistic models for political engagement in the immediate aftermath of the dictatorship. Sharon Magnarelli writes of Alberto Ure's 1984 production of Griselda Gambaro's *El Campo*, in which the nonrealistic staging of a concentration camp supported by a gigantic hand represented human interactions inherent in all political struggles and the ways in which invisible agents regulate power.[10] In 1990, playwright and director Ricardo Bartís staged a free adaptation of *Hamlet* in which the production provoked comparisons between the disingenuousness that Hamlet sees around him in Claudius to the political artificiality and theatricality of the Menem administration's rise to power. Nevertheless, Bartís describes Argentina's initial decade of postdictatorship theatre as "broken," noting that the only recourse for theatrical reinvention was to create an alternative theatre that could be produced in homes, basements, or other nontraditional spaces.[11]

As Buenos Aires's theatre became increasingly impoverished as a result of hyperinflation during the 1980s and early 1990s, a group of artists developed their craft in precisely the sorts of spaces that Bartís envisioned, creating projects that reflected their ongoing frustrations with the nation's sociopolitical and economic difficulties. This new generation of artists, occasionally referred to as *teatro joven*, or the young theatre, worked across performative boundaries, functioning as playwrights, designers, actors, directors, and composers of original music for their productions. Additionally, emerging companies of Buenos Aires theatre makers drew on various aesthetic and structural influences, including clowning, multimedia, video technology, object theatre, collage, and song, to create multidisciplinary performances. Nevertheless, while *teatro joven* artists shared many similarities in terms of production aesthetics, artists and critics alike have rejected the notion that they belong to a collective theatre movement.[12] The productions staged by these theatre makers were often characterized by late-night start times and performances in nontraditional sites such as nightclubs, abandoned warehouses, cultural centers, and other found spaces that offered more economic viability. As a result, these performances were largely attended by an audience of *porteños* in their twenties and thirties who became accustomed to seeing avant-garde performances staged in locations beyond the city's storied Corrientes Avenue theatre district.

Rejecting a unifying ethos or aesthetic, Buenos Aires's performance artists functioned as though their performance spaces were a laboratory for experimentation and exploration of theatre's role in contemporary Argentine society. Theatre scholar Jorge Dubatti recognizes the diversity of these cultural producers and the rich panorama of forms and techniques that are used, while noting that the artists considered part of the theatre's new golden age did share some commonalities.[13] A significant number of emerging playwrights experimented with narrative forms that eschewed Aristotelian structure. Scholar Laura Cerrato argues that many of the nation's emerging dramatists saw the world as a series of discursive fragments that operate on their own rather than fitting within a system or superstructure.[14] Scenically, directors and designers collaborated to create playing spaces that departed from realistic representation and instead created a sense of subjectivity.[15] These artistic choices separated the *teatro joven* playwrights from their more realism-based predecessors.

However, while Dubatti and others suggest that this experimentation makes the work difficult to classify as political theatre, the plays produced by many of these young artists should be read as commentaries on the current state of memory politics in Argentina. The *teatro joven*'s embrace of what is essentially the postmodern calls attention to what Hayden White has pointed out as the ways in which the shaping and presentation of official narratives always result in a fiction that is manipulated and shaped by various modes of "emplotment."[16] Although much of the dramatic literature produced by Argentina's emerging playwrights renounced the traditional binaries of a good protagonist in opposition to an evil antagonist, the theatre makers created texts where conflict arose out of ambiguity or a particularly fraught sociocultural environment. These dramatic shifts positioned the Argentine theatre to emerge from its postdictatorship period of crisis to foreground an environment where artists could explore their aesthetic tastes in addition to highlighting and undermining political strategies that the Menem administration used to shape and control memory narratives.

The plays included in this chapter draw from a selection of artists who emerged from the *teatro joven* of the 1990s to provide counternarratives of collective memory in order to voice their resistance to the Menem administration's official politics of forgetting. By the end of the decade, many of these artists developed a following that expanded their messaging from independent spaces to international tours and productions in Buenos Aires's city-operated Teatro San Martín. Each of the works uses nonlinear dramatic structure and nontraditional theatrical aesthetics to call attention to the artificiality of officialized narratives. However, rather than communicating these ideas solely to theatregoers of the dictatorship generation, the performances make the politics of postdictatorship visible to young Argentine spectators who may not have experienced the Process and to international audiences who might encounter these works on European and American tours.

The playwrights, directors, and theatre artists addressed in this chapter did not didactically produce agitprop dramas that subvert the Menem administration's amnesties and reconciliatory transitional justice strategies. Instead, the works voice opposition to the very nature of state-sanctioned political discourses and the political capital that must be exerted to uphold them. El Periférico de Objetos's *Máquina Hamlet* (1995), an adaptation of Heiner Müller's *Hamletmachine*, relies on spectators' familiarity with Shakespeare's *Hamlet* and the ensemble's staging of the play as object theatre to explore the discourse of cruelty and how hegemonic forces employ violence to uphold particular ways of remembering. Javier Daulte's *Martha Stutz* (1997) foregrounds the fictionalized courtroom proceedings of a true childhood disappearance juxtaposed against *Alice's Adventures in Wonderland*. As testimonies are performed and cross-examined, multiple entities with divergent agendas struggle for narrative authority and the power to impose new interpretations of past events. Marcelo Bertuccio's *Señora, esposa, niña y joven desde lejos* (1998) uncovers the evolving memory narratives and power dynamics of family members who cannot openly communicate with each other about a loved one's disappearance. Finally, Luis Cano's *Los murmullos* (2002) draws from several hundred texts and source materials to raise questions about the very nature of politics, art, and representation.

The authors present complex views of ongoing strategies for constructing memory narratives in ways that are oftentimes ambiguous and contradictory, reflecting the multiple and incongruous approaches articulated by the Argentine government and its citizens. In doing so, these plays require that individual viewers take responsibility for understanding the ways that remembering is ultimately a public and collective act. Although these explorations may seem to play into the hands of those who would deny the dictatorship or question efforts toward transitional justice, the authors believe that addressing memory's unreliability is necessary to deconstruct the memory narratives that facilitated transitional justice policies of amnesty and reconciliation under the Menem administration.

Animating Memory Narratives in El Periférico de Objetos's *Máquina Hamlet*

El Periférico de Objetos acquired international acclaim as one of Argentina's most innovative performance ensembles in the 1990s. The group originated as participants of the Teatro San Martín's puppet group, studying

Bunraku and other techniques for puppet and object theatre performance. When the group broke away from the San Martín and started its own theatre company in 1989, the ensemble began staging works in Buenos Aires's independent theatres, developing a respected reputation for imaginative productions and visually evocative stagings. This success paved the way for the group to begin touring across the globe.

El Periférico's founding members were Ana Alvarado, Emilio García Wehbi, Paula Natolí, and Daniel Veronese, with Román Lamas and Alejandro Tantanian joining and Natolí departing in later years. Individually, they have found success in the contemporary Argentine theatre, but their ensemble received particular acclamation for staging adaptations that used puppets and objects of varying shapes and sizes to foreground sociopolitical concerns in postdictatorship Argentina. Among El Periférico de Objetos's notable creations are several original works and collage pieces, including a dramatization of Alfred Jarry's *Ubu Roi*, a theatrical adaptation of E. T. A. Hoffmann's *The Sandman*, a variation of Samuel Beckett's works titled *Variaciones sobre B . . .* , and *Zooedipous*, an interpretation of the ancient Greek myth that has been read by Brenda Werth "as an evocation of the continuation of the most recent dictatorship into the present."[17] Each of these productions incorporates elements that have become hallmarks of the ensemble's aesthetic, including projections, pastiche, and dolls or puppets made from plastic or porcelain, created specifically for the ensemble's performances.

Scholars interested in transnational reception of the Argentine theatre and artists' roles in critiquing postdictatorship memory narratives can read metaphorically into El Periférico's adaptation of *Hamletmachine*. This variation of Heiner Müller's tour de force ran in Buenos Aires intermittently from 1995 to 1999 in addition to touring internationally as part of the troupe's repertoire. Although Müller's play encourages polysemous interpretations, double meanings, and questions about traditional character representation, El Periférico's history of engaging with the politics of embodiment through object theatre encourages a reading of the production within the context of Argentina's postdictatorship.

The performance can be read as drawing connections between the costs of acquiring hegemonic control of narratives and the effect of oppressing minority stakes in articulating individual traumas. Müller's play has often been read with political power dynamics in mind, as theatre critic Jonathan Kalb suggests that the play's titular character serves as a "symbol for the . . . prevarications, hesitations, and rationalizations in the face of tyranny and terror."[18] Similarly, the character of Ophelia can be read in a way that explores strategies for resistance to the authoritarian governing of gendered bodies and the usage of coded language to frame victims of political violence as illogical and responsible for the abuse inflicted on them. However, much of the present literature on El Periférico, including the text by Werth, focuses on the group's reception within Argentina. Nevertheless, in considering the troupe's place as an acclaimed Buenos Aires company touring and staging the play for Argentine, European, and American audiences, the play becomes more specifically situated as a transcultural depiction of dictatorial violence and the ways in which outsiders bore witness to the trauma that the Process inflicted on Argentines without intervening or implicating themselves.

El Periférico de Objetos originated *Máquina Hamlet* after giving thought to creating its own adaptation of *Hamlet*. With deliberation, however, the company decided that Heiner Müller's text addressed its sociopolitical interests while also allowing the troupe to push itself aesthetically. Upon deciding to stage *Hamletmachine*, the company hired German dramaturg Dieter Welke and the program director of Argentina's Goethe Institute, Gabriela Massuh, to create a new Spanish-language translation of the text and collaborate with the troupe during the first fifteen days of its multimonth rehearsal, as well as in intermittent work thereafter.

Taking inspiration from Müller's text, the ensemble wanted to create a visual language that explored hegemonic control of memory narratives and political violence. Consequently, El Periférico imbued *Máquina Hamlet* with theatrical elements that rendered the discourse of posttraumatic power and control legible in performance. For example, the play's four performers wear military boots, dark pants, and black tuxedo jackets, which evoke both military power and the less visible power of political and financial influence, although later actress and ensemble member Ana Alvarado changes into a red dress.

Most notably, the performers spend the majority of their time onstage manipulating puppets, dolls, dioramas, and other objects of varying sizes. Most of the objects resemble humans, although they are made from different materials, including plastic, porcelain, latex, and wood (fig. 1.1). They range from a just a few inches in height to nearly six feet tall. Some mannequins resemble rag dolls and remain completely limp outside of the performers' manipulations; others feature movable appendages with working joints or have wheels so that they can be rolled around the stage with greater facility.

The smaller figures largely consist of several dozen porcelain dolls with holes in their hollowed-out heads, which allow for the performers to manipulate the objects by inserting their hands into their skulls to move them around the theatre. Lola Proaño-Gomez's essay about *Máquina Hamlet* in *Gestos* suggests that she sees the objects as lifeless and stripped of power, but I would argue that the use of objects instead transfers the power of interpretation away from the performers and into the hands of spectators, who can reflect on their own positionality and potentially alter their subjectivity by assigning an inner life and intention to the figures' movements.[19]

El Periférico creates a performance that produces meaning through a subjective exchange among spectators, artists, and material objects. The production most obviously influences spectators' perceptions through the use of object theatre as the performers interact with the mannequins and dolls to create a scenario in which the actors and the objects they manipulate become two distinct types of media, encouraging their audiences to consider the relationship between the two. The puppet, as an inanimate object, possesses no agency over its words and actions and is wholly subject to manipulation by puppeteers, who exert absolute control over the figure. Nevertheless, spectators are invited to see the actor and the object as different characters. Simultaneously, an object's words and actions are not directly attributable to the person controlling the object, absolving the manipulator from responsibility for the doll's behavior.

Yet Matthew Isaac Cohen notes in "Puppetry and the Destruction of the Object" that from his perspective as an object theatre artist, puppets, dolls, and other figures are "alien others" that evoke Richard Schechner's notions of "not me" and "not not me."[20] In *Máquina Hamlet*, man and object work together as one, which challenges the spectators' sense of what constitutes a body. However, I would expand Cohen's position to suggest that within the context of a touring troupe from Argentina performing for international audiences, an attempt to make meaning of the animate and inanimate bodies onstage has political repercussions. These are explored later in the chapter.

El Periférico's manipulation of objects is always fully visible to the audience. Spectators clearly see the performers grab puppets and maneuver them at will. Nevertheless, several of the play's life-size mannequins look human enough to disorient viewers. Reviewer Amy Strahler's appraisal of the troupe notes that although the smaller dolls feature hollowed skulls and empty eyes so that actors can operate them, the figures look as though

Figure 1.1. Emilio García Wehbi, Alejandro Tantanian, and Román Lamas (*left to right*) pose with one of the life-size mannequins used in El Periférico de Objetos's *Máquina Hamlet*. COURTESY OF MAGDALENA VIGGIANI.

they are characters who just emerged from a lobotomy and are human enough to discombobulate observers.[21] Moreover, when the production uses larger figures, it becomes harder to distinguish between living actor and inanimate object, and the relationship between life and death blurs onstage. For example, in the opening beat of the performance, the production's four actors intermingle with several mannequins in a manner that makes it virtually impossible to distinguish who is living and who is not.

The use of violence in the production also challenges the audience's understanding of the relationship between living and inanimate objects. The members of El Periférico de Objetos roughly manhandle their puppets, which serve as recipients of the majority of *Máquina Hamlet*'s vicious stage violence. The *New York Times* review of the production in its first American performance at the Brooklyn Academy of Music notes that the interactions between the animate and inanimate figures create "a brutalizing sense of paranoia that horror can emerge from any location on the stage."[22] El Periférico de Objetos's presentation insists that audiences recognize that object theatre is fundamentally based on the control that actors hold over their theatrical objects. Although the reaction evoked by the ensemble is not particularly unique to object theatre, foreign audiences' responses to the performers' ruthless handling of the puppets can be seen as efforts to understand the dictatorship's brutality and the trauma inflicted on thousands of Argentines during the Process.

El Periférico de Objetos's exploration of the relationships among performer, puppet, and spectator becomes part of the production's efforts to depict the staging, shaping, and controlling of political discourse. This strategy is initially brought to bear in the play's first scene, titled "Family Album." In his original script, Müller uses the appellation to emphasize what Brian Walsh refers to as "the text's concerns with kinship and memory, and the individual's confrontation with historical fragments that are arranged together, but do not necessarily announce a coherent narrative."[23] This production endows the opening moments with similar emphasis.

The scene begins with life-size marionettes and actors alike crowded behind a long table. Then one of the actors manipulates a full-size mannequin to take a seat in a chair at the table's center, directly facing the audience. The mannequin represents the eponymous Danish prince, who tries to distance himself from his commonly known history as a voiceover states, "I was Hamlet."[24] The amplified voice then describes a first-person renunciation of Hamlet's vengeful past, in which he stopped his father's funeral march and handed pieces of the dead king's remains to the pro-cession's crowd. As in Müller's text, Hamlet proceeds to quarrel with his father's ghost—rejecting the notion of revenge—before imagining himself violently raping his mother. However, as this language is played through the theatre's speakers, two of the other performers onstage use dolls to perform aspects of Hamlet's narrative, including Claudius's poisoning of Hamlet's father and his subsequent marriage to Gertrude. As the Claudius puppet pours poison into the king of Denmark's ear, the murderer is manipulated to look out into the audience and present his chalice to them, bringing the audience into the play's violent action.[25]

The Hamlet mannequin is in a position of privilege inasmuch as he can imagine a world in which he can verbally renounce his family and willfully distance himself from his traumatic past, but he lacks the physical agency to do so. In production, the figure representing Hamlet remains seated watch-ing other puppets reenact the events described in the opening monologue. Moreover, the Hamlet object cannot consider the ways in which he bears cul-pability for the world that he seeks to overthrow. Within the context of the postdictatorship, Hamlet's desire for revolution and the ways his aspirations are undermined by his own passivity take on great resonance. For domestic and international audiences, the opening scene can be read as questioning whether leaders such as Carlos Menem, who express a national directive to forget the past, believe that their decrees truly function as progressive actions that will bring closure to the transitional justice process or whether these statements are passive acts born out of intellectual unease with more radical forms of systemic change and transitional justice. Additionally, in performance, the spectator notices that a puppeteer, whose motives for ma-nipulating the Danish prince must also be questioned, controls Hamlet. Is Hamlet's expressed desire to forget an actual desire voiced by the character, or is it simply the manipulation by a more powerful entity that is personally vested in a memory narrative of reconciliation and impunity?

In opposition to Hamlet's imagined revolution, Ophelia is presented as a character whose dialogue and physical performance facilitate identifica-tions with silenced and oppressed women throughout history. Her intro-ductory scene, "The Europe of Women," begins with a scenic transition in which numerous life-size mannequins are chained against the back wall of the playing space, evoking a connection to Argentine detention camps used during the dictatorship. When the set change concludes, Ophelia emerges from offstage, trapped inside a plexiglass box surrounded by actors in rat masks who dance around her cell. Ophelia is the only human character, played by actress Ana Alvarado, rather than a puppet. The monologue emphasizes Ophelia's gender and Hamlet's repeated misogyny toward women who assert their own sexual agency. Whereas Hamlet longs to disregard his complicity in fostering violence, but his passivity and the puppeteers' control will not allow for such forgetting, Ophelia desires to remember the violence that has been inflicted on her in hopes of inciting revolution. The monologue continues and Ophelia gathers strength as she imagines fomenting a revolution that might allow her to take revenge against those who have inflicted violence upon her:

> I smash the tools of my captivity, the chair, the table, the bed. I destroy the battlefield that was my home … I destroy the windows. With bloody hands I break the photos of the men I loved who used me on the bed, on the table, on the chair, on the ground. I set fire to the prison, I throw my clothes into the fire I wrench the clock that was my heart out of my breast. I walk into the street clothed in blood.[26]

Although the audience watches Alvarado in her plexiglass cell, they hear her monologue delivered in voiceover played via loudspeaker—the character's voice is separated from her body. Text and scenography conjure what Diana Taylor refers to as the constant oppression that women endured as part of a dictatorship whose masculine desire for domination projected a narrative onto women suggesting that feminine bodies desired submission and would willingly sacrifice of themselves for the greater good of the military and country.[27]

Nevertheless, although *Máquina Hamlet* recognizes the ways in which violence is imposed on feminine bodies, this is only one aspect of the character. As the play continues, El Periférico's production empowers Ophelia, and other women by extension, to be destabilizing forces in authoritarian regimes by asserting their physical presence in public spaces. Ophelia is not passive in captivity but instead pounds on her plexiglass entrapment and makes her efforts to escape captivity obvious to the play's spectators. Within the context of Argentina's dictatorship, Ophelia's demands for violence and uprising evoke organizations such as H.I.J.O.S., which as a matter of recourse took the lead in voicing visible resistance to the Menem administration's efforts to elide the painful memories of those for whom the Process was most traumatic by publicly shaming and marking the perpetrators of violence as enemies to the efforts of justice and accountability.

However, Ophelia's calls for revolution in this scene are also tempered by a failure to engage with the structural imbalances that allow for such sexual and gender-based inequities.

Máquina Hamlet's third scene, titled "Scherzo," relies heavily on silent object manipulation and mime in departing from the previous scenes' fragmented deconstruction of Shakespeare's characters, yet the action that El Periférico de Objetos employs continues to question the construction and control of memory narratives in a post-traumatic situation. In El Periférico's production at the Teatro San Martín, the ensemble has configured the stage to resemble a cabaret hall with several tables surrounding a dance floor. Life-size puppets are placed at each of the tables, positioned to watch a mannequin perform a *danse macabre* with one of the human performers. The dance is aggressive, violent, and physically uncomfortable to watch as the doll is sadistically and repeatedly flung around the stage. As the action transpires, a human actor watches over all the seated mannequins, in a performance that suggests that the figures cannot intervene in the dance without risk of punishment. The viciousness continues to build as one of the life-size figures seated at a cabaret table is brutishly dragged onto the dance floor and manipulated to plead for its life before one of the play's actors shoots the mannequin in the head, places the dummy on an upstage wall, and throws several darts at the lifeless figure. The action concludes, and the living actors encourage *Máquina Hamlet*'s audience seated in the theatre's house to throw darts at the upstage mannequin and applaud for the puppets that they have just witnessed being assaulted onstage.

If Hamlet's and Ophelia's monologues imagine the possibility of revolutionary action, then "Scherzo" serves as a reminder of hegemonic power's ability to silence through sheer cruelty. The scene underscores the relationship between narrative control and political impunity, particularly within the context of the Argentine postdictatorship by implicating spectators for their failure to act. Whether performed in Argentina or elsewhere, the play places audience members in a position of determining whether they will throw darts, applaud, or otherwise intervene through a conceit that challenges assumptions that what happens in other countries has nothing to do with foreign populations. Hegemonic forces have always been mindful of how they regulate memory narratives through transitional justice policies and extralegal threats of violence. El Periférico's production creates a rich metaphor for what anthropologist Lesley Gill describes as the ways that impunity curbs the public's ability to constrain violence and hold perpetrators accountable for their wrongdoings.[28] The violence that spectators witnessed discomforts their passive viewing of the production, while the constant threat of military monitoring prohibits citizens from intervening in the play's action.

The Hamlet mannequin returns for the play's fourth scene, in which the titular character continues the process of negating his identity: "I am not Hamlet. I no longer play that role. My words no longer say anything . . . My drama no longer has a place."[29] Rather than fully abnegating his sense of identity, however, the Hamlet mannequin envisions a revolutionary uprising in which he is working with and against the masses, "My drama, if it ever took place, would be at both sides of the front, between the front lines, over and between them."[30] Hamlet dreams of a man speaking rebellious words on top of a government building while other subversives storm buildings and hurl stones at officers riding tanks and wielding bulletproof shields. As the monologue continues, the prince grows nauseated by his imagination and the realization that he no longer has the will to participate in acts of resistance even if they would accomplish the transformation of memory narratives that he claims as a goal. The mannequin longs for a redemptive future, but in describing what it might look like, he is sickened and rendered helpless.

Müller's original text allows Hamlet to disappear into an ice age, but El Periférico de Objetos's production envisions a different ending for Hamlet. As the actor manipulating Hamlet's mannequin delivers the monologue, two performers remove the figure's clothing before dismembering the object. The human actors revel in separating the mannequin's shoulders, followed by his knees, his face, and finally his head, before turning their attention toward other objects onstage. The performers punch and physically assault their inanimate castmates before the act concludes with a projected montage of images from the Argentine dictatorship, concentration camps in Germany, and the first Gulf War. Hamlet cannot participate in imaginary utopian counternarratives of rebellion before the authoritarian control that the puppeteers exert on him makes him nauseous, and he is dismembered limb from limb for his subversive thought. The combination of actors, objects, and video projection complicates the spectators' ability to passively witness the production by overwhelming their ability to find cohesion among the production's varied images.

Máquina Hamlet concludes with Ophelia redirecting her violent energy away from the Hamlet narrative, assuming the role of Electra by way of references to Greek tragedy, Lady Macbeth, European terrorist groups, and the Manson family.

> I am Electra. In the heart of darkness. Under the sun of torture to the cities of the world. In the name of victims. I eject all the sperm I have received. I turn the milk of my breast into lethal poison. I take the world I gave birth to. I choke with my thighs the world I gave life to. I bury it in my sex. Death to the happiness of submission. Long live hate, contempt, rebellion, death. When she walks through your bedrooms carrying butcher knives, you'll know the truth.[31]

In performance, El Periférico's staging enhances Ophelia's violent language. The character enters the performance stage, and as the actress speaks, puppeteers reenact the entirety of *Máquina Hamlet* using hand puppets on a miniature model of the theatre's proscenium. In this restaging of the play, the power dynamics between subject and object are made more significant because of the size disparity between the actors' bodies and the objects manipulated onstage. Spectators are also included in the small-scale performance as varied headless dolls are seated in front of the action as witnesses to the restaging of violence. The small-scale repetition emphasizes the ways audiences perceive and reperceive political violence and trauma at various distances, depending on their proximity to the violence.

Ophelia does not allow this miniature performance to conclude; rather, she uses a lighter to incinerate the miniature sets and actors. This concluding moment is a significant departure from Müller's script, which imagines Ophelia set ablaze. In El Periférico's production, the stage lights fade as Ophelia is dragged off the stage while the conflagration burns. But while Lola Proaño-Gomez wonders whether this concludes the production on a note of pessimism that mirrors the act of disappearing, I read the scene as a moment of optimism suggesting that Ophelia has the potential to disrupt the repeated patterns of violence so that something new might rise out of the ashes that remain onstage.[32] The conclusion offers promise for future revolutions staged by those seeking political justice. Ophelia's language and actions destroy Hamlet's narrative altogether, eradicating the visible reminders of her oppression with the language of resistance and active subversion that finally upends hegemonic control. In this final act, El Periférico de Objetos envisions an anarchic strategy that might be enough to upend decades of governmental control over postdictatorship memory narratives.

The question remains, however, whether the international spectators who witnessed the production share Ophelia's revolutionary vision of structural upheaval or see the production as perpetuating dictatorial violence. Although nothing specific to the production sets *Máquina Hamlet* in Argentina, numerous reviewers instinctively make the connection between the play and the Argentine Process. Amy Strahler's review of the production at Brooklyn Academy of Music refers to the violence as "revealing of a culture still grieving in the aftermath of the Dirty War." Pat Donnelly of the *Montreal Gazette* also links the production to the disappearances. Diana Taylor warns that conflating Latin American theatre with performances that resist political violence can create a limited view of the region's performance offerings. Moreover, Josette Feral's work on international theatre festivals notes that South American performances staged at international festivals almost always seem to elicit political readings from elite global audiences that are read as presentations of third-world terror for first-world audiences.[33]

However, the international tours and receptions of El Periférico de Objetos's adaptation of *Hamletmachine* strike me as an opportunity for international audiences to become aware of their own complicity in the political violence that has occurred in Argentina and other parts of the world. The production's ambiguity and lack of narrative create gaps that spectators fill in for themselves. El Periférico de Objetos's production of *Máquina Hamlet* encourages the audience to think about the possibilities for revolution in the aftermath of the postdictatorship and envision a world in which state-sanctioned violence and hegemonic control are eradicated. Visually representing the ferocity of hegemonic violence plays an important role in this adaptation of *Hamletmachine*, but it is important to note that the ensemble does not offer any specific solutions about how Argentines or any other citizens may prevent such oppressive acts shy of massive structural upheaval. Instead, the ensemble projects a dystopian meditation on the ways memory narratives are controlled and regulated by hegemonic bodies that apply visible and invisible pressure on publics and the ways the past is collectively remembered and subverted. Argentina's relationship to history is important to El Periférico de Objetos and also to Heiner Müller, whose work reminds spectators that, as Kalb puts it, "history is a perennial bloodbath . . . guilty shadows with whom the living have a bloody obligation to grapple."[34]

Allegory and Judicially Imposed Memory
Narratives in Javier Daulte's *Martha Stutz*

Javier Daulte seems to have been a part of the Buenos Aires theatre community almost since his birth in 1963. The acclaimed playwright and director
began studying with Ricardo Monti, Mauricio Kartun, and others from a
young age and was writing his first plays as a teenager. In his twenties, Daulte
rose from acting at Buenos Aires's Teatro Payró to assuming the position of
artistic director, serving in that role until 1998. In spite of Daulte's early and
frequent successes, one of the most important artistic events of the artist's
life may have been born of failure. In 1995, Juan Carlos Gené, acting manager
of the Teatro San Martín, proposed that the theatre hire several of Buenos
Aires's leading young dramatists to write works with themes that would
resonate with young actors who were struggling to engage with the theatre's
more adult repertoire. The eight playwrights chosen to launch this project
were relatively unknown at the time, but at present they read as a roster of
some of the nation's best dramatists, including Daulte, Alejandro Tantanian,
Rafael Spregelburd, Ignacio Apolo, Jorge Leyes, and Alejandro Zingman.

Unfortunately, Gené's project was doomed from the start because of
the space's financial woes and poor communication between the venerated
yet traditional artistic staff and the aesthetically ambitious playwrights.
Consequently, within five months, the project was abandoned. Undeterred,
Daulte and his fellow playwrights continued developing their work together under the auspices of the University of Buenos Aires's Ricardo Rojas Cultural Center, calling themselves the collective Caraja-ji. Although
these playwrights shared many different approaches to writing, the artists
collectively railed against traditional realist models of Argentine theatre
set in a family's living room or other domestic spaces. The playwrights
instead chose to create modern productions set in numerous locations
that told stories from multiple perspectives and eschewed linear narratives
while exploring linguistic fragmentation and other forms of wordplay.
Members of Caraja-ji began to stage their plays in nontraditional spaces
in addition to Buenos Aires's burgeoning alternative theatre community,
earning respect that would later bring many of these artists back to the
Teatro San Martín as well as national and international festivals. Although
the collective separated after two years together, they paved a way forward
for experimentation and for new models of play development for Buenos
Aires playwrights.

Javier Daulte's work is particularly known for its playfulness and referentiality. *Criminal*, the 1996 play that emerged from the development process with Caraja-ji, draws inspiration from the psychological thrillers of Alfred Hitchcock. Scenes shift between two psychologists' offices, constantly playing with dramatic space, audience perceptions of characters, and the psychological concept of transference. The play ran successfully for several months at the independent Teatro Payró. *Criminal*'s success enabled Daulte's next play, *Martha Stutz*, to receive a production at the Teatro San Martín, where director Diego Kogan staged the play in the Cunill Cabanellas Room. Although Daulte had been fired by the theatre only two years before, his work with Caraja-ji drew enough critical acclaim that he was invited to perform in the theatre's smallest space, a room reserved for experimental performances where audiences knew they would see material that differed from the canonical classics of European and Argentine theatre that graced the performance venue's larger stages. Additionally, the political nature of *Martha Stutz* may have made the play an easier sell to theatre administrators who found themselves in political opposition to the Menem administration. In *Martha Stutz*, the playwright continued his experimentation with intertextuality, narrative ambiguity, and shifting multiple character perspectives by adapting one of Argentina's great true crime murder mysteries into an allegory about power, narrative control, and corruption in postdictatorship Argentina.

Allegory functions as a major literary device in post-traumatic Latin American literature. Ana Elena Puga cites Ricardo Monti, Roberto Cossa, Carlos Manuel Varela, Mauricio Rosencof, Marco Antonio de la Parra, Juan Radrigán, Augusto Boal, Gianfrancesco Guarnieri, Chico Buarque, and Oduvaldo Vianna Filho as having been part of a lengthy tradition of writers who lived during military dictatorships in Argentina, Uruguay, Chile, and Brazil and used allegory as a way of voicing resistance to oppressive governments.[35] In the theatre, Argentine playwrights often created allegories as a means of subverting the dictatorship. Jean Graham-Jones analyzes several plays from 1976–83 and writes that playwrights frequently used common metaphors in their dramatic writing. For example, houses and apartments symbolized the country, patriarchal figures represented tyrants, and playground activities concealed what Graham-Jones calls "ritualized violence."[36]

In times of political crisis, allegory makes sense as a form of artistic expression because it is a form of literary production that does not directly impugn but rather suggests the recourse of an imagined space that will alter the status quo. Yet the allegories that both Puga and Graham-Jones write about have a fixed one-to-one correspondence between the symbols that they produce and the objects in reality that they are supposed to represent. Although these allegories may make sense within the construct of subverting authoritarian oppression, they are less useful for engaging in the abstract systematic and structural critiques of power that are multivalent, such as the control of memory narratives. Instead, perhaps Javier Daulte and Argentina's *teatro joven* produce a new model of allegory that draws on their own playwriting techniques. Within the discourse of memory narratives and performance, these contemporary texts employ multiple viewpoints and shifting perspectives that reflect the complicated process of understanding memory in the postdictatorship. Narrative authority is viewed with uncertainty as theatre makers and human rights activists ask what particular factors allow state-supported narratives to accumulate widespread cultural acceptance.

Javier Daulte's *Martha Stutz* functions as an allegory about memory and narrative, but it is enhanced with the modern Argentine theatre's use of shifting dramaturgical perspectives, nonlinear playwriting, and intertextuality, embedding numerous references to Lewis Carroll's *Alice's Adventures in Wonderland* and *Through the Looking Glass* within the play script. Daulte's script also takes inspiration from Carroll's use of simulacrum and parallelism. The play explores political injustices and official strategies for shaping memory narratives through a courtroom drama investigating the 1938 kidnapping of a Córdoba-born girl named Martha Stutz. The adolescent's disappearance captured national attention, becoming a media sensation and a political cause célèbre. A local criminal named Antonio Suarez Zavala faced indictment for Martha's kidnapping and murder, but the absence of the young girl's body prevented a conviction.[37] Daulte's script envisions a grotesque public trial in which the facts of Martha's case are presented before a judge and his assistants. Unfortunately, testimony from multiple perspectives renders each witness's account unreliable. Additionally, actors in the performance take on multiple roles at a moment's notice, further disorienting the audience's ability to follow the play's narrative.

Parallels between Stutz's kidnapping and the numerous disappearances that occurred during the dictatorship are easily read. The script references the Process and appropriates Stutz's kidnapping as an allegory that attests to the problems of searching for justice through the judiciary system, the difficulties of constructing accurate memory narratives in the face of hegemonic support for impunity, and efforts toward meaningful transitional justice policies in the aftermath of traumatic events.

Martha Stutz's dramaturgical configuration marginalizes its titular character from the start. Daulte's framing of the play as a courthouse drama structures the performance around several witness who take the stand to provide testimony from their accounts of the evening that Martha disappeared, even if most saw the young girl only in passing. As statements are enacted onstage, a character named Woman/Girl performs Martha, although the actress who plays her also appears as Alice from Carroll's novels and as an anonymous child prostitute as the performance continues. As a disappeared body, Martha lacks the agency to determine how others shape her life's narrative. Instead, the actress represents Martha, in an oftentimes passive or unwilling performance, as a cipher in the testimonies that others construct about her. Like Carroll's Alice, Martha is mutable depending on the needs of particular narratives. Through this conceit, Daulte creates a discernible understanding of how missing bodies often have specific meanings imposed on them.

Martha is not the only character envisioned from multiple vantage points. Accused kidnapper Suarez Zabala is played by two different actors, referred to in the text as Suarez Zabala 1 and Suarez Zabala 2. In the Teatro San Martín production, director Diego Kogan cast two actors made easily distinguishable through significant differences in height and weight.[38] The two characters also embody divergent aspects of the accused's persona in Daulte's script. Suarez Zabala 1 is timid and frail, maintaining his innocence throughout the courtroom proceedings, whereas the second Suarez Zabala openly proclaims his guilt and revels in aggressive and unchecked lust for underage girls. Spanish literature scholar Sharon Magnarelli, writing about the ludic quality of *Martha Stutz*, notes that the division of the defendant into multiple selves "flies in the face of our traditional concept of character as a composite of consistent traits."[39] However, within the historical context of Menem's political maneuverings for transitional justice policies of impunity and forgetting, Daulte's depiction of character as inconsistent and multivalent takes on political significance that Magnarelli does not ascribe to the play. Daulte foregrounds the notion that memory narratives contain numerous perspectives that should not be reduced to one unyielding interpretation. A thoughtful layering of multiple subjectivities in *Martha Stutz* reflects the many viewpoints vying for control of postdictatorship collective memory.

Kogan's 1997 staging also reinforces the fragmentation and shifting narrative perspectives that play a central role in Daulte's script. Oria Puppo's set highlights the artificiality and theatricality of constructing narratives, framing the play in what the author refers to as an "empty space, a theatrical space."[40] Sharon Magnarelli suggests that this scenic design is "self-conscious of the theatrical act" and openly acknowledges that the audience is about to partake in an act of "re-presentation."[41] As lights rise on the performance space, actors bring jurors' benches into the tennis court style theatre and place them in front of the audience. Simultaneously, El Conductor, the judge of these theatrical proceedings, takes his place at a podium carried onto the stage by the two assistants. The performer, who dons heavy makeup and a powdered wig, opens the inquiry into the investigation of Martha's kidnapping with a self-aware theatricality, performing to maintain control of the courtroom proceedings but also to engage the play's audience. Kogan's dramatization of the opening moments positions the characters as both performers and observers, while also situating the spectators as witnesses to these judicial proceedings. Moreover, the fluidity of this opening scenic transition reinforces the notion that theatrical performance creates scenarios that are constantly subject to change.

The play's first scene features two courtroom attendants who introduce the events of Martha's 1938 disappearance to the audience, informing spectators that the case has been heretofore closed for lack of physical evidence. The actors speak directly to the audience as if they are presenting testimony to a jury and courtroom gallery. During the attendants' expository information, they call the Woman/Girl onto the stage to model as Martha in order to describe her attire on the evening of her kidnapping. Their efforts at displaying evidence do not proceed as planned.

> Woman/Girl steps forward. She stands firmly and extends her hand. She holds this gesture until Assistant 1 understands and approaches rapidly. He places a prop dollar bill in her hand. The Woman/Girl looks at her outstretched hand and leaves it extended. The assistant, somewhat disoriented, pauses for a moment and then delves into his pocket finding a couple of coins that he deposits in the hands of Woman/Girl. She looks at her hand and with the other hand counts the coins and bills that she has acquired. Satisfied, she smiles at the assistant and closes her fist.[42]

Woman/Girl's solicitation of a bribe underscores the flaws of assuming that the judiciary can produce and validate knowledge through the presentation of legal evidence. Seemingly straightforward testimonies remain subject to manipulation in a juridical proceeding where absent bodies cannot participate in or contest the narratives that others impose on them.

After the courtroom assistants introduce the case, El Conductor continues the trial, seizing control of the theatricalized courthouse. As witness testimonies continue, the judge demonstrates his ability to control the spectatorial gaze within the playing space. Daulte's script empowers El Conductor to modify the stage lighting's intensity and focus throughout the performance. At several key moments in characters' statements, the judge looks toward the theatre's lighting booth and gestures to illuminate specific areas of the stage that draw attention away from or toward the person testifying. The actor's visible manipulation of focus asserts a relationship between hegemonic power and public reception of evidence. The ability to control discursive focus ultimately determines what is made visible and invisible. El Conductor's ability to control the courthouse narratives gains particular significance in the historical context of the Menem administration as the president faced accusations of manipulating and undermining Argentina's judicial system through his pardoning of the dictatorship's leaders and accusations of packing Argentina's Supreme Court.[43]

To this point in the plot, *Martha Stutz* has maintained some degree of similarity to traditional courtroom plays. The dramatic action has consisted of witnesses testifying before a judge. However, Daulte diverges from the tropes of the form to expand his allegorical exploration of hegemonic control and the shaping of memory narratives when witness testimony is interrupted by the sudden intrusion of *Alice's Adventures in Wonderland*'s White Rabbit, who scurries onto the playing space. The rabbit creates a major disruption in the proceedings, frightening the Woman/Girl and causing other characters to comment on this intrusion as evidence that El Conductor cannot maintain order in his courthouse. Although the White Rabbit's interference appears to be a non sequitur, the creature's entrance serves as a reminder that outside forces beyond the judiciary's control can interfere with unearthing knowledge and efforts to perform the legal process. The rabbit's entrance also anticipates another intrusion that occurs later in the play when Daulte introduces Gonzalez, a fictitious journalist who has researched Martha's disappearance.

Gonzalez interrupts the trial, intervening on behalf of Suarez Zabala, who he believes is being rushed toward a hasty and unjust conviction for Martha's kidnapping and disappearance. The reporter introduces evidence and raises questions that complicate El Conductor's prosecutorial narrative. Although the judge desires to resolve the trial without further delay, he acknowledges that Gonzalez's information holds the possibility of challenging and altering the jury's impression of Suarez Zabala's guilt. Yet Daulte undermines Gonzalez's authority before he arrives onstage so as not to privilege one effort to control the memory narrative of Martha's disappearance over another. Javier Daulte's program note takes the extraordinary measure of informing readers that although Gonzalez has carefully studied the facts surrounding Martha's kidnapping, he did not witness Martha's disappearance and should not be considered an authority.[44] Gonzalez's information is based on journalistic inquiry, but it is incomplete.

Gonzalez's credibility is further undermined when Risler, a prostitute scheduled to testify against Suarez Zabala, implies that Gonzalez began a homosexual relationship with the accused while conducting investigative work about Martha's kidnapping. The play does not affirm or deny the relationship between the two men, but once Risler offers this information to the El Conductor, the judge calls for further testimony about the two men's relationship, transitioning the play away from the courtroom proceedings momentarily to present a scene between Gonzalez and Suarez Zabala in which the accused confesses fear of unjust persecution before turning to the journalist for legal aid. In turn, Gonzalez offers to assist the defendant. Contradictory interpretations of the past reinforce the play's thesis about the unreliability of memory narratives derived without forensic evidence.

Consequently, El Conductor's control of the courthouse and the likelihood of Suarez Zabala's prosecution slips further away. As the trial spirals out of control, one of the judge's assistants tries to prematurely adjourn the proceedings. In performance, the lights dim for a few seconds so as to suggest that the case will be closed, but this is a brief feint, and when the characters refuse to vacate the playing space, the trial continues. The moment can be read as a commentary on the belief that although the Argentine state and its institutional structures insist on promoting certain memory narratives that uphold preferred transitional justice policies at the expense of others, alternative memory narratives will continue to seek public access. Contradictory narratives continue to overlap and accrue until El Conductor makes an exasperated call for a recess, which signals the play's intermission. In *Martha Stutz*, however, this interval is not a break for spectators. As the courtroom adjourns, the actors transform the playing space, carrying tables covered in porcelain china onto the stage and assuming roles as characters from *Alice's Adventures in Wonderland*. The characters enjoy high tea, sharing cakes and conversation about the nature of names and their absurdity, speaking to the futility of imposing a single narrative on events that contain multiple subjectivities.

The characters return from this staged intermission and continue to reenact testimonies and possible variations on Martha's disappearance. Actors perform and reperform testimonies, offering overlapping evidentiary claims that further obfuscate the conditions and events that led to Martha's disappearance. In one of the most notable testimonial reenactments, Suarez Zabala's wife, Pascuita, performs as the prostitute Risler to take pictures of the defendant with the half-naked Woman/Girl. Following the reenacted prostitute's haunting statement, Gonzalez demands to see Risler's photographic evidence of the relationship and receives blank paper, as the photographs do not exist. The scene raises interest in its continued exploration of individual's multiple selves, but Daulte also offers a critique of physical evidence itself as a narrative device. Images and other documents can be distorted and manipulated as a means of controlling narratives, and they are not irrefutable and infallible. Under these scenarios, evidence becomes another tool at the disposal of hegemonic forces to shape memory.

In the play's climax, El Conductor's efforts to convict Suarez Zabala of involvement in the death of Martha Stutz advance toward prosecution, until Gonzalez decides to seize control of the courtroom through violence. Gonzalez shoots El Conductor, murdering the master narrator so that he can assume control of the trial's conclusion. The journalist takes possession of the podium and uses the same body language and hand signals as El Conductor to call for a drastic shift in lighting before exploring another variation of the evening that Martha disappeared. Gonzalez's appropriation of El Conductor's authority may shift control of the memory narrative, but there is no evidence that this particular narrative is any more grounded in fact than El Conductor's proposition. Gonzalez's personal relationship with the accused child molester and murderer is vested. Moreover, the violent nature of the journalist's takeover suggests to the audience that even revolutionary attempts to take control of a corrupted narrative are grounded in unreliable assumptions that obfuscate the ability to come to terms with traumatic historical moments and the transitional justice process.

Martha Stutz concludes with a conversation between Suarez Zabala 2 and the Woman/Girl that accentuates the difficulties involved in creating wholly accepted memory narratives. The two speak about the silent *h* in

Martha's name (the *h* is silent in the Spanish language). Suarez Zabala references the Cheshire Cat from *Alice's Adventures in Wonderland* as a way of linking the *h* in Martha's name with a fictional character who is similarly present without being visible to those in the vicinity. The conversation creates one final moment of recognition about the ways Martha has lost agency of her own narrative, leaving control in the hands of hegemonic bodies that choose what remains silent or invisible. If the play begins by positioning the audience as jurors who must decide what has become of Martha's body, it concludes by admitting that without seeing the invisible biases underneath a narrative, it is impossible to move toward a position of justice that might bring about a healing of the body politic.

At the conclusion of the play, spectators know nothing more about the reality of Martha's kidnapping than they did upon entrance. In demonstrating their competing viewpoints, the play's characters have revealed the biases that reside within those perspectives. Moreover, without the possibility of continued investigation into the facts of the case, the audience is wholly dependent on hearsay and conjecture. Nevertheless, this has not been a wasted evening. Daulte and Kogan have created a production that demonstrates the ways memory narratives are manipulated and controlled by powerful actors. Conflicting interests can even obfuscate something as supposedly unbiased as the judicial process. The best that a viewer can hope for is to tie different perspectives together to create a multifaceted understanding of the past.

Argentines living under the postdictatorship must also navigate through multiple competing discourses. While Menem may promote an official narrative of reconciliation and forgetting, other pathways for engaging with the nation's past are equally compelling. Beatriz Trastoy reminds her readers that Alice could return through the looking glass and understand that her adventures were nothing more than bad dreams.[45] Conversely, the Argentine dictatorship's unpunished crimes cannot be eluded. Daulte informs his audience that as much as official narratives seek closure to ease the ongoing national trauma, no true understanding of the Process is attainable with a single-minded reliance on official memory narratives.

Genealogical Memory in Marcelo Bertuccio's
Señora, esposa, niña y joven desde lejos

Although Marcelo Bertuccio is not as acclaimed as many of the members of Caraja-ji, the playwright has created a significant career for himself in the Buenos Aires theatre. Born in 1961, Bertuccio studied playwriting with Susana Torres Molina before staging his plays in alternative theatre spaces throughout Buenos Aires. His most renowned play, *Señora, esposa, niña y joven desde lejos* (*Mother, Wife, Daughter and Young Man from Afar*), opened in Buenos Aires's Abasto neighborhood at Callejón de los Deseos, a theatre known for staging experimental works for an audience of young Argentines looking to discover the city's emerging playwrights. After the production ran at the Callejón in 1998 and later at the Ricardo Rojas Cultural Center from 1999 to 2000, it took a European tour, playing in Germany and Austria.

Unlike many of his peers, Bertuccio frequently addresses the aftermath of the Process directly and without prevarication. For example, his 1996 play, *Eugenia*, explores the relationship of a man and woman, named He and She, who are separated by a cell. The play reveals that She is twenty years older than He, who was disappeared. Each character longs to keep their relationship alive, but He's disappearance has placed their relationship in a permanent state of inertia. Such themes of postdictatorship stasis are prevalent in other works by Bertuccio as well, including *El Joven Jorge*, *Naufragio en nocturno* (*Shipwrecked at Night*), and *Y el miedo enorme de morir lejos de ti* (*And the Great Fear of Dying Away from You*). Although several of his works address feelings of loss among family members separated by Argentina's political violence, *Señora, esposa, niña y joven desde lejos* is Bertuccio's most-discussed play.

Brenda Werth suggests that the work's potency lies in its ability to allude to traditional and modern forms of media and communication, such as photography, radio, and the Internet, "to recontextualize individual and collective identities ... and juxtapose past and present paradigms."[46] While I agree with this assessment, I'm interested in the ways that both Bertuccio's playwriting and Cristian Drut's staging use techniques of the period to communicate how post-Process memory narratives are constructed and regulated by powerful forces in the home as well as in the upper echelons of government. Additionally, I consider Bertuccio's reception in Austria and Germany, creating linkages between the play's explorations of intergenerational memory in postdictatorship Argentina and their resonances in post-Shoah nations.

Argentine theatre scholar Beatriz Trastoy observes that the forced disappearance of bodies during the Process influenced the contemporary theatre to explore new forms of representation.[47] However, for much of the postdictatorship, many plays drew on psychological explorations of power and control in the relationship between governmental forces and individuals who worked to resist them. These themes can be found in plays of the 1980s, such as Jorge Goldenberg's *Knepp*, Griselda Gambaro's *Antigona furiosa*, and Eduardo Pavlovsky's *Pablo*, as well as in the public discourse surrounding human rights organizations such as the Mothers of the Plaza de Mayo, who were framed as fearless advocates challenging the Argentine government's desire to forget the *desaparecidos*. The plays largely read as critiques of the nation's failure to properly mourn its citizens.

Transitional justice policies certainly play a major role in how nations remember the victims of political violence. However, localized disputes over strategies for remembering disappeared loved ones also play out at the family level. Psychologists Inger Agger and Søren Buus Jensen write about the effects of political violence in South America, cataloguing emotional trauma for families who have lost family members at the hands of dictatorship. Their studies conclude that as strategies for remembering the disappeared coalesce, usually as a result of an edict from the family elder, relatives who choose commemorative tactics counter to the approved family strategy of remembrance lose contact with their kin and tend to withdraw from their extended family.[48] This phenomenon is not exclusive to Latin America, as Holocaust scholar Eric Santner notes that commemorative tensions also impeded familial communication in the aftermath of the Shoah and other instances of state-supported violence.[49]

Marcelo Bertuccio's *Señora, esposa, niña y joven desde lejos* explores contested memory narratives and control of those discourses within a family dynamic. The play centers on the mother, wife, and daughter of a young man disappeared during the dictatorship and their varying approaches to remembering him. Play and production experiment with static staging and linguistic aphasia to create a performative framework that investigates the relationship between representation and absence. Additionally, Bertuccio text's explores hegemonic structures for preserving specific memory narratives and how the trauma that those discourses provoke intergenerationally can emotionally paralyze a family.

Bertuccio initially sought to explore the disappeared's absence by creating a performance piece that rendered all bodies invisible to the audience. The playwright subtitled *Señora* as a "work for listening," conceived as a radio play in which the script enveloped the audience in a world without movement. After developing the piece in a series of staged readings, however, he realized that it might attain deeper resonance as a live play. Collaborating with director Cristian Drut, Bertuccio began to find the visual imagery necessary to make the play comprehensible to his audience.

In performance, house lights fade and the theatre turns silent as the Young Man's disembodied voice fills the space, delivering a lengthy monologue in complete darkness.[50] This is the first of five monologues that the central character performs from offstage, situating the audience in what *La Nación* critic Alejandro Cruz refers to as a solemn and reflective state that induces claustrophobia.[51] The Young Man's monologues create a state of timelessness that gives the character agency to assert control of his own memory narrative, but as he speaks, the audience realizes that he exists in a liminal space where he faces inevitable erasure. The character describes his offstage environment as cold place where the task of remembering becomes increasingly difficult. He conjures a description of his mother frying *milanesas* in his childhood home, recounting the battering and frying of cutlets in great detail in hopes that this reminiscence might trigger additional memories à la Proust's madeleine, but as the monologue continues, he cannot recall other aspects of his life. Additionally, the Young Man cannot pronounce *memory*, repeatedly using the fabricated "momeria" instead of the proper Spanish *memoria*.[52] The very act of naming memory eludes the play's invisible protagonist.

When the monologue concludes, stage lights rise slowly to reveal three women sitting in chairs looking directly at the audience. The actors play the Young Man's mother, wife, and daughter. Bertuccio's stage directions request that the women remain still and look toward the audience, with only occasional glances at each other. The production's static staging has drawn comparisons to photographs. Brenda Werth asserts that the stillness of the production suggests characters "frozen in a photographic image" that inquires into the role of art in the "representation and politicization of trauma and memory discourse in postdictatorship Argentina."[53] This connection between the production and still images makes sense as relatives of the disappeared such as the Mothers of the Plaza de Mayo and curators of commemorative spaces such as Buenos Aires's Memory Park have regularly used photographs as a means of remembering those presumed murdered during the Process. Children of the disappeared particularly rely on photographic materials to look for physical similarities and shared traits as a means of reclaiming their history.[54] To my eye, the staging in this opening tableau evokes comparisons to an evolutionary chart rather than reflecting a traditional family portrait. In Drut's staging, the three women sit side by side, and each women sits taller and more upright than her older relative.

The three women remember the Young Man on his birthday, each making an effort to commemorate him in her own way. The Wife participates in the Mothers of the Plaza de Mayo's weekly march, while the Mother stays home to make *milanesas* to memorialize her son. Meanwhile, the Daughter asks whether her father will return home from what she believes to be an extended trip and if his birthday celebration will include cake and singing "Happy Birthday to You." When the Wife informs her daughter that neither of those events is appropriate to this particular occasion, the Daughter declares the entire affair to be "the saddest party."[55] In fourteen lines, Bertuccio highlights how the dictatorship created ruptures that atomized the family as commemorative strategies privileged particular narratives of remembrance and memory over others.

In performance, the characters' stillness and flattened vocal patterns suggest that the Young Man's disappearance has created emotional strain for his surviving family. Additionally, spectators can take insight from the Daughter's inquisitive personality and her disappointment that the family cannot move beyond their state of solemnity to change the chosen memory narrative about her father. Each interaction explores competing strategies contesting the ideal means of remembering the Young Man, while reinforcing that such memory is controlled by the living and enforced by entities and individuals in positions of perceived authority.

Bertuccio explores the disappeared's inability to control the narratives surrounding their postdictatorship absence through the Young Man's linguistic aphasia and its development over the five monologues that he delivers throughout the play. In each instance, meaning becomes less intelligible, words become mispronounced, sentences run together, and syntactical structure becomes altogether unrecognizable. The character's vocabulary notably deteriorates as the production proceeds. In his second monologue, the Young Man states that he no longer remembers how memory, which he still mispronounces as "momory," functions, while acknowledging that his attention span is waning. The audience realizes that the character is losing not only his ability to remember but also his ability to properly form and conjugate words. The monologue concludes with a series of repeated words as the young man struggles to articulate his desire to be remembered fondly: "Restart it. Retrieve it. Recognition. Recognize me. Recognize it. Enjoy. Ennjoy it. Ennjoy. Desappearance."[56]

Human rights abuses and subsequent efforts to create a narrative of impunity and forgetting create an organized destruction of meaning that undermines the public's ability to understand the violence inflicted on them. The Young Man's struggle to reclaim the words that have disappeared from his memory and recognition is particularly striking in its suggestion that he is no longer capable of finding the very words that express the act of retrieving memory.

In the Young Man's final monologue, he has lost all semblance of coherence. Ivana Costa's review of the performance for the Argentine newspaper *Clarín* suggests that the character's linguistic deterioration devolves from a slight slurring in the opening monologue to such garbling of words as to produce a complete breakdown of meaning.[57] Language disintegrates into phonemes and complete incomprehensibility: "a a a ya yo quín vene quín a yo vene yo a quí vene a yo vene vene quí vene yo lu qui on supa ma ma mi no no ne gle pi yudi ol ong cres d d d m ou ll m f f f."[58] The Young Man loses the capacity to form words, causing his ability to articulate his own memories to finally disappear in the same way that his body vanished during the Process. The violent acts of the dictatorship have rendered him incapable of presenting and controlling how others will remember him. As the audience listens to the fragmented sentences of the Young Man and his attempts to reclaim memory, spectators must fill in the character's vocabulary gaps through their own attempts to construct meaning, drawing from their repertoire of experiences to understand the narratives that cannot be expressed.

If the disappeared Young Man lacks agency to control how others remember him, the Wife and the Mother compete to determine who will have greater influence over how the family memorializes. Scene five heightens tensions between the two, focusing on a conversation that occurs before the Young Man's spouse departs to participate in the Mothers of the Plaza de Mayo's weekly march. The Wife asks why her mother-in-law never accompanies her on the marches, leading the Mother to explain her grieving process:

> I do not accompany you because I don't know what I will find there turning and turning in silence with a bunch of strangers . . . He was my son. Only mine. I am not obligated to share my pain with a bunch of strangers.[59]

The Young Man's disappearance and the erasure of his corpse have functioned to prevent the mobilization of a memory narrative that the family can agree on. The Mother chooses to internally carry her trauma, finding refuge in the family home and avoiding public mourning. Her memory narratives of her son are privately felt, yet nevertheless palpable and profound, even as they exacerbate tensions within the household.

Contrarily, the Wife actively participates in the Mothers of the Plaza de Mayo's marches, lending her name and her husband's memory to public discourses about the dictatorship designed to facilitate public remembrance. While the Wife engages in this public process of creating collective memory, she also bears culpability for the fragmented memory discourses about her husband that exist within the family's household. For example, the Daughter asks a series of questions about her father's whereabouts, noting that she has written to her father and wants to know where he has traveled and when he will respond to her letters. As the scene progresses, Bertuccio's language makes clear that the Daughter does not understand the truth about her father's disappearance. The Wife refuses to answer her daughter's questions about the Young Man's location, suggesting that her father is on a trip. The Wife publicly marches with the Mothers of the Plaza de Mayo to commemorate her husband, yet within the privacy of her home, she paradoxically works to avoid discussion of his death. Her actions function as an inverse of what anthropologist Michael Taussig refers to as public secrets—information that everyone knows but that cannot be articulated, or in some instances thought, for fear of disrupting the status quo once the secret becomes open.[60] The Wife can perform her role as the spouse of a *desaparecido* in the public sphere, but speaking of her pain within the privacy of her home would disrupt the façade of domestic normalcy that she is trying to preserve. In this household, the Wife repeatedly tells her child that the Young Man is not dead and evades her daughter's sharp questions. As a result, the family's private secret inhibits their ability to accept their anguish and meaningfully address their trauma through the creation of a memory narrative that might provide psychological healing.

As the play continues, the Wife's relationship with the Mother deteriorates further. The two women begin to openly display their loathing for the other's mourning methods, calling each other names and making threats toward each other. By the play's final scene, the Wife has kicked her mother-in law out of the family home. Ultimately, the two women are never able to find common ground in memory narratives of the Young Man. Instead, they allow their contested discourses of remembrance to break the family bond. When the two elder generations of women fail to find commonalities, the Daughter tries to maintain family ties, but she lacks authority within the household to participate in shaping memory narratives and the knowledge of her father's disappearance necessary to activate her own process of commemoration.

The costs of denying collectively agreed-upon memory narratives are paid through the damage inflicted on the Daughter throughout Bertuccio's play. As Argentine literature scholar Judith Filc notes, the dictatorship's infliction of trauma reconfigures the family structure by rearranging generational roles so that younger generations must engage not only in self-reflection and introspection but also in a process of historicization that leads to a simultaneous construction of ancestral and future selves.[61] The Daughter's attempts at settling differences between her mother and grandmother fail, so she must turn to her own methods of constructing her father's memory narrative in a way that is accessible to her understanding. Bertuccio enables this process dramaturgically, by giving the girl monologues through which she can articulate her limited understanding of her father's circumstances. These monologues create a structural connection between father and daughter, both of whom fail to fully comprehend the events of the dictatorship because of their inability to construct or understand narratives that might clarify their reasoning.

In the first of these monologues, the Daughter wishes her father a happy birthday while begrudgingly noting her mother's refusal to bake a cake. As the monologue continues, spectators learn about the girl's understanding of her father's existence. The Daughter speaks of her experiences accompanying her mother several months earlier to the Plaza de Mayo, where she understood the march to be a ceremony for the dead and noticed her mother wearing a picture of the Young Man on her coat, but she could not reconcile these images with the notion that her father is away on a journey. While the Daughter does not understand the reasons for her father's disappearance, she is also skeptical of mother's and grandmother's explanations of the situation, noting that she searches for information about him on the Internet and wondering aloud whether he has an e-mail address where she can write to him.

In the play's final scene, the Daughter decides to look for her father by leaving home and entering the dark space. Before she leaves the stage, however, she tells her mother, "Don't carry my photo to the dangerous plaza. I want to pass unnoticed except by those who loved me like you or grandmother."[62] As she exits offstage, her language begins to deteriorate and she also loses the ability to remember and form language. Her final words to her mother are the last words of the play:

> Before I lose my senses do me a favor. Send me an e-mail ... I'm already forgetting, mom. Remember me. Now I'm seeing. Something. Confused. Still. Parts. Other. Parts. Daughter. Father. Grandma. Mom. Here. I am. Daughter. Here. Father.[63]

The Daughter understands that as long as she allows her mother and grandmother to shape her father's memory narratives, she will never know him. The erasure of her father's body and the denial of his disappearance have turned the Young Man into a void outside of the Mother's and the Wife's presentations of him. With no recourse, the Daughter must enter the dark space to construct her own process of grieving and remembering. Unfortunately, her move into the liminal area does not allow her to reclaim her father's memory. Instead, she loses her ability to remember while eradicating all possibilities of unifying family memory narratives.

The play's exploration of memory narratives as constructed within familial spaces received significant critical acclaim in Buenos Aires. Reviews from major newspapers *Clarín* and *La Nación* applauded Bertuccio's ability to combine the aesthetics of Buenos Aires's *teatro joven* with postdictatorship politics. However, the production's universality in its exploration of postgenerational memory became most apparent from reviews after Drut's production played for audiences in Vienna and Berlin. The European press frequently commented on the play as an example of the significant aesthetic changes taking place within the Buenos Aires theatre and linked the play's narrative to the politics of dictatorship. Reviews also mentioned that the play held particular resonance for post-Shoah audiences, who likewise felt the trauma of intergenerational contestations of memory. Lora Chernel's review in the Viennese newspaper *Weiner Zeitung* noted that the play's exploration of family politics could be felt by any audience facing the sudden and traumatic death of a loved one and that the resonances spoke deeply to Austrian audiences.[64] Similarly, Frido Hütter's review in *Berliner Zeitung* suggested to audiences that the play's relevance needed to be separated from Argentine politics of the 1970s.[65] The critics' ability to draw connections between the production and national concerns speaks to the power of the contemporary Buenos Aires theatre's ability to create visual languages that could transmit political messages about the postdictatorship to international audiences.

Ultimately, *Señora, esposa, niña y joven desde lejos* communicates that memory narratives are not objective renderings of past events. Rather, they are shaped through social exchanges that give form to ways of remembering. Bertuccio's play asks the spectator to think about how intergenerational communication allows for family members to work through trauma by constructing unified memory narratives. In turn, the spectator must make the logical leap to recognize that Argentina and other nations exist as states whose multiple memory narratives have created fissures in the national psyche. *Señora* explores multiple strategies for constructing mourning and remembrance narratives in the aftermath of trauma. Yet the play is also evasive, speaking toward the need to construct memory narratives of the disappeared, while also warning against the dangers of holding those narratives too tightly and restricting future inquiries into the past. Argentine theatre critic Federico Irazábal notes that Bertuccio's work moves beyond the traditional divide between form and substance to create a work in which the very aesthetics of the performance create meaningful political discourse.[66] This assertion proves true in *Señora, esposa, niña y joven desde lejos* as Marcelo Bertuccio uses a fragmented structure, non-naturalistic language, and a minimalist depiction of character to create a visceral feeling of the halting and often frustrating attempts of multiple generations of family to engage in meaningful discourse after the traumas of the dictatorship.

Intertextuality and Narrative Ambiguity in Luis Cano's *Los murmullos*

Luis Cano studied playwriting and acting at Buenos Aires's Metropolitan School of Dramatic Art and the University of Buenos Aires before launching a career that has earned numerous awards. His productions have toured internationally after playing in many of Buenos Aires's independent theatres. Cano has developed a reputation for creating rich metatheatrical texts filled with intertextuality, nonlinear plotting, and variations in tone that range from parody to tragedy within the same scene. Throughout his twenty years of working in the theatre, the playwright has questioned whether art can play a meaningful role in constructing or countering memory narratives without getting caught up in self-aggrandizement.

He explores these ideas in his 2002 play, *Los murmullos*, by creating a fragmented narrative loosely based on Dante's *Inferno*. The vaguely constructed plot centers on the daughter of a disappeared Argentine who searches for her father's presence in the detention center where he was held.

Cano opts for an intertextual approach to playwriting and performance that explores the boundaries of theatrically representing the disappeared. *Los murmullos* draws from hundreds of sources ranging from personal testimonies to children's cartoons to literature and film to create a series of disjointed images designed to provoke bewilderment and aggravation by questioning whether it is possible for performance to assist in recovering the memories of disappeared ancestors and whether the construction of memory narratives holds meaning altogether.

Cano's play constitutes part of what Osvaldo Pellettieri refers to as the theatre of disintegration—a late twentieth- and early twenty-first-century mode of theatre making marked by linguistic fragmentation, intertextuality, and montage—essentially categorizing the work, like so many of the other plays from the *teatro joven* era, as postmodern.[67] Additionally, performances such as those within the theatre of disintegration take meaning out of artists' hands and place interpretative responsibilities on spectators. The central question of postmodernism is how spectators understand performative fragments and how such performances encourage audiences to apply their own meanings to the dramatic event. Within the context of the Menem administration's efforts to structure, regulate, and legislate the postdictatorship to ensure a national discourse of forgiveness and reconciliation, the ability to infuse the self, to re-create history, and to play is an opportunity to dismantle the master narratives in place. Cano's take on the theatre of disintegration can be read as an effort to resist narrative construction of any sort, since it creates memory narratives that are as false as any efforts to construct a historical truth.

Los murmullos disorients efforts to understand the dictatorship's effects on contemporary Argentine society. Spectators must construct meaning from the assortment of narratives and intertextual references presented throughout the play. When the author comes to the stage in performance, he admits that his own memories of the dictatorship are fragmented and cannot possibly be transmitted to spectators eloquently.[68] Consequently, Cano develops a play designed to challenge the audience's acceptance of memory narratives and encourage viewers to take responsibility for constructing their own understanding of the dictatorial past and its violence without assuming a collectively shared experience. Part of Cano's strategy lies in an examination of language and how it has changed post-Process. *Los murmullos* actively borrows from more than two hundred texts written by a diversity of authors and sources, including Ovid, Evita Perón,

Ronald Reagan, Octavio Paz, e. e. cummings, Hannah Arendt, William Shakespeare, Diego Maradona, and *Pokémon: The Movie 2000*, making no distinction between material appropriated from high and low art.[69] The author includes his works cited list in the program, admitting to having freely borrowed from these texts without citing where they are used in the play. The numerous literary and cultural references interrupt the spectator's viewing of the performance. Critic Silvina Diaz suggests that because the play borrows so liberally from familiar authors, the references lose their original context.[70] Although I respect Diaz's work as critic, I would reframe that assertion. Instead, the texts accumulate and advance the idea that memory is not only viscerally experienced but also interpreted through the images and texts encountered in daily living.

While Cano's texts borrow from a number of cultural referents, director Emilio García Wehbi and scenic designer Norberto Laino evoke the dictatorship's horrors in the play's scenic design.[71] García Wehbi's 2002 staging of the play in the Cunill Cabanellas Room of the Teatro San Martín transforms the theatre into the ruins of a former detention center. Debris fills the playing space, the floor strewn with dirt, rocks, and litter. As the audience enters the theatre, they walk in on a young woman seated center stage, bloodied and tied to a chair. The actress's face is covered by a large porcelain doll's head used as homage to director García Wehbi's work with object theatre ensemble El Periférico de Objetos. Spectators enter a world where they are immersed in what reviewers have described as "a spectacle of decay and degradation" that visually reinscribes the horrors of Argentina's detention camps as a counternarrative to Menem's discourse of forgetting (fig. 1.2).[72]

Cano's text does not aim to solely condemn notions of impunity and amnesia, however. Structurally, the play directs its attention toward its protagonist, Rosario, as she searches for information about her father and hopes for a richer understanding of the dictatorship's horrors in a mysterious underground world. A guide named Botero, whose name translates as "Ferryman," evoking Charon guiding bodies across the River Styx, navigates the protagonist through her journey. Botero and Rosario row across the stage in a makeshift sailboat constructed from debris onstage. As they sail through a sea composed of the intestines and viscera of the dead, the ferry guide describes Rosario's father dying a slow and painful death.[73] The river guide uses this noxious environment as proof that man is not artistic material, positing instead that violent actions create the best

Figure 1.2. Alberto Suárez and Maricel Alvarez perform in Luis Cano's *Los murmullos*, staged in Buenos Aires's Teatro San Martín. COURTESY OF CARLOS FURMAN.

art and concluding that art must be paid for with life.[74] Cano's grotesque description of the dead not only challenges the Menem administration's narratives of forgetting and reconciliation but also proposes an alternative viewpoint to the sacred imaginings of the *desaparecidos* facilitated by human rights organizations by describing the disappeared's viscera and remembering these individuals as human beings made of literal blood and guts. Additionally, the text inquires into art's limits in creating memory narratives of the Process, challenging the theatre's efficacy to do more than recirculate the horrors of violence.

The play's third scene, "Dead Father Speaks," reunites Rosario with her father, but the reunion is destabilized by several conditions beyond the family's power. Rosario's father appears as a hand puppet controlled by Botero in the scene. Additionally, the conversation between father and daughter raises tempers, as Rosario uses the conversation as an opportunity to confront her father about abandoning the family, asking, "Why didn't you stay dead for good?" before determining that he cannot help her work through the traumas created by his disappearance.[75] The strained conversation between generations deconstructs the narratives of the disappeared as sacrosanct or mythical figures, and in doing so, the play critiques the memory narratives put forth by human rights activists. Their mythification of the disappeared is as much an act of narrative construction as the Alfonsín and Menem administrations' efforts toward promoting forgetting and impunity. Moreover, Rosario's exchange with her father, portrayed as a conversation between the living and a representation of the dead, suggests that the framing of absent bodies and the imaginings that their loved ones impose on them are acts of theatricality that ring hollow. The scene evokes and challenges other representations of the disappeared that scholars such as Diana Taylor have noted turn the disappeared into icons.[76] Instead, Cano's text suggests the possibility that unearthing the *desaparecidos* can create additional and meaningful emotional trauma.

After conversing with her father, Rosario's objective changes from genealogical exploration to a fuller effort to understand the effects imposed on her by the dictatorship and the various strategies for remembrance that exist in postdictatorship Argentina. Rosario and her ferryman proceed to an underworld space, where they find the fairy-tale character Snow White encased in her glass coffin, awaiting Prince Charming. With Botero's prodding, Rosario feeds coins into a slot just outside the box, and Snow White awakens, reciting a love letter to her beloved that urges him to join her in the coffin so that they can begin their honeymoon. She tells him of the beautiful birds resting on her body and the pleasure she takes in the children who view her corpse, before stopping midsentence and saying "insert" to request another coin.[77] Cano once again demonstrates the falsehoods that come with efforts to remember the dead and disappeared. Snow White's stops and starts as she asks for more coins suggest the ways that representations of the dead are often commercialized to capitalize on specific strategies of remembrance.[78] The image of Snow White encased in the glass coffin holds particular relevance for Argentines who witnessed the appropriation and iconization of Evita Perón, similarly laid to rest, memorialized, and commodified.[79]

Following their encounter with Snow White, Botero leads Rosario to the site of an "official" press conference. In this scene, four actors don masks of Che Guevara, Karl Marx, Juan Perón, and Evita, while strobe lights flash and music plays throughout the theatre, underscoring a montage of audio clips ranging from an announcer's call of Argentina's game-winning goal in the 1978 World Cup to Martin Luther King Jr.'s "I Have a Dream" speech.

This juxtaposition of sound and images continues for nearly ten minutes, and then Botero delivers an address to Argentina's youth in which he refers to the nation as a great butcher that uses and kills its own offspring.[80] The ferryman speaks of the Argentine military's willingness to drug its citizens and quotes military officers who asserted that the Process would destroy the weak, then the indifferent, and finally the timid.

This scene is immediately followed by the enactment of a ghoulish game show in which Rosario must demonstrate her knowledge of the new meanings that certain words acquired following the dictatorship. Marguerite Feitlowitz writes that the dictatorship's appropriation of several common words has made them intolerable to many Argentine citizens.[81] Cano addresses these linguistic tensions and forces the audience to confront the slipperiness of language. As the game show concludes, the audience is asked, "What would become of us without the guilt? / Without this sucking of pain?"[82] Both the montage and game show question the way political actors and human rights activists both anchor the political ideologies of memory in language that necessitates decoding. Cano is deliberately antagonizing the audience, but rather than doing it as a means of alienating spectators, he is exploring how contemporary Argentine discourse might be able to historically contextualize the full scope of the dictatorship in a less politically driven manner than the memory discourse of the Menem administration or its human-rights motivated adversaries.

When Cano himself takes the stage in the play's ninth scene, he begins a dialogue between creator and spectators, asking his audience to consider theatre's role in shaping memory narratives. Most of the author's monologue is critical of his audience and of memory politics altogether, insulting spectators before claiming that nothing in his text deserves applause.[83] After berating the audience, the playwright begins to critique the nation and memory politics itself:

> We Argentines . . .
> We are the delusions of grandeur . . .
> All this talk
> we do not understand . . . We are afraid
> Afraid of history.[84]

Cano speaks rapidly and clearly as he wonders out loud whether art has a role in helping the public understand and work through periods of historical trauma and whether that risk is worth the potential dangers of

perpetuating the traumatic event through a repetitive cycle of reenactment and narration. Yet as the author articulates these frustrations, the
performance of the play undermines his assertion that his work is futile.
Cano clearly grapples with the notion that his work does not contribute
to the recovery of memory, yet he chooses to stage his play and to directly
address the audience with his concerns. In doing so, he complicates his
critique and challenges the audience to investigate their own memories and
to understand how theatrical representations of the past can transmit some
understanding of the dictatorship's horrors in a way that runs counter to
discourses of forgetting and amnesty.

The relationship between performance and narratives of the dictatorship
entangle further when Botero abuses the author after his lecture. The guide
notes that the author worries about his representation of the dictatorship
yet only cites other people's texts, before pointing a gun at Cano and repeatedly forcing the author's head into a bucket of dirty water. Alejandro
Cruz notes that the scene's violence radically departs from the play's largely
comic tone.[85] Indeed, the act of putting a captive's head in a bucket of water carries particular significance, since this act of violence, known as the
submarine, was one of the most common techniques that military officers
used to torture the disappeared. However, by staging this visceral moment
of torture, García Wehbi and Cano force their spectators to confront the
brutality of the Process's violence. After Cano is nearly drowned, Botero
forces him into a metal cage upstage. Theatre and performance may not be
perfect vehicles for exploring memory and working through the trauma of
violent political actions, but efforts to prevent forgetting the past can mean
that future political violence might not go unchecked. Botero's violent act
ultimately undercuts Cano's intellectual self-doubt.

Once Botero locks Cano away, the guide tells Rosario that she will return
to her home tomorrow and encourages the play's protagonist to sleep. She
dreams about the history of late twentieth-century Argentina as a boxing
match between two puppets. The river guide's puppet represents a history
of governmental action, while the other represents revolutionary forces.
As a military march plays in the background, Rosario's father recounts
the battle between revolutionary forces and military oppression, from the
presidency of Juan Carlos Onganía in 1966 to the economic crisis of 2001,
with the rapid and syncopated enunciation of a sports commentator. The
dialogue consists of newspaper headlines and political slogans through
five rounds of staged action. Ultimately, this battle of hand puppets proves

to be fixed when revolutionary forces appear to have the upper hand, but then Botero pulls out a gun and points it at the revolutionary puppet, forcing puppet and puppeteer to the ground via pistol-whipping. Cano again undermines the notion that art has no place in the postdictatorship memory discourse. The scene began as a comic battle between two puppets, yet by the end of the match, the production reinforces the ways that those in positions of hegemonic authority can use the force at their disposal to upset equitable positions.

Los murmullos concludes with a final conversation between Rosario and her father. They say their goodbyes and Rosario prepares to leave the underworld when her father makes a final request of his daughter—to leave him and abandon hope of coming to a comprehensive understanding of the dictatorship's horrors. Lorena Verzero writes that for Rosario, the journey to reclaim her ancestral past has only led her to understand that his existence has made her life unbearable.[86] As the play concludes, there is not much that the audience knows with certainty. Cano addresses questions of self-reflection and memory politics in order to blur the boundaries between the two. The author may not believe that the theatre can effect change as an adequate medium for shaping memory discourse, but he certainly feels that the theatre can become a space for critical reflection. Moreover, Cano does not want spectators to feel complacent. Instead, he prompts them to speak out even if they do not agree with him. Cano often stood anonymously in the theatre's lobby to listen to the conversations and whispers of his audience, and he included an e-mail address in the production's program so that spectators could write to him about the experience of watching the play. Thus Cano proves to be invested in exploring whether his fellow spectators want to take the risk of rebuilding their memories of the past.

Ultimately, the Menem administration's politics of forgetting had the paradoxical effect of multiplying memory discourse by refusing public recognition of the disappeared, allowing the desaparecidos' families and human rights activists to continue debating the past, even as an economically challenged Argentina turned toward the twenty-first century. Anthropologist Antonius Robben suggests that Argentina's continued efforts to create narratives of resistance that challenged the Menem administration's amnesty policies "led to a polyphonic reconstruction of the past which pushed conflicting memories of violence and trauma to the forefront of each group's political concern."[87] The theatre became a space in which playwrights and directors could challenge memory narratives as a way to fight political authority visibly for national and international audiences. As the Menem administration came to a close at the end of the twentieth century, groups acting on behalf of the disappeared transitioned from debates of justice versus impunity and directed their attention toward advocating for legislative transitional justice strategies and new legal tactics that would guarantee greater control of memory discourse.

2

Teatroxlaidentidad:
The Right to Memory and Identity

TRANSITIONAL JUSTICE ADVOCATES CALLING for greater access to information about governmental practices argue that declassifying military and intelligence records and storing these materials in a public space would provide greater transparency about the extent of dictatorial-related violence and individual officers' culpability. Héctor Levy-Daniel's *El archivista* (2001) challenges this assertion through its staging of an ongoing tête-à-tête between an archivist and Ana, a woman who wants information about her biological identity. I'll discuss the play at greater length later in the chapter, but here I want to note a particular staging device. In a repeated action performed throughout the production, the archivist sits silently in front of his visitor, pouring water from a pitcher and drinking from his glass while waiting for Ana to leave the repository in frustration at her failure to find the answers that she seeks or to pass out from exhaustion. The onstage action serves as a metaphor for the ways access to publicly held information can be controlled and regulated when suppression serves state interests.

The interventions on forgetting enacted by Scilingo, H.I.J.O.S., Argentina's emergent generation of playwrights, and human rights organizations successfully shifted national memory narratives away from an acceptance of the Menem administration's transitional justice policies of impunity and toward a desire to see the disappearances redressed. As memory activists continued to publicly explore the dictatorship's legacy of violence with renewed vigor, they necessitated new strategies for engaging the Argentine public and politicians who might pursue a different line of transitional justice legislation.

Although Alfonsín's amnesty laws and Menem's pardons largely hamstrung criminal prosecutions, advocates for the disappeared and their families began to propose alternative strategies to redress the dictatorship's brutalities. Rather than continue to cast doubt about the construction of memory narratives, human rights organizations began to create discursive strategies that could have come out of the hands of a more traditionally conservative policymaker's playbook. Activists began to pursue archival evidence and appropriate the language and sentiments of family bonds to advocate for a shift in postdictatorship memory politics. On an evidentiary front, proposals included pursuing symbolic criminal prosecutions in international courts, altering Argentina's constitution to outline additional freedoms that would reverse or circumvent previously enacted amendments, and developing new forensic techniques that might help identify the *desaparecidos*' remains. In addition to backing new documentary approaches to create legible proof of the Process's cruelty, organizations began to collaborate with cultural producers to develop a coherent and unified political message that might help Argentines understand how the dictatorship's kidnappings appropriated children from their biological families in ways that irreparably broke family bonds. As an alternative, human rights advocates began speaking to ideas such as family origin, biology, and genetics as necessary tools for Argentines to restore national unity and develop a fully realized sense of self.

Initial efforts to circumvent the Alfonsín and Menem administrations' absolutions and exonerations materialized though efforts to prosecute the dictatorship's leaders and military officers in foreign courts. Domestic and international legal groups sympathetic to the disappeared provided legal aid and financial resources so that families of *desaparecidos* who held dual citizenship could file criminal charges internationally. Argentina's large immigrant population and Europe's lax dual-citizenship laws made finding victims with twofold nationality relatively straightforward. Legal organizations argued that because domestic prosecutorial efforts were not viable in Argentina, international trials might provide censure for political crimes against the nation's citizens. Arguments proved persuasive, and by the 1990s, France, Germany, Italy, Sweden, and Switzerland had agreed to open judicial proceedings.

The most prominent of these trials was that of Argentine naval captain and intelligence operative Alfredo Astiz, sentenced in absentia to life imprisonment by a French court in 1990 for his involvement in the disappearance of two French nuns who marched alongside the Mothers of the Plaza de Mayo. Legal proceedings in other countries soon followed as Spain and

Italy took a particularly active role in trying Argentine soldiers for military-sponsored political violence. Approximately six hundred expatriates and Argentines of Spanish and Italian descent pursued prosecutions and trials of military leaders, which most notably led to Spanish Judge Baltasar Garzón indicting and filing an international arrest warrant for junta leaders Jorge Videla, Emilio Massera, and nearly one hundred other officers accused of genocide, unlawful arrest, murder, torture, and kidnapping in November 1999.[1] Although the Menem administration refused to extradite citizens, these foreign hearings and their rulings demonstrated that judicial bodies could find a preponderance of evidence necessary to prosecute and convict Argentina's military for criminal offenses committed during the Process, which in turn enabled human rights activists to continue shaping memory narratives that might persuade politicians to pursue judicial and legislative transitional justice measures domestically.

In addition to working toward international legal action, human rights activists in Argentina creatively lobbied for domestic judicial efforts that would establish popularly supported individual rights that might shine a light on the dictatorship's abuses while also preventing future atrocities. Argentina's Center for Legal and Social Studies (CELS) asserted that although amnesty laws blocked criminal proceedings from moving forward, family members of the disappeared retained the legal right to pursue information regarding their loved ones' locations. CELS further asserted that the state held a lawful obligation to assist families through the use of any and all of its resources.

CELS advocated for what it defined as a right to truth, which entitled victims of state-enacted violence, or the executors of their affairs, to seek information about the totality of circumstances surrounding a prisoner's captivity. In the event that such information could not be produced easily, the courts would require the state to hold hearings and investigations that might satisfactorily produce resolution.[2] In 1995, a Buenos Aires federal appeals court considered the center's legal argument and acknowledged an individual's right to truth and the state's obligation to aid individuals who wished to pursue this matter, ordering the minister of defense as well as the Argentine Army and Navy to find and provide files on disappearances. Argentina's Menem-supporting courts held the case in appeals until 1999, when the Inter-American Commission on Human Rights, a permanent body that examines abuses of civil liberties across the Western Hemisphere, negotiated a settlement with Argentina in which the nation agreed to uphold the appeals court ruling and admitted a responsibility to exhaust "all means to obtain information on the whereabouts of the disappeared."[3]

In the aftermath of this accord, Argentina began holding truth hearings in cities across the nation. These judicial proceedings compelled public witnesses, military officers, and relatives of the disappeared to testify and face cross-examination under oath—albeit in a legal setting devoid of defendants or the possibility of conviction. Unlike the CONADEP hearings held in the years after the dictatorship, these inquiries were not charged with determining the scope of wrongdoing committed as part of the Process but were instead authorized with obtaining information about specific disappeared individuals. Although political scientist Francesca Lessa questions the hearings' impact on bringing quantifiable results to the *desaparecidos'* families, she notes that the procedures amassed physical evidence and testimonies that proved invaluable to the state when criminal prosecutions for dictatorial-related crimes resumed in 2006.[4] The right to truth ultimately represented what Argentine legal scholar Leonardo Filippini refers to as a transitional justice "compromise between the commitment to finding the truth, and the context of impunity."[5]

The pursuit of these judicial measures marks a shift in human rights organizations' ability to procure the proof needed to demonstrate Argentina's culpability for the Process and its violence. One essential component for the success of these projects is access to reliable and well-organized documentation. Diana Taylor notes the ways that the archive "sustains power," working across temporal and geographic boundaries to store accumulated knowledge so that it might remain present for future interpretation.[6] Although the interpretation of these archival materials may shift over time, CELS and other legal associations were able to use courtroom rulings and files turned over by the military as evidence for continued development of transitional justice policies. However, other human rights organizations began to pursue documentary evidence that might hold greater weight in the eyes of the public than legal briefs and other governmental records.

The Grandmothers of the Plaza de Mayo have proven themselves trailblazers in advocating for transitional justice legislation, pursuing advancements in criminal forensic technologies that assist in identifying the disappeared, and collaborating with cultural producers to devise effective memory narratives that might persuade Argentina's courts and legislature to aid in the recovery of their disappeared grandchildren. The association's founders, who met in the Mothers of the Plaza de Mayo's weekly marches, heard rumors about military leaders murdering women in detention centers who had recently given birth and giving the newborn babies to political sympathizers who promised to raise the children as their own. From these conversations, thirteen women established an NGO charged with reuniting birth families with the babies kidnapped during the Process, in addition to helping individuals and families with questions or concerns about their identity find the resources necessary to determine biological ancestry.[7] The organization's membership has worked tirelessly for forty years, pursuing information about the estimated five hundred children separated from their families during the dictatorship.[8] As of August 2017, because of their efforts, 122 individuals have learned that they are the progeny of *desaparecidos*.

The Grandmothers' mission relied on innovations in forensic science and DNA testing that can determine a person's biological genealogy with 99.9 percent accuracy. In the early 1980s, Rita Arditti's comprehensive history of the organization revealed that the group provided financial and legal support to ensure that noted forensic anthropologist Clyde Snow could exhume mass graves to identify individual remains and determine whether disappeared children were buried with their parents.[9]

Empowered by these scientific advancements, the organization also lobbied politicians to support legislation that would affirm biological identity as a nationally approved human right. In 1987, the Grandmothers successfully petitioned for the Argentine legislature to begin a national genetic database where families of the disappeared could register DNA samples at no cost. Additionally, the Grandmothers collaborated with the Argentine Ministry of Foreign Affairs to draft Articles 7 and 8 of the United Nations Convention on the Rights of the Child treaty in 1990. These articles affirm a child's right to information about identity, nationality, name, and family relations with state support and without unlawful interference. Similar provisions were passed into Argentine law and later the national constitution. The universal declaration placed an imperative on the state to ensure and enforce the law's enactment. This provision held particular importance because military officers were not granted immunity for kidnappings committed during the dictatorship. As noted by political scientist Michelle Bonner, The Grandmothers of the Plaza de Mayo used this loophole to work with prosecutors to file criminal charges against the Process's leaders in unsolved cases regarding missing children.[10]

The Grandmothers forcefully advocate for their efforts using the rhetoric of blood and genetics, which they posit as insoluble, as their discourse of resistance to transitional justice policies of impunity. They argue that understanding biological ties helps one further develop a sense of national unity and that a knowledge of one's family background is essential to an individual's process of self-actualization. This belief system has led some leftist organizations to critique the Grandmothers on the charge of legitimizing essentialist notions of identity that reinscribe and legitimate definitions of family, selfhood, and the importance of blood ties as essential to national strength and unity through logistical justifications similar to those that the dictatorship used to rationalize its own political actions. I'll return to this critique later in this chapter; however, scholars such as Argentine sociologist María Teresa Sánchez argue that the Grandmothers of the Plaza de Mayo's linguistic turn is simply a matter of reappropriating language, in the same way that the Process changed the meaning of words during the dictatorship.[11]

To alter the lexicon to allow room for new considerations of family, selfhood, biology, and other determining indicators to become part of this archive of knowledge about the disappeared, the Grandmothers of the Plaza de Mayo needed to turn to what Taylor names "the repertoire of embodied performance" to teach the Argentine public their terminology and how to employ it as a memory narrative for the advancement of new transitional justice policies.[12] The Grandmothers' most visible contribution toward engaging the public in understanding the importance of biology and genetics as determinants of identity was the development of acts of cultural production designed to raise awareness of the organization's resources and advance the group's agenda to change the tone of national memory narratives away from impunity and forgetting and toward a discourse of recovery and restitution grounded in blood ties. Brenda Werth observes that by the 1990s, the Grandmothers recognized that the children for whom the organization had advocated had reached the age of legal adulthood and were capable of taking agency for efforts to understand their personal backgrounds and biological identities.[13]

Subsequently, the group's leaders began to envision the creation of cultural events that would call attention to the ongoing efforts to find the five hundred children of the disappeared and would remind Argentines that if they had questions about their birth origins, they had a legally mandated right to uncover pertinent information about their blood relatives. By 2001, the Grandmothers had created a series of events designed to draw attention to the organization and advance the concept of genetic identity. These events, called "Rock for Identity," "Dance for Identity," "Film for Identity," "Sports for Identity," and more, became easily recognizable sites of cultural engagement that targeted the adults in their twenties the organization wanted to interact with. It was in this framework of political and cultural action that *Teatroxlaidentidad* (Theatre for Identity) emerged. This project began as a single theatrical event staged in Buenos Aires in 2000, but since its inception, it has evolved into a play festival and performance workshop that is considered a major theatrical event and has generated national and international media attention, involves cross-country tours, and draws audiences that number in the hundreds of thousands.

Teatroxlaidentidad: Origins and Foundations

The *Teatroxlaidentidad* festival was not the first time that the Grand-mothers of the Plaza de Mayo had provided support for artistic projects, nor was it the first time that the Argentine theatre explored narratives about the kidnapped children of the disappeared. Eduardo Pavlovsky's 1985 play *Potestad* (*Power*) depicts a dialogue between a doctor who separated a child from her birth parents and the young woman who had grown up and confronts him after reaching adulthood and discovering her birth identity. In 1997, the Grandmothers commissioned acclaimed playwright Roberto Cossa to write *¿Vos sabés quién vos?* (*Do You Know Who You Are?*) as a fund-raiser staged at the Teatro Nacional Cervantes, the na-tional theatre. The production, which presented the narratives of three pregnant women along with testimonies from recovered children, drew on the Grandmothers' messaging about the importance of maintaining and preserving biological ties and hereditary knowledge.

The production's successful performance led the Grandmothers to con-sider the possibility of a play festival, but the idea remained unfulfilled until theatre artists Patricia Zangaro, Daniel Fanego, and Valentina Bassi saw the opportunity to collaborate with each other on a politically significant project. The trio met with the Grandmothers to determine the logistics of devising a play for the organization that would bear witness to the kid-nappings and appropriations of children that occurred in Argentina's de-tention camps and speak to the importance of biological identity. Director Daniel Fanego writes about his conversation with the Grandmothers as a transformational moment in his life in which the organization helped him understand its widely held belief that when one person's identity is in a state of flux, the entire country's knowledge of self is in question.[14] During the discussion, Fanego, Zangaro, and Bassi committed to constructing a production supported by the organization, and the Grandmothers provided the ensemble with oral testimonies, audiovisual materials, and primary documents that playwright Zangaro used to write the script for their play. Titled *A propósito de la duda* (*With Regard to Doubt*), it was directed by Fanego and featured Bassi in performance.

The Grandmothers instructed the ensemble that they were to create a half-hour-length play that would speak to the importance of genetic identity and inform the audience about the dictatorship's history of kidnapping the disappeared's babies. With this prompt, the author decided on a dramatic approach that merged direct address inspired by individual testimonies of familial reconciliation, with techniques drawn from *escraches* and other street protests that would heighten the narrative's dramatic urgency. As the script developed, Zangaro created a text that filled the theatre space with nearly thirty actors and musicians; including members of the political protest group H.I.J.O.S. Under Fanego's direction, the actors rehearsed once a week, working late into the evening with little compensation, united by a desire to create meaningful political theatre. *A propósito de la duda* opened on July 5, 2000, at the University of Buenos Aires's Ricardo Rojas Cultural Center with a scheduled run of five performances.

Before the production, Werth writes, both the Grandmothers and the artistic team involved in creating the work believed that the play would have a well-attended run, before closing and becoming a small yet critical moment in the organization's history.[15] To the surprise of all involved, however, the play resonated deeply with the University of Buenos Aires's primarily student audience, which included many spectators who were within the target ages indicating that they might have been children of the disappeared. As word of mouth about the performance began to spread, the production transferred to the Recoleta Cultural Center, where nearly sold-out performances ran through November 2000. Ultimately, some eight thousand spectators saw this production, and the Grandmothers reported that seventy people approached the activists to participate in DNA testing that might provide new information about their genetic identities.[16] Furthermore, seven of those participants discovered new information about their biological pasts and genetic relation to the disappeared.

A propósito de la duda's success inspired the Grandmothers to think about cultural production as a larger part of their mission and also caught the attention of other theatre artists looking for an opportunity to make a political impact on post-Process memory narratives. Shortly after the production closed, the human rights organization announced plans to launch a festival of new plays concerned with the dictatorship's kidnapping and appropriation of babies and the questions of identity evoked by those acts. In setting this goal, *Teatroxlaidentidad* (TxI) was founded and positioned as one of largest and most significant performances of political theatre since Argentina's restoration of democracy. This theatrical event has inspired significant scholarship from a number of academics, such as Brenda Werth and human rights scholar Kerry Bystrom, who rightly note the political success of the festival in identifying children who were kidnapped from their parents during the dictatorship and in recruiting advocates for transitional justice policies committed to remembering the disappeared and the horrors of dictatorship.[17]

This chapter contextualizes the *Teatroxlaidentidad* festival's significance as a theatrical catalyst for social change, looking at the festival's symbolic and spiritual connections to the *Teatro Abierto* festival staged in Buenos Aires during the dictatorship's final years in the early 1980s and giving consideration to why it behooves TxI to claim itself as a descendant of the earlier project. Following this historicizing, the chapter turns to an analysis of the Grandmothers' event during its earliest and most impactful years (2000–2002). The production's growth and development into an international phenomenon is chronicled by noting the ways that the plays produced for the event develop multiple aesthetic approaches and artistic strategies for creating memory narratives that articulate the importance of kinship, blood relations, and biological identity as essential to constructing a self-actualized Argentine body.

Moreover, I note how the performances brought increased awareness to the Grandmothers of the Plaza de Mayo's varied public services and political initiatives. Additionally, I look toward moments in the festival's history where dramatists have subtly critiqued the discourse of genealogical heredity and complicated some of the Grandmothers' fundamental assertions about the right to identity and kinship's role in creating restitution for Argentina's dictatorial past. To enact this progression, I engage in close readings and theatrical reconstructions of three of the festival's key productions—Patricia Zangaro's *A propósito de la duda* (2000), Héctor Levy-Daniel's *El archivista* (2001), and Mariana Eva Perez's *Instrucciones para un coleccionista de mariposas* (2002)—to explore the playwrights' strategies for writing about the nature of identity while also reflecting the Grandmothers' views on the perpetrators who kidnapped infants, the individuals growing up without knowledge of their biological identities, and the families who continue to search for their lost loved ones after some forty years.

Connections to *Teatro Abierto*

Political theatre staged in Buenos Aires over the past four decades owes significant debt to the *Teatro Abierto* (Open Theatre) festival, initiated in 1981. This event, organized as an act of resistance to the dictatorship during the Process's waning years and Argentina's return to democracy, served to reaffirm the theatre's vitality in a period of political censorship.[18] Organizers staged twenty plays featuring hundreds of actors, designers, technicians, and directors working without financial reward from July to September for an estimated audience of twenty-five thousand spectators. When organizers continued to stage the event after the hosting theatre, Teatro Picadero, burned under mysterious circumstances amid the threat of political violence, the festival's reputation only grew, earning it increased reverence and political importance. *Teatro Abierto* ran annually from 1981 to 1983 and then returned for a final year in 1985. During its four years of operation, the play cycle produced scripts written by some of Argentina's most important twentieth-century dramatists, including Osvaldo Dragún, Carlos Gorostiza, Ricardo Monti, and Griselda Gambaro. As a cultural signifier marking the dictatorship's final years, the cycle received critical acclaim for developing what Jean Graham-Jones calls a renewed sense of importance and national pride within the Argentine theatre.[19]

Teatroxlaidentidad has positioned itself as an heir to the *Teatro Abierto* festival since emerging as a multiplay cycle in 2001. Like its predecessor, TxI has included plays written by some of the nation's most established playwrights, including Gambaro, Susana Torres Molina, and Ariel Dorfman. However, Argentine theatre scholar María de los Ángeles Sanz writes that the festival also served as an introduction to Argentina's emerging generation of playwrights, actors, and directors, who gave their time and labor for the cause without compensation.[20] Aesthetically, both festivals have relied heavily on one-act plays with a typical running time of twenty to thirty minutes and stagings that favor small casts and minimalist sets to more easily facilitate the performance of multiple shows nightly. Additionally, each of the events is fundamentally rooted in creating memory narratives that resist the Argentine government's official statements and positions about the dictatorship's place in the national psyche.

Although there are both significant and superficial connections between TxI and *Teatro Abierto,* the current festival's founders make conscientious efforts to position themselves as descendants of the theatrical proceedings of the 1980s. Daniel Fanego claims to have been directly inspired by the productions as a young man, and he cited *Abierto* in numerous public speeches during the original festival and in subsequent years.[21] The Grandmothers have released press statements linking the two events. Similarly, scholars such as Grisby Ogas Puga, María de los Ángeles Sanz, and others have written about *Teatroxlaidentidad*'s spiritual, aesthetic, and ideological efforts to maintain continuity with *Abierto.*[22] Although it makes sense for the later festival to position itself as part of the earlier festival's legacy in attempting to cement its place in Argentine theatre history, it is not a stretch to suggest that the claim of descent from *Teatro Abierto* is also an effort by TxI and the Grandmothers to assert the importance of understanding the role of heredity in one's identity construction. Perhaps these claims of inheritance play a role in discomforting some critics and scholars, such as Grisby Ogas Puga, who attempts to diminish the current festival in comparison to the historical events of the 1980s.[23]

In spite of the attempts to create a link between the two events, the festivals do distinguish themselves from each other in ways that merit consideration. To begin with, although both performance cycles engage in political acts of resistance, *Teatro Abierto* primarily developed through collaborations among theatre artists looking for a way to reassert the primacy of Argentina's national theatre at a time when the number of productions and spectators were falling rapidly and when the national dramatic academy eliminated courses in Argentine theatre. *Teatroxlaidentidad,* on the other hand, clearly served as a vehicle for disseminating messages on behalf of the Grandmothers of the Plaza de Mayo. Few of the plays staged as part of *Abierto* advocated for direct action in support of particular political organizations or causes. In comparison, audiences could not help but be inundated with requests to support the Grandmothers and to get genetic testing if they had any doubts about biological identity during messages delivered before, after, and during productions staged as part of TxI.

Additionally, Graham-Jones notes that part of the reason for the current festival's continued success in comparison to the short-lived status of *Teatro Abierto* lies in financial support from the Grandmothers, but the *Teatroxlaidentidad* also has a built-in network of spectators who are tied in to the organization and numerous other human rights activists.[24] These audiences created a word-of-mouth buzz that led to additional attendees, providing financial sustainability. An examination of the theatre's website also reveals that the festival operates under a highly bureaucratic structure, which was not in the case with *Abierto*'s organizational model. Ultimately, it serves the present organization economically and politically to claim this heritage to the past, even if there are marked differences in political goals and sponsorship.

Genetic Identifications of Self and Nation in Patricia Zangaro's *A propósito de la duda*

When the Grandmothers of the Plaza de Mayo decided to collaborate with theatre makers Patricia Zangaro, Valentina Bassi, and Daniel Fanego, the Grandmothers took great effort to ensure that the theatrical production created affirmed the organization's values and mission. Zangaro and her collaborators met with founding members of the group, who provided the trio of artists with dramaturgical materials that included historical documents pointing toward the dictatorship's kidnapping of children from pregnant *desaparecidos* and delivering them to military supporters, documentary films that addressed the dictatorship's political aims, and recorded testimonies from family members who described the emotional trauma of losing their children and grandchildren before the Grandmothers reunited their families to great joy and fanfare.

While many critical studies of *A propósito de la duda*, including works by Monica Botta, María Luisa Diz, and Brenda Werth, note the archival trove of materials that the play's creators had at their disposal, there is a gap in articulating why the organization felt the need to provide the play's creative staff with so many resources.[25] Given the Grandmothers of the Plaza de Mayo's decades of labor pursuing forensic advancements, genetic testing, and investigations into the whereabouts of the *desaparecidos*' children, it can be understood that while the Grandmothers felt as though personal testimony played a role in the construction of memory narratives, they did not feel as though individual statements could sufficiently communicate the importance of assessing and uncovering biological identity. Consequently, there was an imperative for Zangaro to avoid reinscribing what Araceli Mariel Arreche suggests is a prevalence of Argentine postdictatorship theatre that privileges individual testimonies of state-sponsored violence that overlook documentary materials.[26]

Although the Grandmothers' preference for data over personal anecdotes precedes the book's publication, their rationale calls to mind Beatriz

Sarlo's *Tiempo Pasado,* a seminal work on memory politics in Argentina. Sarlo, like the Grandmothers, explores the limits of personal testimonies and witness narratives for fear that they rule out deeper historical reflection on the dictatorship.[27] Although Sarlo does not wholly dismiss the merits of testimony, she posits that testimony must be compared and contrasted with archival evidence in order to analyze it as though it were another's experience.[28] With *A propósito de la duda,* Zangaro and Fanego created a theatrical production that feels grounded in the personal testimonies of the hundreds of individuals searching for their disappeared loved ones and those who do not know their biological identities, but it also explores the importance of examining archival documents, genetic materials, and other forms of produced knowledge. In doing so, the playwright and director created a play that claims evidentiary authority yet ultimately constructs a narrative that supports the Grandmothers of the Plaza de Mayo's political ambitions.

Monica Botta notes that staging *A propósito de la duda* drew on epic theatre techniques inspired by Bertolt Brecht.[29] The production's employment of these techniques works to remove the emotional connection that spectators might have with the play's characters and instead engage the audience in a larger conversation about the dictatorship's appropriation of the disappeared's children and how these actions necessitate the right to identity. Within the text, Zangaro incorporates direct address as a way of bringing the play's political message more immediately to observers. Additionally, the author deliberately avoids presenting the characters' backstories or incorporating explicit expositional material in hopes of creating performers onstage whom the spectators might view as what Brecht describes as "types who encounter specific situations and assume them with particular attitudes" without regard to psychological motivation.[30]

As a further literary device, the playwright opts to refer to the characters as types rather than provide them with proper names. The play is populated with Appropriators, Grandmothers, and Youth, which enables the actors to function as metaphorical figures who can call attention to the search for the missing children and the restoration of their biographical pasts. Moreover, *A propósito de la duda* includes musical interludes that disrupt the dramatic action of the scene through chants and *murga,* carnival music often used during the H.I.J.O.S.'s *escraches.* In directing the work, Daniel Fanego opts for a minimalist scenic design that also enhances the Brechtian elements of Zangaro's script. He uses a largely empty stage, populated by only a handful of plastic chairs, and he costumes the actors in contemporary dress to create a sense of estrangement between the spectators and the performance.

A propósito de la duda begins with an anonymous boy tossing a ball, before the sound of a helicopter plays through the theatre's speakers. The helicopter's blades grow louder, at which the boy becomes scared of the noise and leaves the stage.[31] The ball lies on the proscenium floor until three members of the Grandmothers of the Plaza de Mayo pick it up, share a knowing look, and begin to examine it together. From the outset, the play presents itself as the story of a young boy's disappearance, including the use of a sound effect that would clearly hold emotional resonance for spectators familiar with the recent confessions about disposing of drugged bodies by tossing them out of an airplane, before turning to the Grandmothers' efforts to determine the boy's location. However, rather than allowing the emotional weight of a potential disappearance to take the audience's attention, Daniel Fanego shifts the spectators' gaze toward the Grandmothers, who are inspecting the ball in hopes that it might provide some forensic knowledge about the boy's identity or whereabouts.

As the scene continues, lights rise on the tableau of a man and woman, each in possession of a full and thick head of hair, seated next to a hairless character listed in Zangaro's script as the Boy. The three Grandmothers observe the family and note that baldness is hereditary, introducing the concept of heredity, and project their judgments with increased volume until the Boy's father, listed in the program as the Male Appropriator, rises from his seat and delivers a monologue with the objective of claiming paternity. In making his declaration of parentage, the Male Appropriator claims to have birth certificates and other legal documentation assuring that the bald child is his biological son. However, the alleged father initially refuses to submit his son to a blood test, suggesting that a genetic exam could be manipulated, before identifying himself as a police officer.[32] The Male Appropriator's dialogue immediately positions the character as a villain whose attempts to obfuscate information about his employment and his alleged son's background are easily read by the audience as efforts to undermine the search for justice. The language is designed to echo the public statements used by military officers who attempted to publicly deny their wrongdoings to cast aspersions on human rights organizations.

The Male Appropriator's monologue also expresses the potential perils that kidnappers may derive from the Grandmothers of the Plaza de Mayo's efforts to raise doubt about relying on documentation of parental lineage over genetic testing. The Male Appropriator argues that he possesses documentation that the bald Boy is his son, but his desire to cite legal documentation rather than use genetic information that carries 99.9 percent certainty to confirm this leads the audience to speculate that the certification may be forged and to reject argumentation that privileges politically motivated forms of identification over scientific knowledge of truth. Argentine journalist Luciana Peker writes that the only irrefutable truth that a man needs in life is the knowledge that his son is his own, yet in practice, the prospect of DNA testing undermines the Male Appropriator's certainty in a way that might destabilize the social or psychological relationships that he has formed with the child he has raised since infancy.[33] Zangaro's script further undermines any efforts that the spectator might take to sympathize with the character when a Grandmother turns to the audience and states that as long as one person has his identity stolen, the entire nation lives in a state of doubt and uncertainty. In this case, the play's production of skepticism toward legal paperwork in favor of hereditary markers and genetic testing generates greater self-reflection and contemplation about the dictatorship's offenses.

The Male Appropriator's efforts to claim paternal rights over the bald Boy are followed by an appeal from the Boy's purported mother, listed in the script as the Female Appropriator. Instead of using documentation to appeal to the Grandmothers, the character attempts to plead with the women on an emotional level. She speaks of the years that she has raised the boy as her own, caring for his physical and mental health, before reciting a poem that the Boy wrote to her when he was ten years old. Nevertheless, the supposed mother's emotional entreaties also rely on claims that carry less authority from the Grandmothers' perspective than genetic confirmation. The Female Appropriator speaks of the act of caring for a loved one in a way that privileges emotional subjectivity over definitions of identity that can be objectively determined. Such behaviors facilitated the military's faithful following of superior officers' orders during the dictatorship and are fundamentally antithetical to the Grandmothers' goals of determining objective proof of hereditary identity. Fanego's staging of both the Male and Female Appropriator's monologues creates the appearance of a dialectic, positioning both of the Appropriators on one side of the stage and the Grandmothers on the other; however, it is clear that the sympathies of the director and playwright are with the elderly women through the play's use of language and because of their organizational sponsorship.

The Appropriators' statements are followed by a pronouncement from the Boy, who delivers a homophobic and violent monologue in which he claims absolute certainty about his lineage based on the privileges he has enjoyed through his highly affluent socioeconomic upbringing, including a boast of romantic prowess with women, which mirrors the character's perceptions of his father. The Boy conjectures that his father was also bald before buying a hair implant and says that he too will acquire one as he grows into adulthood. As the monologue continues, the character turns his attention to others who might be bald like him, noting that both he and his father believe that bald men look like "faggots who should have their balls seized and busted," whereas once he gets his implants, he'll be able to "fuck everything and rule the world, busting the balls of the bald men [he] encounters."[34] In identifying with his alleged father, the Boy has lost his own sense of individual decency and assumed the attitudes and beliefs of a violent individual awash in misogyny, homophobia, and consumerism without reservation. This implementation of language echoes what Patricia Devesa sees as the discourse employed by the military during the dictatorship, assimilating the perpetrator's justifications into his lived experience.[35] The Boy's verbiage also evidences concerns documented by political scientist Ari Edward Gandsman, who writes that the Grandmothers have often worried that kidnapped children professed sympathies for their appropriators as a form of Stockholm syndrome.[36]

After exploring the horrors of the Boy's life as a child living with the Appropriators, Zangaro introduces characters who have recovered their biological identities. A character listed as Young Woman 1 begins to speak to the audience and the Boy alike, describing the only memento that she has of her mother, a video recording of a birthday party in which the only words that the character's mother speaks are "Give me the fork."[37] As the performer recounts her mother's detention at the notorious *Pozo de Banfield* detention center and her own appropriation by a police officer, she notes a deep feeling of not belonging to the place where she grew up. Although the Young Woman does not explain how she uncovered the truth about her identity, she expresses a desire never to speak to the policewoman who kidnapped her again, stating, "If somebody lies about something as simple as who you are and where you come from . . . How can you not doubt every word she says?"[38] She concludes by noting that presently she joins her biological grandparents for weekly meals, and when she dines with her family and asks for a fork, she feels a deep connection to her mother. The resolution of the character's monologue reflects several of the Grandmothers of the Plaza de Mayo's dominant assumptions, including the convictions that knowledge of genetic truth holds therapeutic value and that biological lineage is determinant of more abstract formulations of identity, including behavioral characteristics and the soul. The Young Woman's description of a wholesome family dinner with her biological kin serves as a counter to the Boy's problematic attitudes toward women and homosexuals.

A propósito de la duda follows this scene by presenting actors who describe eyewitness accounts of their children's and grandchildren's disappearances, before a planted audience member begins shouting at the actors onstage, interrupting the play's momentum. The spectator identifies himself as a soldier who transferred captives from the Campo de Mayo detention camp to other sites around the country, including military hospitals. He describes delivering a pregnant woman to a military hospital, where she gave birth and a military officer took possession of the child while the mother was killed, but the spectator denies feelings of culpability because he was only following orders. The spectator's public confession is shocking in performance, suggesting that dictatorship sympathizers live among the onlookers, where they show little repentance for their complicity in the appropriation of babies across Argentina. As he finishes, however, a group of protesters storm into the theatre's house, where they stage an *escrache* that lasts for several minutes before the spectator is removed from his seat among the audience, while the demonstrators encourage the audience to chant along with them. While this moment brings awareness of those Argentines who continue to sympathize with the dictatorship, the staged protest also implicates the production's observers in the process of recovering identity by encouraging them to remain vigilant and to intervene in instances where they find military supporters disseminating misinformation. *A propósito de la duda* trains future allies of the Grandmothers in addition to educating them.

As the demonstration takes place in the theatre's house, Fanego's direction calls for the Boy to start to leave the stage, when he is stopped by the child whom the audience saw bouncing a ball at the play's start. This youngster is joined by several other youths who describe memories of separation from their parents and subsequent efforts to find their missing relatives as several other actors begin to chant, "Do you know who you are?" to the sound of beating drums.[39] The actors' dialogue builds to a crescendo of personal testimonies and efforts to link individual behavior with the beliefs and values of the restored youths' disappeared parents. Each statement slowly begins to lead the Boy to question his sense of selfhood. At last the cacophony of voices and sound concludes when a very pregnant woman appears before the Boy and describes her captivity, subsequent torture, and the experience of giving birth before being separated from her baby in a prison cell. The Young Woman expresses a deep desire that her experience as a captive might somehow remain in her son's soul so that he will take the initiative to look for her someday. *A propósito de la duda* concludes with a group of youths turning toward the audience members and asking whether they are certain that they know about their own identities, as the stage lights fade to black.

Zangaro's play ultimately presents multiple narratives about kidnapping, torture, and appropriation that call to mind Tzvetan Todorov's assertion that one's knowledge of self depends on an understanding of identity.[40] The production imagines a world in which the appropriators and repressors who supported the dictatorship historically and in the present act in perpetual opposition to the human rights activists who work to creative recuperative transitional justice policies through affirming the right to identity. And yet, while the play holds an important place in Argentine theatre history, it is important to acknowledge the restrictions that arise because of the company's collaboration with the Grandmothers of the Plaza de Mayo and the ways the play's argumentation consequently moves toward the didactic.

The Grandmothers imagined their collaboration with Zangaro and Fanego as part of a specific effort to engage with college-age Argentines who had reached the age at which they might begin to doubt the narratives of their upbringings and look for their families. The Grandmothers had already collaborated with playwrights and literary figures on previous occasions, but they envisioned this partnership as an event that would mark a decided effort on their part to encourage and support artistic production as a strategy for reaching their target audience. Consequently, as I mentioned in the book's introduction, members of the organization regularly attended rehearsals and invited other human rights groups to attend as well, although both Zangaro and Fanego insist that their rehearsals were open to all interested parties and that such a public process did not alter their creative ambitions.

This supervision from the human rights organization also regulated the play's message. The Grandmothers have spent the better part of four decades positing that neither an individual nor a nation is whole until each individual understands his or her true identity. However, identity as defined by the organization is largely framed as one's remembered knowledge of one's personal background and genetic ancestry. This definition is a very limited presentation of the notion of personal identity, in which a person develops a sense of who they are through what philosopher Sydney Shoemaker refers to as a variety of markers, including sexual orientation and personal relationships with friends and family.[41] Additionally, the Grandmothers' definition ignores forms of social identity such as race, gender, and religion. In spite of these qualifications, *A propósito de la duda* holds an important place in twenty-first-century Argentine theatre as one of the most influential political plays staged during the postdictatorship. The production speaks to the marriage of individual testimonies and forensic evidence as coconveyors of memory narratives that resist hegemonic discourses. For over fifteen years, the play's influence has constantly informed the dramatic works selected for *Teatroxlaidentidad* by the festival's jury and selection committee.

Privileging Genetic Identity over the Written Archive in Héctor Levy-Daniel's *El archivista*

A propósito de la duda's successful five-month run inspired the Grandmothers of the Plaza de Mayo to take advantage of the play's momentum to expand the project by proposing an ambitious and extensive new-play festival to Buenos Aires's theatre community. In November 2000, the organization launched a call for unpublished plays that focused on identity as viewed through the dictatorship's appropriation of children. The Grandmothers' efforts produced 115 proposals from artists who understood that selected plays required minimal design elements and that the staged productions needed to procure their own financing. After soliciting the proposals, the Grandmothers put together a committee featuring some of Argentina's most established playwrights, including Daniel Veronese, Mauricio Kartun, and Susana Torres Molina, alongside many other theatrical luminaries with experience dating back to the *Teatro Abierto* festival and beyond. Again, the organization released press materials that labored to establish a lineage with the *Teatro Abierto* plays. The esteemed panel selected forty-one new works from emerging and established writers.

Although the plays were united through the Grandmothers' proposed theme and minimalistic staging demands that reflected the scarcity of production resources, the selection committee created a program that drew from a number of different approaches to commenting on the dictatorship's kidnappings and the construction of biological identity as necessary knowledge for understanding the self. Some, like Marta Betoldi's *Contracciones* (*Contractions*) or Franco Gabriel Verdoia's *D.N.Y.*, imagine conversations between parents and their progeny told through mediums such as diaries or photographs, with intergenerational memory transmitted through objects and artifacts in addition to genetic information. Other plays, including Griselda Gambaro's *El nombre* (*The Name*), Ariel Barchilón's *El que borra los nombres* (*He Who Erases Names*), and Gastón Cerana's *Radiomensajes* (*Radio Messages*), use metaphors that communicate the uncertainty of identity as well as the uncertainty with which individuals must act to balance the lives they have known with newly discovered understandings of their ancestral selves. Additional dramatic works borrow from documentary-style presentations of facts and figures (*Sorteo*, by Posse, Laragione, Molina, and Winer), choral performances of grieving and loss (*Viudas*, by Ariel Dorfman), ghost stories (*Método*, by Silvia Aira), and travelogues of discovery (*Blanco sobre blanco*, by Mateo, Scaramuzza, and Rosenbaum). The aesthetic diversity of plays designated for production speaks both to the eclecticism of the *Teatroxlaidentidad*'s 2001 play selection committee and to the wide variety of playwrights who wanted to participate in this cultural phenomenon.

The 2001 festival commenced on March 26 with a massive ceremony at Buenos Aires's Teatro Liceo. Following a remounted performance of *A propósito de la duda* during the opening ceremonies, the festival staged forty-one plays in fourteen theatres throughout the Argentine capital every Monday evening at 9:00 from April to June. At each theatre, three plays were performed weekly to packed houses that received free admission. Argentine theatre scholar Kerry Bystrom notes that the festival's synchronized start times across multiple theatres fostered a community among audiences who could imagine themselves identifying with each other, the actors, and activists by coming together and empowering themselves through performance.[42] However, while Bystrom envisions a utopic community, I want to reemphasize that the community that the festival's spectators are imagining themselves to be a part of is limited to a particular understanding of dictatorial terror and the right to identity as articulated by the Grandmothers to disseminate the particular memory narratives viewed as necessary to create changes in Argentina's transitional justice policies. Although many human rights supporters and countless young adults who belonged to the same age demographics as the kidnapped grandchildren attended the festival, they were supporting a framing of identity dependent on heteronormativity and the infallibility of genetic bloodlines.

Nevertheless, the festival was a resounding success by any measure, as nearly three hundred actors and hundreds of directors, designers, and theatre artists participated in the extravaganza, with an audience of forty thousand spectators over the three-month run. Because of *Teatroxlaidentidad*'s success, the Grandmothers of the Plaza de Mayo received a special citation from the María Guerrero Awards, Argentina's equivalent of the Tonys.

While one could consider any number of plays to get a sense of the 2001 cycle's offerings, this chapter examines Héctor Levy-Daniel's *El archivista* (*The Archivist*), which follows in *A propósito de la duda*'s footsteps in exploring the concept of biological identity as emotionally and physically restorative. It also offers a way forward for engaging with memory and identity that empowers spectators to remain analytical about their own recollections and lived experiences, privileging embodied experiences over state-provided textual documentation.

El archivista opened in April 2001 under Marcelo Mangone's direction. The two-person play explores a woman's efforts to recover information about a biological family she vaguely remembers at a state archive whose opacity and bureaucratic red tape deny a fuller understanding of her biological lineage. The play's conflict reflects what Diana Taylor refers to as the tensions between the archive and the repertoire, particularly in how the archive all too often undermines the ephemerality of lived experience rather than working in collaboration to determine the ways both recorded evidence and transient occurrences might transmit accumulated collective memory.[43]

An investigation of this interaction between the archive and embodied retention resonates particularly in Argentina and other former dictatorships where official records of totalitarian regimes are not publicly accessible or where critical information about political and military action is redacted from the public record. The Grandmothers of the Plaza de Mayo, the Center for Legal and Social Studies, H.I.J.O.S., and countless other human rights organizations have all claimed that Argentina's postdictatorship administrations have deliberately concealed critical records that might assist in locating the disappeared's discarded remains, the whereabouts of appropriated children, and the full extent of criminal actions committed during the Process under military order. Levy-Daniel's play uses repetition and fragmentation as aesthetic devices that represent the national archive's employment of bureaucratic formalities and nebulous regulation to maintain hegemonic control of Argentina's history.

El archivista's four scenes encourage spectators to question the authority of state-sponsored memory narratives and the roles that archives and embodied experiences play in our shared understanding of past, present, and future. Simultaneously, the production also advances the Grandmothers' goal of serving as a watchdog against the state to keep national politicians accountable for passing transitional justice measure that will uncover the truth about the *desaparecidos*' whereabouts and their children's appropriations. Moreover, it articulates the need for independent forensic and genetically based record keeping, such as the autonomous national DNA databank developed as a result of the Grandmothers' pleas and petitions for transparency. The activists' work functions as a viable alternative to a dilatory and obfuscating governmental bureaucracy.

Spatially, designer Jorgelina Herrero Pons's set consists of five scenic flats decorated as the file cabinets of a massive archive.[44] In an interview with Argentine theatre scholar Paola Hernández, Levy-Daniel says that the staging of *El archivista* must include the representation of a large storage space whose presence looms over the play's characters and the spectators' imagination. Hernández notes that this massive presence evokes the physical closeness of a truth that one can never fully comprehend.[45] Although the limitations of staging the play as part of the *Teatroxlaidentidad* festival prevented the creation of the all-consuming archive that Levy-Daniel might have imagined, the production's manipulation of space is clearly central to the performance's visual language. The scenic design also includes a chair and the shrunken representation of a counter, both of which create physical barriers to archival access. Pons's design keeps documented knowledge just within arm's reach, while also at enough of a distance that it provides an obstacle for Ana, the play's protagonist.

El archivista's first scene introduces Ana, a daughter of *desaparecidos* in her twenties, who searches for information about her biological family—particularly the whereabouts of her brother—as she sorts through individual and personal memories that her adopted family does not possess. The lights rise to find the young woman in a massive archive, where she is having her blood drawn and conversing with Felix, the attendant who works at this site. As the archivist draws blood, he asks his counterpart to remember everything she can about her childhood in hopes that it might reveal some information that could help him locate information about her birth family. Ana can only recall images of a patio garden and a fishbowl that has never existed in her current household, which she offers as unhelpful evidence of a life lived before separating from her parents.[46] These recollections of memories evoke Maurice Halbwachs's distinctions between autobiographical and historical memory, the former of which can seem limited beyond the individual who experiences them.[47] During Felix and Ana's conversation, the two characters appear friendly and familiar with each other, but as the scene progresses, the duo's interaction veers toward disquiet. As Ana struggles to recollect additional information about her upbringing, the topic changes to Ana's blood as she inquires why the archivist has drawn so many samples from her body. In Mangone's staging, the characters' rapid banter awkwardly pauses, before Felix asserts that he has never drawn her blood before.

El archivista continues its turn toward the foreboding as Felix pours a glass of water from a tall jug and takes several lengthy drinks. Ana, parched from her recent blood withdrawal, asks for a drink, but the archivist denies her on the grounds that he has only one glass, before suggesting that she might be able to quench her thirst if she leaves the facility. Ana rejects the notion, observing that Felix has suggested this action on multiple occasions to rid himself of her presence.

Before the conversation can continue further, however, a loud scream sounds from behind the file cabinets. Initially, the archivist denies hearing the cries, but after further inquisition from Ana, he attributes the noise to nearby neighbors throwing a massive party. After another staged dialogue pause, in which both characters evaluate each other's statements, Felix again notes Ana's visible fatigue and urges her to leave the archive so that she might eat and rest, comparing her behavior to that of his childish daughter who refuses food and stays up too late. Ana expresses befuddlement over her foil's statement, as she recalls previous conversations when the archivist mentioned a college-aged son. However, Felix denies her statements and instead urges her to continue recalling the hazily held memories of her childhood. Ana cannot recollect additional information, but she does show the archivist a photograph of the house where she spent her youth, noting that she has provided the archivist with multiple copies of this image and others during the indeterminate time that they have spent together. The scene concludes as the government employee examines the images and expresses optimism that they will uncover the truth before the archive closes. Nevertheless, the mere mention of closed collections resolves the scene on a pessimistic note.

Levy-Daniel's introduction of Ana and Felix pits the former character's desire to reach a more complete understanding of her memories through supplementation with archival materials against the mechanisms of state bureaucracy designed to protect a discourse of forgetting. Luis Roniger and Mario Sznajder's study of memory politics in Argentina and Uruguay notes that it behooves governments to encourage the forgetting of autobiographical memories advance their own memory narratives.[48] The characters' competing objectives do not develop out of a deep-seated personal or ideological antagonism, but rather they are both pursuing goals that are not amenable to each other's intentions.

The scene calls to mind Louis Bickford's inquiries into human rights organizations' assertions that postdictatorship transitional justice policies enacted under the Alfonsín and Menem administrations similarly enabled military sympathizers to seal and otherwise obfuscate physical materials that advocates of the *desaparecidos* might uncover to understand the full extent of the dictatorship's actions.[49] The state's ability to control and regulate memory narratives that might undermine changes in transitional justice policy manifests through Felix's well-meaning bewilderment. The titular archivist appears before the audience as a minor figure in the archival space's hierarchical structure, making several references to his superiors throughout the play's first scene. In spite of his lowly position, his control over Ana's access to the archive can be read as oppressive. Levy-Daniel writes the archivist as an obstacle to Ana's search for truth about her biological identity, but rather than outright refusing her access to documents and other materials, Felix engages in subtle performances of power designed to heighten Ana's emotional agony and neutralize her will to procure information about her past.

One of the most visible ways that Mangone and Levy-Daniel's production of *El archivista* demonstrates Felix's efforts to exert control over Ana is through the production's manipulation of physical space and onstage objects. As the play begins, the archivist draws his counterpart's blood in the repository, but the young woman never questions why this withdrawal is taking place amid file cabinets and dusty boxes rather than in a medical facility or genetic storage site, such as the locations supported by the Grandmothers of the Plaza de Mayo. Ana's desire to discover the truth about her biological identity is so great that she allows the archivist to take whatever measure he deems necessary if it will lead to the information that she seeks.

As the scene progresses, other objects such as the chair, water jug, and glass also become items that Felix can use to control Ana and assert the state's power over her. The archivist's chair becomes a deterrent to Ana's willpower because Felix possesses the ability to rest his body while Ana must stand throughout the play. Typically, standing signifies strength onstage, but in Ivana Duarte's performance of Ana, the actress shows the exhaustion that accompanies multiple blood withdrawals though the slumped physicality of her upright position. Similarly, Felix's jug of water and drinking glass also represent mechanisms of power. Water could replenish Ana's blood-deprived body, but the archival clerk refuses to allow the young woman to drink, claiming that he lacks the proper materials to bring comfort. Although the archivist could take extraordinary measures to provide Ana with what her body needs by allowing her to drink directly out of the jug or by sharing his glass, the mechanisms of state power do not encourage such creativity. Rather as French philosopher Michel Foucault puts it, they "disindividualize" the representative of state power and anyone who might challenge that person's authority.[50] Levy-Daniel uses this dramatic action to call attention to the ways that state power refuses to make exceptions in providing archival information for individuals regardless of need.

Felix's oppressive actions attempt to eradicate Ana's agency, leaving her exhausted, upended, and thirsty as she waits for the archival clerk to provide her with the critical evidence that she needs to uncover her biological identity, but the young woman remains in control of the memories and experiences she possesses from early childhood before being appropriated from her parents. This embodied knowledge provides a seeming contrast to Felix, who hears screaming coming from behind the archive and tries to deny its existence before attributing the sounds to an irrational source. As an employee of the state, Felix cannot acknowledge information that deviates from hegemonic narratives of the postdictatorship, but so long as Ana remains capable of transmitting and articulating her own lived experiences, she can attempt to construct a path that will enable her to continue seeking truthful information about her ancestral lineage. Felix suggests to Ana that she might find the comforts of the outside world by leaving the archive, but doing so would end the character's search for truth and runs counter to the Grandmothers' belief that an individual cannot truly exist in a state of peace without certain knowledge of their genetic selves.[51]

Scene 2 returns to Ana and Felix in the archive after an unspecified period of time in which neither character has made progress in achieving his or her objectives, and their interactions remain unchanged. As Felix observes the woman's ongoing exhaustion, he expresses sympathy and states the desire to offer her a chair, but nevertheless he regrets that he cannot provide one because his superiors removed all of the archive's resting places in years past as fewer people visited the space over time. The archival attendant also laments that he cannot offer Ana his own chair, because his feet ache from walking back and forth amid the various files. In performance, the admission draws laughter because Felix has remained seated throughout most of the play. As the archival caretaker finishes his rationalizations, pained screams sound from behind the archive's files yet again. Once more the archivist denies hearing the noises, before hypothesizing that they may be coming from a dysfunctional family whose members constantly argue with each other. Later in the scene, when the shrieks are heard again, Felix will attribute the clamor to students performing at a nearby acting studio.

When the noise diminishes, Levy-Daniel's antagonist informs Ana that he is not able to uncover any additional information about her biological identity based on the photographs and personal memories that she has shared. As the character conveys this information, however, he chooses to express skepticism about Ana's memory and its role as a valid tool to be used in uncovering the past. The archival employee expresses doubt about the young woman's stories and tells her that he does not see any resemblance between Ana and the numerous faces of the people in her photographs, before suggesting that the search for her missing brother might be born out of the sort of loneliness that might also lead a person to spent countless hours in an archive. Such scenes hark back to accounts cited in Diana Taylor's *Disappearing Acts* in which the authoritarian state referred to human rights activists, especially women's accounts of dictatorial trauma, as born out of emotional and mental instability and loneliness.[52]

Ana continues to share her recollections of early childhood in hopes that they might provide some information that leads to documented information about her family and their whereabouts, but Felix refers to these recollections as hypotheses and finally concludes that visual evidence and orally transmitted memories do not compare to factual documentation as legitimate sources of knowledge. After taking in Felix's words, Duarte plays Ana as particularly stricken with disappointment, while Luis Campo's portrayal of Felix evolves from benign to belligerent. Once again, Felix pauses to pour himself several glasses of water, taking deep drinks before asking if Ana is thirsty. When she answers in the affirmative, the archivist directly states that if she is thirsty, she should leave the facility, and perhaps he might be able to find some additional information in her absence. When Ana chastises him for constantly suggesting that she vacate the space, however, the clerk once again turns antagonistic and posits that it's only a matter of time before the archive is closed. The scene concludes when Ana proposes that her blood samples might provide vital genetic information about her ancestral history, but Felix denies ever having drawn blood before, suggesting that he could do so if she thought it might be helpful. This interaction between the characters concludes with a physically weakened Ana providing yet another blood sample as Felix tells her about his child, who is now described as a five-year-old daughter.

Ana and Felix's relationship may appear identical in *El archivista*'s first and second scenes, but as Felix observes Ana's weakened condition, his ambivalence to her well-being and unwillingness to offer the comfort of his possessions suggests that the young woman's persistent search for information about her genetic history has become a threat to the archival clerk's efforts to control memory narratives and documented knowledge. Felix recognizes the considerable amount of time Ana has spent in the archive and has observed her long enough to note that she does not eat or sleep well enough to maintain her health, but he is not capable of providing her with items that might bring her greater physical relief. Again the text notes the state's hesitance to provide services that exceed its minimal obligations. In doing so, the dramatic action validates the Grandmothers' efforts to fight for dictatorial-related human rights and to pass legislation regarding the right to identity.

Furthermore, Levy-Daniel provides information in the script suggesting that Felix received visitors before Ana's arrival, but over time, the site's guests dwindled, causing his supervisors to remove all of the collection's public seating. Felix delivers this information as a suggestion that other Argentines have grown tired of looking for archival information connected to the dictatorship's kidnappings and other criminal acts, but it also reveals what Louis Bickford reads as the fact that state-sponsored repositories of memory relied on time's passage as a strategy for obscuring information about the dictatorship to maintain democracy.[53] These temporal constraints influenced the extent and quality of national memory narratives and transitional justice policies.

In calling attention to the limitations of state-sponsored archives, *El archivista* supports the Grandmothers of the Plaza de Mayo's aspirations by creating a contrast between nationally supported archives and the reposito-ries of information curated and organized by nearly a dozen human rights organizations throughout Buenos Aires, including the Grandmothers. The organization's headquarters maintains a small collection of oral histories and legal records that contains detailed information about missing grand-children, including legal documentation and biographical details about each kidnapped victim. Although the Grandmothers' offices are often un-derstaffed, Levy-Daniel's critique of national archives presents a scenario in which the organization's archives might serve as an alternative space where individuals curious about their biological identity might begin the process of discovering information about their pasts without fear of obstruction.

Nevertheless, it is important to note that neither Levy-Daniel nor the Grandmothers of the Plaza de Mayo suggest that archival information alone provides the certainty that will enable an individual to remove doubt about his or her background and ensure self-actualization. Ana's childhood memories once again play a major role in the scene, as the protagonist must defend her recollections against Felix's accusations that they are fabricated out of loneliness. According to Argentine social scientist Emilio Crenzel, a complaint that emerged from the aftermath of Argentina's truth and reconciliation hearings was that state-enacted memory narratives view individual testimonies with suspicion and doubt, and they had to be verified through physical and textual evidence that attested to proof of criminal action.[54] The state's expression of uncertainty was a deliberate tactic during the postdictatorship to immobilize family members of the disappeared and kidnapped children and prevent them from taking action.

Although documentation and individual memories can provide the impetus to search for identity, Ana insists on having her blood analyzed so that she can be certain about her biological heritage. Genetics now take priority over other archival documentation of identity. This prioritization is evident in the Grandmothers' work, as Arditti observes that the organiza-tion's literature speaks of a tacit knowledge or implicit suspicion individuals have that they are children of the disappeared. Intuitive knowledge can be deceptive, and hereditary technologies can resolve doubt with almost absolute certainty.[55] Ana believes that the only way she can learn the truth about her identity is to remain in the archive and continue to work with Fe-lix in hopes that he might find documentation or genetic evidence that will prove her biological heritage with certainty. Consequently, the character chooses to remain in the archival space despite her physical and emotional discomfort. Levy-Daniel, on the other hand, crafts the rapidly devolving situation between Felix and Ana as a warning that the state's bureaucratic control of memory narratives creates physical and psychological anguish akin to torture, using deliberate delay tactics to weaken identity seekers' resolve to learn about themselves.

In scene 3, the tension heightens between the play's two characters as the archivist informs Ana that he has received an order to close the archive because of her refusal to leave the facility. Felix claims that civic officials who outrank him have passed the orders down, and in spite of his own efforts to keep the space open, he must ultimately follow directives. Ana is devastated by this news, but Felix suggests that the facility's closure is positive, as it affords her the opportunity to find life outside of the archive, choosing to play, laugh, dance, and find fulfillment in the world like a normal person.

Ana resists Felix's counsel and makes multiple efforts to persuade him to search for evidence about her background with the information that she has provided, but the archivist tells her that there is nothing to be done and that he will never be able to provide her with her biological surname or verification about her brother and birth family. As a last resort, Ana asks Felix about the blood that she has provided, but here Felix exposes the archive's limitations in record keeping and analysis, noting that he simply kept the samples in files because he lacked the resources to analyze them. Felix's description of boxes of Ana's dried blood sitting in test tubes is meant to provoke Ana into leaving the facility. The offstage screams are heard again, and Felix's entreaties turn into intimations of violence as he states that the hidden shouts and cries do not come from neighboring parties or acting studios, but rather from other people like Ana who refused to leave the archive and who have been haunted into madness. Ana nevertheless refuses to leave the site, and the scene ends with the two at a standstill, when Felix threatens to call his superiors but Ana refuses to exit this space of memory.

Scene 3 reveals the full extent of each character's efforts to attain his or her objectives. Felix no longer pretends to have interest in helping Ana recover the documentation or genetic samples that would establish her biological identity, and the reasoning that he offers refutes his own culpability in causing Ana suffering while simultaneously blaming the young woman for the archive's closure because of her desire to learn the truth about her past. Felix's justifications immediately evoke the military's rationalizations for political violence in the dictatorship's wake. The archivist's behavior takes on a particularly insidious quality as he describes the collections of test tubes filled with dried blood, indicative of the state refusal to engage in the process of recovering memory. *El archivista*'s imagined scenario forecasts the dissembling and withholding of information that justified the Grandmothers of the Plaza de Mayo's efforts to procure autonomous testing sites, such as the National Genetic Data Bank, and led the Grandmothers and other nongovernmental organizations to develop their own archives that might help interested Argentines uncover the truth about their identities.

Ana insists on learning the truth about her hereditary self, and when Felix can neither provide documentation that might finally let her know her family history nor return analysis from the blood samples that she has provided, the character must exert considerable willpower to remain in the archive, where she continues to perform resistance to the state's efforts to promote forgetting. The play's protagonist demonstrates the physical and mental effort that one must exert to gain the true sense of self-actualization that comes from certainty about one's identity. Ana becomes part of the practice of reconstructing history and recovering identity as a symbol of the Argentine people.

El archivista concludes with a short scene in which Ana sits alone behind the archive's counter, having successfully seized control of the space and the chair that might bring comfort to her weary body. Felix no longer has a place in the archive, and Levy-Daniel's play script does not provide information about him or his whereabouts. In performance, Ivana Duarte drinks plentifully from what was Felix's water glass, and after quenching her thirst, she begins to voice memories from her childhood. Initially, she vocalizes remembrances about the patio and fishbowl that she mentioned in earlier scenes, but as the action progresses, Ana begins to remember images of brown pants, the sounds of cries, and the actual occurrence of her kidnapping. With the entirety of the archive at her disposal, Ana acquires the means to organize her memories in a way that might allow her to combine both biological knowledge and the repertoire of her lived experience to reach a fuller understanding of herself. Ana may not know her surname yet, but she has limitless access to navigate the archive in search of information that the hegemonic powers would have preferred remain hidden, and the play ends on an optimistic note that the character will be able to find a truer and richer understanding of her past.

El archivista serves as a representation of the plays selected for the 2001 *Teatroxlaidentidad* cycle because of the work's exploration of biological identity and the loss of self-actualization brought about through the dictatorship's kidnappings and subsequent denial of those acts. The script directs spectators to understand the reasoning behind the Grandmothers of the Plaza de Mayo's political efforts to lobby for the legal rights of children of the *desaparecidos*, while also alluding to the organization's creation of alternative archival spaces such as the National Genetic Data Bank and its own small collection of files located at the association's headquarters. However, the play presents a more complex message than *A propósito de la duda* by contributing to a larger conversation about the state's efforts to control postdictatorship memory narratives and human rights organizations' efforts to reconstruct collective memory. Héctor Levy-Daniel writes of the importance that he places on political theatre in his essay "Theatre: Sense and Politics," in which he presses his fellow theatre artists to avoid didacticism if it comes at the expense of testing new aesthetic forms that might open up unorthodox strategies for theatrically engaging in acts of political opposition.[56] *El archivista*'s script provides a model for political theatre and for TxI that supports the Grandmothers' strategies for raising awareness about biological identity.

Unexpected Consequences in Mariana Eva Perez's *Instrucciones para un coleccionista de mariposas*

Argentina's 2001 economic collapse threatened to derail preparations for *Teatroxlaidentidad*'s 2002 festival, but the Grandmothers persevered, expanding their call for new plays to explore identity in broad terms that did not necessarily require engagement with the appropriation of babies during the Process. This new directive allowed playwrights greater flexibility in the works that they could submit, while still allowing the Grandmothers to keep their focus on scripts that advanced memory narratives of genetic selfhood as essential to the development of a unified Argentine body and a shift in transitional justice practices. As a point of fact, the dramatic pieces selected for the 2002 festival did explore identity politics more diversely than did plays of the previous cycle. For example, Araceli Arreche and Amancay Espíndola's *Crónica de las Indias* (*Chronicle of the Indies*) addressed gender identity through the exploration of three women's relationships to each other on the day of a wedding taking place during the Spanish Conquest of the Americas, Gastón Cerana's *El señor Martín* considered class identity through the depiction of a middle-class Argentine youth navigating his way through an elite British prep school, and Norberto Lewin's *El piquete* (*The Picketers*) addressed Argentina's growing unemployment and the changing status of the nation's poor during the financial crisis.

Teatroxlaidentidad's selection process largely mirrored that of the 2001 cycle, with a panel of Argentine theatre luminaries deciding among 225 proposals of self-financed plays that did not exceed a half hour in length.[57] Spatial and financial limitations allowed for the acceptance of only twenty-one plays, but on July 15, 2002, the second edition of the festival opened in a ceremony at Buenos Aires's Teatro Lorange. The cycle's traditional Monday evening 9:00 curtain saw eight separate theatres perform two to three plays interspersed with personal testimonies shared by appropriated children who had been properly identified and other supporters of the Grandmothers' organization. The festival ran in Buenos Aires from July 22 to October 21, but newly formed variations also began to play for audiences in Córdoba and Mar del Plata.

Although the festival's scope expanded, most selections still alluded to the dictatorship's violence and its ramifications for those who carried the weight of biological uncertainty about their parentage. Works staged during the cycle that explored stories of appropriation and the recovery of biological identity include Ariel Barchilón's *El Manchado* (*The Stained*), Cristina Merelli's *Humo de leña verde* (*Smoke of Green Wood*), and Juan Sasiaín's *Una buena afeitada* (*A Good Shave*).

Nevertheless, even within TxI's traditional explorations of heredity and identity, playwrights began to develop new approaches to this narrative model that allowed for richer criticism and conversation about the Grandmothers' belief in biological determinacy. For instance, Mariana Eva Perez's *Instrucciones para un coleccionista de mariposas* (*Instructions for a Butterfly Collector*) explores the playwright's familiarity and personal history with the Grandmothers of the Plaza de Mayo organization to challenge its idealized messaging about the healing powers of restitution. Perez drew from her personal experiences as the daughter of *desaparecidos* and the biological sister of an appropriated child in writing *Instrucciones para un coleccionista de mariposas* at the age of twenty-five. Raised by her grandparents, she worked with the Grandmothers of the Plaza de Mayo from an early age to search for her brother, born in captivity at ESMA. After locating her brother in early 2000 and meeting with him, Perez realized that their relationship did not develop as human rights activists might have imagined. The complicated feelings that arose from her unfulfilled expectations led her to write an open letter to her brother in the Grandmothers' monthly newsletter, to honestly articulate the realities of locating a sibling who rejects his restored biological identity.[58]

Assorted public responses to Perez's letter and the success of the 2001 *Teatroxlaidentidad* festival inspired the author to adapt her biographical account into a one-act play for the 2002 cycle, working with director Leonor Manso. The production uses minimal staging to draw attention toward actress María Figueroa, who performs as María, a fictitious character based loosely on Perez, who recites a missive to her recently identified brother. The scenic design consists of a single black acting cube, a shadow box, and the accoutrements necessary to preserve a large, blue butterfly whose presence informs the play's conceit.

The performance begins as María enters the playing space accompanied by the sound of a ticking clock.[59] After taking the stage, the character presents the dried remains of a large, blue butterfly, which she holds in her hands while acknowledging that she should use forceps. She notes that the animal is her first catch and that she feels compelled to hold it in her bare hands so that it feels real (fig. 2.1). Before delving too deeply into lepidoptery, however, the protagonist abruptly changes subjects, observing that before learning the difficult work of insect preservation, she used to pass her time by holding conversations with an imaginary friend who she pretended was pulled from her mother's arms as a baby before being given to another woman. She names her imagined addressee Rodolfito, and as she describes him, the audience learns that this was the name that would have been given to her brother in memory of their father's deceased friend.[60] In these opening moments, Perez lays out the play's central narrative. María's preservation of the butterfly functions as a symbol for the character's static conception of her missing baby brother. The need to collect and identify insects fulfills a deeper emotional need. At first glance, Perez's script appears as though it will function similarly to other plays of the *Teatroxlaidentidad* festival, depicting the emptiness that a protagonist feels when unable to connect with a disappeared relative and reinforcing the Grandmothers of the Plaza de Mayo's belief in the relationship between biological identity and personal fulfillment.

María continues reciting her letter to Rodolfito, describing memories of experiences and feelings that she believes they would have shared, including walks to school, a local church's cold temperatures, the itch of mosquito

Figure 2.1. María Figueroa displays her newest acquisition in Mariana Eva Perez's *Instrucciones para un coleccionista de mariposas.* FILM STILL FROM RECORDED PRODUCTION STAGED AS PART OF THE 2002 *TEATROXLAIDEN-TIDAD* CYCLE.

bites, tactile sensations of jumping in puddles, the smells and tastes of cream, pastries, and chocolates bought by the grandparents who would have raised them. The character's verbal descriptions do more than represent María's own lived experiences; they communicate bodily experiences that evoke what Alison Landsberg refers to as prosthetic memories in the spectator, provoking an empathetic connection to the character through a performative mechanism that allows the character's memory to be viscerally felt rather than purely experienced as an act of representation.[61] María extends the metaphoric connection between Rodolfito and the butterfly, redirecting her focus on the winged insect and applying a relaxing fluid to the animal so that she can manipulate its wings for mounting and preservation, noting the butterfly's delicate body and voicing her fears that the creature could turn into dust after too much contact with the environment.

Perez's play develops in unexpected directions that resist the ties between biological identity and self-actualization when María begins performing another letter to her brother. In this correspondence, the actress informs the audience that she learned that her brother was still alive when she was nine years old. Instead of becoming a celebratory occasion, however, the revelation creates extraordinary stress. The character speaks of the need to remember every detail about her life and the lives of her parents and grandparents so that she could fill in her brother's knowledge gaps about their shared biological family should they ever meet. In performance, Figueroa's eyes well with tears as she tries to explain the impossibility of recalling details about a beloved puppet lost in a movie theatre or her grandfather buying *dulce de leche*. Additionally, María describes the burden of memory that arises when she realizes that her recollections are no longer hers alone—they are also testimonies that she feels compelled to share with her brother. This monologue echoes feelings that Perez voiced in the open letter to her brother, noting that before finding him, his absence occupied all aspects of her thoughts and daily existence.[62]

The performer articulates the burden of remembering on behalf of absent bodies, but in doing so, the play begins to challenge some of the fundamental assertions that inform the Grandmothers of the Plaza de Mayo's quest to restore the identity of the disappeared. Arditti observes that the human rights organization has advocated for the recovery of all appropriated babies as an inherently necessary act that would help heal the wounds of dictatorship while also fostering a more open and truthful Argentina.[63] María's testimony complicates the Grandmothers' narrative by conveying the emotional toll that accompanies upholding memory in anticipation of finding a lost sibling. Paul Ricoeur notes that the only way to maintain memory is to pass it along from generation to generation.[64] But within the context of postdictatorship Argentina, the task of knowledge transmission creates a strain on those who carry the weight of remembering.

As the letter continues, María resumes describing personal experiences that further depart from the Grandmothers' preferred messaging about genetic identity and self-actualization. The character begins to explain her parents' efforts to resist the dictatorship as members of the Montoneros, a leftist guerrilla organization that attempted to destabilize the dictatorship's rise to power. As she describes hazy memories of her mother and father, María notes that her mother's only flaw was being a member of this political organization, while her father's only failing was sleeping with an arsenal of weapons within arm's reach. She wonders why these two otherwise ideal parents would catch "Montonero fever" when they saw the violence inflicted on their friends and loved ones, including the man in whose memory they named their firstborn son.[65]

Traditionally, human rights organizations have avoided criticizing the Montoneros. According to Argentine historian Ana Laura Pauchulo, this conscientious choice materialized as an effort to prevent the military from demonizing the organization to justify the dictatorship's oppressive measures.[66] Although María does not critique the group's purpose and later expresses fear that her brother's military upbringing will lead him to disrespect her parents' commitment to the insurgent group, the performance's spectators would recognize the playwright's questioning of her parents' participation in the guerrilla group as a transgressive act. María's ambivalence about the act of preserving memories that she should share with her brother becomes more apparent when she turns her attention to the butterfly again and realizes that although the insect looks blue in most lights, it looks black in the performance space. She compares her preserved acquisition to a kaleidoscope. Just as the protagonist's visualizations of a relationship with her sibling begin to grow increasingly complicated, so does her ability to define the butterfly's color.

María's final letter to Rodolfito describes the anguish of waiting for a DNA test that proves their shared genetics, as well as the character's feelings after the test confirms their genetic linkage and the siblings finally meet. As the Grandmothers describe these interactions, ties between appropriated children and their kidnappers collapse as the information about biological identity emerges, but as sociologist Ari Edward Gandsman notes, the process of building relationships between biological relatives takes time, as the individuals who have been recovered must grapple with dual identities and twofold relationships with the members of the family they were born into and the parents who raised them.[67]

María and Rodolfo's reunion depicts the ambiguity of these interactions. The actress describes her initial impression on finding him shooting tequila at a bar, noting the differences that arose between the young man, proud of his military upbringing, and his estranged sister, who holds leftist views, studies political science at the University of Buenos Aires, and listens to punk rock. During their conversation, María's sibling rejects the name Rodolfito, by which she has always identified him. Additionally, the young man refuses to embrace his biological identity, stating that he had provided a blood sample only because he wanted to know if he had a sister, while simultaneously positing that if given the choice, he would choose to live his childhood with the parents who adopted him all over again.

The scene counters the Grandmothers' accounts of reconciliation by indicating that relationships are not forged solely through genetic knowledge but also by establishing emotional ties. Although *Instrucciones para un coleccionista de mariposas* takes some fictive detours, the play's plot does reflect ideas that Perez recalls in the letter published in the Grandmothers' monthly newsletter. In that essay, she describes the process of discovering the limits of her own ability to connect with her brother and her growing comprehension that she must accept her sibling for who he is, rather than as the imagined figure she invented during her childhood.[68] The play continues by noting that the two siblings do not completely dismiss the possibility of establishing a relationship with each other, although María cannot help but feel resentment toward her sibling and the couple who raised him.

The young woman's letter concludes with an expression of uncertainty as to whether she will ever be able to truly know her brother, but she also tempers her critique of the Grandmothers of the Plaza de Mayo's narrative by acknowledging that even if she does not continue to meet with her sibling, she has personally undergone a process of knowing herself better, recognizing that although her reunion experience was painful, acquiring the information was better than living her life with the anguish of uncertainty about her brother's existence.

The final moments of *Instrucciones para un coleccionista de mariposas* find María returning her attention to the butterfly, whose body is now prepared for mounting. As the young collector forces a needle through the desiccated butterfly's thorax and places it in a shadow box, she comments on the insect's beauty while also lamenting its death. As she makes her final adjustments to the butterfly's position inside the glass encasement, María creates a particularly evocative linkage between the animal and her sibling. The woman who once imagined a cheerful reunion with her sibling must now leave her idealized relationship with "Rodolfito" behind, pinned inside a glass case where she can gaze on the memory of what might have been while still acknowledging that her yearnings for restitution must remain locked away. As the stage lights fade to black, the sound of a ticking clock emerges from the theatre's speakers, and the audience leaves with an understanding that idealizing the past and reuniting with an appropriated relative do not ease the burden of carrying memory narratives in the present.

The Grandmothers of the Plaza de Mayo have tirelessly advanced the cause of human rights in Argentina by expressing the need for every citizen to know his or her biological identity as an effort to heal the nation's remaining postdictatorship wounds. As part of this effort, the organization has demonized the appropriators who removed babies from the nation's detention camps. Their labor has shaped public memory narratives and led to the passage of transitional justice measures that have granted additional rights to Argentina's growing population and enabled new forensic technologies to confirm genetic identity. In spite of these efforts, the Grandmothers' ambitions occasionally fail to account for the psychological and emotional anguish that comes from decades spent searching for a loved one who may never be found. Additionally, the association's public discourse does not acknowledge the possibility that an individual might not want to build relationships with blood relatives after a matching DNA test. In Grisby Ogas Puga's essay on *Teatroxlaidentidad*, the scholar notes that unlike the instructions that a butterfly collector may follow to properly mount the insect in a display case, the family involved in recovering a disappeared youth does not receive proper training in bringing a relationship to resolution.[69] However, while Ogas Puga's essay suggests that the play speaks to the festival's lack of clarity in creating coherent political messaging, I would posit that the work instead highlights the frictions within the Grandmothers' idealized memory narratives and their fervent appropriation of the language of blood and genetics.

The organization has continued to struggle with this messaging in recent years, most notably in the case of Marcela and Felipe Noble Herrera, the adopted children of media magnate Ernestina Herrera de Noble. In 2001, the Grandmothers suggested that the children were appropriated from *desaparecidos* and given to Ernestina in exchange for favorable media coverage of the dictatorship. After a decade-long struggle over DNA testing, results revealed that Marcela and Felipe were not biologically linked to any of the disappeared, but the legal struggles and political battles surrounding the case undermined the family's right to privacy and the siblings' ability to choose their own familial identities. Similarly, Mariana Eva Perez's lived experiences speak to the uneasy tension in using genetics as the dominant force in constructing familial identity.

Instrucciones created significant conflicts between Perez and the organization, and in the fallout from the original production, the playwright was expelled by the organization. Nevertheless, Perez's relationship with the Grandmothers from childhood to adulthood enabled her to write about the recovery of her sibling in a play that ends with her own enriched self-awareness, even if the process of acquiring that knowledge created an unnecessary rupture between the playwright and the organization that had supported her throughout her youth. *Instrucciones para un coleccionista de mariposas* refrains from the good and evil dualism found in many *Teatroxlaidentidad* plays and instead creates a rich and viscerally felt portrayal of the questions and emotions that accompany recouping the past.

Sponsorship, Expansion, and Institutionalization

Teatroxlaidentidad's 2002 cycle marked a turning point in the festival's scope and ambitions. In the festival's initial years, the performances ran as self-financed spectacles supported by volunteer labor from the creators who proposed them, logistical assistance from the Grandmothers of the Plaza de Mayo, and a handful of donations from theatre spectators, usually obtained by passing around a hat postperformance to encourage munificence. Additionally, TxI focused on presenting work in Buenos Aires, where theatre artists have long found a supportive audience for political theatre. As the Argentine economy began to stabilize following the economic crisis, the 2003 festival deviated from producing a play cycle that repeated the patterns established in 2001 and 2002. Instead, the TxI board enacted a plan to increase the geographic scope of the performances by hosting itinerant shows in Buenos Aires's provinces. In light of these changes, the organization opted to forgo its annual new play solicitation to focus on known quantities that could travel easily. The 2003 cycle staged eleven plays from the 2001 and 2002 cycle, enacted in various theatres across Córdoba, Tucumán, and other provinces from June 8 to July 7. This decision expanded the Grandmothers' cultural reach while introducing several of *Teatroxlaidentidad*'s playwrights to new audiences.

In 2004, the organization journeyed internationally, staging plays in Barcelona and Madrid, where more than 150 artists presented twelve scripts from previous cycles of the festival and eight theatrical pieces developed in workshops. By 2005, the festival began to transition into hosting developmental projects in multiple cities across Argentina while simultaneously expanding its outward reach into the United States by presenting a series of plays at the University of Connecticut. As the organization's ambitions enlarged, TxI began to secure funding from government sources, drawing a subsidy from the city of Buenos Aires to build a new headquarters and additional monies to stage the 2004 cycle.

Argentine theatre scholar María Luisa Diz claims that the board's willingness to seek and secure public funding from 2003 onward marks a shift for the play cycle in which the festival nationalized, favoring approaches to storytelling and accounts of violence and state oppression that worked in conjunction with the political efforts of newly elected president Néstor Kirchner, whose alignment with human rights organizations marked a distinct shift from the Menem administration.[70] During the early years of the Kirchner administration, numerous theatres received financial resources and institutional support from the National Theatre Institute, Buenos Aires's *Proteatro* subsidies, and the Theatre Council for the Provinces of Buenos Aires.

In exchange for these funds, however, the state has taken a greater interest in theatrical endeavors, demanding a higher degree of professionalism and the formation of administrative structures. These organizational changes began to manifest in the *Teatroxlaidentidad* festival; in the first two iterations, artistic director Daniel Fanego had personally signed authorization on all major decisions, but now the administration's executive committee began to sign directives. Diz reads this shift as reflective of the theatre's institutionalization.[71] Nevertheless, as the festival transitions into its second decade, the work produced continues to fulfill the Grandmothers' political goals and aspirations while also answering to other stakeholders, whose demands may grow louder as they contribute a growing pool of resources to the foundation.

Argentina's status as a leader in enacting transitional justice strategies that appealed to multifaceted constituencies remained in place through the end of the twentieth century. Following Scilingo's confession, human rights activists engaged in acts of cultural production and performance designed to shift public sentiment away from cynicism and toward the government's policies of amnesty and forgetting. Instead, they proposed collaboration with human rights organizations and other NGOs that wished to transform Argentina's transitional justice policies at their core. The staging of cultural events, which include the Grandmothers' *Teatroxlaidentidad* collaborations, invited citizens to actively educate themselves through artistic engagement and to participate in resistance to policies of impunity. As a result, the demand for newly articulated memory narratives grounded in relitigation efforts and requests for increased articulations of personal freedoms helped bring about constitutional changes that incorporated international law, the use of international trials to undermine Argentina's domestic amnesty policies, and the creation of newly formed individual rights, such as the right of forgetting.

In sum, Argentina began the process of accepting culpability for the Process's atrocities. These legislative and discursive shifts enabled the nation to move into the next phase of its postdictatorship transitional justice process, with efforts to relitigate those unpunished by the dictatorship, make meaningful symbolic and commemorative reparations for those families afflicted by the Process, and create commemorative spaces designed to remind future generations of Argentines about the dictatorship's horror while serving as instructive reminders of how such brutality could flourish in hopes that state-sanctioned violence would never occur again.

3

Reparation, Commemoration, and Memory
Construction in the Postdictatorship Generation

DESPITE HIGHLY ORGANIZED EFFORTS to shape transitional justice policies, occasionally significant changes emerge from what appears to be little more than chaos or random happenstance. In Lola Arias's seminal play *Mi vida después* (2009), a sixty-year-old turtle appears onstage. Actor Blas Arrese Igor explains that the turtle belonged to his father and that both father and turtle were born sixty years ago. As Igor imagines a world in which the turtle and his father live into their hundreds, he notes that the hard-shelled creature has had several near-death experiences, including surviving a flood, being run over by a car, and taking numerous falls. He states that his mother, who is an astrologer, believes that turtles can predict the future, and he writes the words "yes" and "no" on the floor. Another member of the cast asks whether Argentina will have a revolution in its future. As the video camera captures the turtle on the projection screen, it moves toward "yes" or "no," depending on the night.[1] The reptile cannot be manipulated into giving the desired prediction. Instead, this uncontrolled prognostication of what the future may hold speaks to the unforeseen consequences of political change. Although performers and spectators can be mindful of strategies for constructing memory and aware of the ways archival materials can be manipulated, it is impossible to know how this knowledge might alter the future.

Similarly, the years following Menem's 1995 presidential reelection saw economic disarray devolve into a series of short-term presidential administrations whose duration ranged from one week to two years. After working to eradicate national debt in his first term, Menem began to reduce taxes in an effort to win provincial support during his second term. However, budgetary shortfalls in addition to economic crises in Russia, Mexico, and other Latin American countries negatively affected Argentina's GDP. The nation's fiscal troubles created popular unrest, leading to the 1999 election of opposition party leader Fernando de la Rúa. The new president attempted to form a political coalition to create immediate and long-term solutions to the nation's economic troubles. However, de la Rúa inherited a financial calamity that could not be fixed through stopgap measures, and his alliance fractured as a result of political infighting, a government bribery scandal, and public perception that austerity measures were not leading to a visible fiscal recovery. De la Rúa resigned in 2001 amid riots in the streets of Buenos Aires and historically low approval ratings.

Adolfo Rodriguez Saá, appointed interim president by Argentina's legislature, proposed a new currency before announcing a national debt default. Politicians and the national public alike did not take kindly to these proposals from the interim president, and after a week in office, Rodriguez Saá was replaced by Eduardo Camaño, who held office for just two days before Argentina's legislative committee appointed Eduardo Duhalde to the presidency in January 2002. Duhalde served as president for a year but decided not to run for a full term in office during Argentina's officially scheduled 2003 elections. Throughout this precarious period in Argentina's history, national legislators engaged primarily in efforts to resolve the country's financial crisis, paying little heed to the politics of human rights.

In 2003, however, Néstor Kirchner, little-known governor of Argentina's Santa Cruz province, won election to the presidency. During his term (2003–7) and the subsequent terms of his wife Cristina Fernández de Kirchner (2007–15), the politicians used the platform of their tandem presidencies to institute a series of legislative and judicial reforms, as well as restitutive transitional justice policies that promoted accountability for dictatorial violence and commemoration of the disappeared. First, Néstor Kirchner positioned himself as an ally of human rights activists, domestically and abroad. Second, he enacted executive orders and other political measures to advance highly visible human rights measures that would revoke previous administrations' impunity policies. Finally, he and Cristina developed strategies for restitution and commemoration that brought greater awareness of efforts to remember the disappeared in order to accept nationwide culpability for the state's actions during the 1970s and 1980s.

One of Kirchner's first acts in office was to meet with members of the human rights community in Argentina, including leaders of the Grandmothers and Mothers of the Plaza de Mayo, as well as H.I.J.O.S. In an interview conducted by Francesca Lessa, a member of the Mothers recalled the president's empathetic words to the gatherers, as Kirchner reflected on the disappearances of several of his friends, before recounting his own brief period of detention.[2] Rather than use these experiences as a call to forgiveness, as Menem did, Kirchner signaled that he would bring about a reversal of Argentina's transitional justice policies to ensure that the perpetrators of violence did not go unpunished. The president's efforts to align himself with organizations opposed to political violence also manifested in public statements performed on the global stage. On September 25, 2003, Néstor Kirchner delivered an address to the United Nations General Assembly, stating:

> The defense of human rights occupies a central place in the new agenda of the Argentine Republic. We are the children of the mothers and grandmothers of the Plaza de Mayo, and we therefore insist on permanently supporting the strengthening of the system for the protection of human rights and the trial and conviction of those who violate them. All of this is based on the overarching view that respect for persons and their dignity arises out of principles preceding the development of law, whose origins can be traced to the beginnings of human history. Respecting diversity and pluralism and relentlessly fighting impunity have been unwavering principles of our country ever since the tragedy of recent decades.[3]

The president continued to affiliate himself with families of the disappeared in speeches delivered across Argentina and the world, repeatedly referring to the membership of these organizations as his brothers, sisters, mothers, and grandmothers.

Kirchner also used his executive authority to enact changes to military hierarchy, firing the joint chiefs of staff and forcing the resignations of twenty-seven army generals, thirteen navy admirals, twelve air force brigadier generals, and several captains of the federal police. To contextualize the significance of these changes, these numbers equate to nearly three-fourths of all the nation's generals and half of the navy and armed forces' senior leadership. In their place, the president promoted several young officers who had not begun their service during the years of dictatorship, thus severing ties between his administration and the military sympathizers who threatened the Alfonsín and Menem presidencies.

Additionally, Kirchner asked Congress to impeach several Supreme Court justices on grounds of political corruption. The commander in chief particularly targeted justices added during Carlos Menem's practice of court stacking at the start of his administration. Within a year, five of the nation's justices had resigned and were replaced with adjudicators who signaled support for overturning policies that granted military officers and their subordinates amnesty. These maneuvers were followed by the advancement of judicial actions that nullified the impunity measures passed by previous administrations. In 2003, Kirchner reversed Argentina's nonextradition policies for all crimes against humanity, ordering cooperation with international extradition requests for those officers not facing charges in Argentina. In 2004, federal judges struck down the dictatorship-era pardons issued by Menem, declaring that crimes against humanity are not pardonable by presidential decree.

Finally, in July 2005, the Argentine Supreme Court voted to overturn the Due Obedience and Full Stop Laws by a margin of seven to one, with one abstention, in a sweeping statement that drew on international humanitarian and war crime laws to declare Alfonsín's legislation unconstitutional. At the present moment, prosecutions for dictatorial-related crimes are not a regular occurrence throughout Argentina, but at the end of Cristina Kirchner's presidency in December 2015, nearly two thousand individuals had been accused of crimes against humanity, and several hundred had been condemned to jail sentences or house arrest. Additionally, several extradited military figures had been convicted of crimes and sentenced to prison in Europe.

The final phase of Kirchner's efforts to transform transitional justice policy was the enactment of several symbolic acts of reparation and commemoration designed to memorialize the Process's victims. On March 24, 2004, the twenty-eighth anniversary of the coup that began the dictatorship, the president, standing alongside his newly appointed army commander and several members of his cabinet, ordered that the National War College remove the portraits of dictators Jorge Videla and Reynaldo Bignone from the institution's walls. That same day, Kirchner held a ceremony announcing ESMA's conversion into a memory museum, where Argentina's leader asked the families of the disappeared for forgiveness on behalf of the nation for its silence in the years following the dictatorship. Today the former Naval Mechanics School is divided into commemorative spaces run by several human rights organizations, including the Founding Line of the Mothers of the Plaza de Mayo and H.I.J.O.S., and also serves as the primary site for Argentina's National Archive of Memory.[4] This repository holds government documents connected to the years of dictatorship in addition to oral testimonies from the victims of political repression and families of the disappeared.

Before the end of his term, Kirchner converted several other detention centers into commemorative spaces operating with support from human rights organizations, including Buenos Aires's Club Atlético, El Olimpo, and Automotores Orletti, in addition to sites in Córdoba, Chaco, and other cities throughout the nation. Neighborhoods in Buenos Aires and elsewhere also marked several former centers with *baldosas*, ceramic tiles placed on the grounds of former torture sites, designating the unassuming locations as sites of memory. In the president's final year in office, Kirchner unveiled the Monument to the Victims of State Terrorism at the Parque de la Memoria, a sculpture park and memorial along the banks of the Río de la Plata designed to serve as a monument to the *desaparecidos* and the legacy of memory.

During her terms in office, Cristina Fernández de Kirchner continued to advocate on behalf of human rights activists and enacted policies that would further reduce the likelihood of political impunity for perpetrators of state-enacted violence. The president increased the number of judges committed to prosecuting dictatorial-related crimes, erected additional monuments to the victims of the Process's violence across Argentina, mandated DNA testing in all kidnapping-related cases, ordered the declassification of political and military documents written during the dictatorship, and in May 2010, worked with Argentina's Chamber of Deputies to produce a resolution declaring efforts to pursue truth and justice an absolute right.[5]

Collectively, the two presidents admitted the state's culpability for the dictatorship's crimes to unify public opinion on the need to nullify the pardons and restrictions on justice passed by previous administrations. The end result of these actions is an increased recognition of the need to remember the disappeared, as evidenced by a July 2012 survey conducted by Argentine newspaper *Página 12*, in which 83 percent of respondents affirmed that the violence enacted during the Process qualified as an act of genocide, while nearly 90 percent supported the conviction of military officers, police, and even civilians who aided and abetted the dictatorship.[6]

Nevertheless, the Kirchners' advancement of transitional justice policies has not gone without criticism. Several former military officers who remain supportive of the dictatorship have argued that current transitional justice policies are unnecessarily vindictive and self-serving. Former president Carlos Menem has echoed this position. Meanwhile, human rights activists have questioned whether the presidents' commitments to human rights were genuine. Francesca Lessa's monograph on transitional justice practices in Argentina includes interviews with politician Graciela Fernández Meijide and academics Vicente Palermo and Daniel Lvovich, who observe that the Kirchners did not actively engage in challenging the Menem administration's transitional justice policies before assuming the presidency, nor did Néstor collaborate with activists while holding office in Santa Cruz.[7]

Additionally, the development of commemorative sites such as ESMA have drawn mixed reactions from human rights organizations. The Association of the Mothers of the Plaza de Mayo and H.I.J.O.S. both posit that the creation of memorials to reflect on the disappearances marks the *desaparecidos* as dead, whereas the organizations wish to frame their relatives as alive in the public memory to prevent their causes from being consigned to history. ESMA was scheduled for destruction before Kirchner's intervention, and many feel that the space should have been demolished. Likewise, Andreas Huyssen observes that the development of the Parque de la Memoria has provoked debate over its proximity to ESMA and resistance from those who continue to advocate for national policies of forgetting.[8] These reactions serve as a reminder that although the Kirchners enabled many advances in Argentina's transitional justice policies, the memory narratives that prompted these actions are not homogenous, and the debate over Argentina's memory politics continues to provoke passionate reactions from human rights activists and advocates for impunity.

Staging the Self in the Argentine Theatre

Although changes in Argentina's presidency, military, and judiciary transformed the nation's transitional justice policies from practices of impunity to a pursuit of justice and an acknowledgment of governmental wrongdoing on behalf of the state's victims of oppression, Buenos Aires theatre artists continued to create memory narratives designed to engage audiences in the politics of the postdictatorship. The nature of this discourse shifted, however, from raising awareness of identity and legal rights to projects designed to reconstruct the post-Process generation's understanding of their own self-reflective and subjective accounts of history and the ways that archival materials have informed those understandings.

Several theatrical performances staged during the Kirchner administrations confronted the realities of a generation of Argentines who grew up as small children under the dictatorship and were affected by the Process regardless of their family's connection to the disappeared or their understanding of the dictatorship during the late 1970s and early 1980s. Additionally, numerous plays and productions that did not specifically reference the dictatorship touch on the process of self-documenting to prevent the possibility of disappearing without leaving critical information about the self behind for future generations. Sociologist Gabriel Gatti writes that the generation of Argentines born during and immediately after the years of dictatorship experienced an erasure of their pasts that he refers to as a "catastrophe of meaning."[9] The Argentine public's inability to address the dictatorship in a unified way prior to the Kirchner administration created a memory void that young theatre makers navigated through the creation of cultural productions that consciously engage with the past to document lived experiences and speak to the construction of personal and collective memories for the future.

With the political stakes lessened from the heated years of the Menem administration and the early years of the *Teatroxlaidentidad* festival, the theatre could move away from narratives that advanced the pursuit of new transitional justice policies and venture toward an aesthetically focused conversation about theatrical strategies for representing memory and the self. During the Kirchner administrations, numerous productions explored the act of recording and preserving as a tactic for averting the possibility of future memory gaps by developing documentary performances, installations, or plays grounded in the aesthetics of constructing memory.

Buenos Aires–based theatre scholar Oscar Cornago posits that Argentine cultural production across theatre, television, film, and literature has emerged from an effort to mark the presence of the real in a time when formations of the self were being debated and contested in the nation's politics.[10] For example, Viviana Tellas is perhaps the most renowned of Buenos Aires's twenty-first-century documentary theater artists. Much of her career has explored the theatricality of Argentines' quotidian experiences and their relationship to history. In 2002, Tellas devised a series of plays known as *Proyecto Archivo* (*The Archive Project*). These performances, which were staged from 2002 to 2008, empower people without a performance background—including three philosophy professors, her mother and aunts, and a local disc jockey—to narrate performances based on their daily realities to create a richer understanding of the lives they lead. In an interview with Argentine literary critic Alan Pauls, Tellas contends that "every person has, and is, an archive: a reserve of experiences, knowledge, text and images," and that to address the possibility of extinction for ways of life, the productions seek to preserve some trace of the present.[11] The series allows the playwright-director to continue finding ways Argentine citizens can draw on their own archive to create performance.

Other recent documentary pieces include Cecilia Szperling's *Confesionario* (*Confessional*) (2004–present), in which public figures confess past transgressions onstage and in recorded performances using personal diaries, e-mails, and other artifacts to share their stories. The goal of each performance is to convey the impression that the person speaking has added a new revelation about his or her personal life into the public record to alter collective perception. Similarly, Fernando Rubio's *Hablar. La memoria del mundo* (*Talk. The Memory of the World*) (2007) saw the playwright create a video installation in which he asked more than a hundred individuals, many of whom were fellow theatre artists, politicians, and human rights activists, to each remember the happiest moment of his or her life and then analyze what it was about that particular recollection that created such joy. The work, which has been presented in Buenos Aires and Madrid, encourages audiences to hear both famous and unknown Argentines testify to their happiness and be seen as united with each other in their shared ability to articulate individual instances of pleasure.

In addition to documentary performances that illustrate the realities of living Argentines, the theatre also began to use personal artifacts, including clothes, photographs, and other belongings, in conjunction with multimedia technologies to devise performances that explore the construction of memory, combining text and bodies with what Carol Martin refers to as "the technological postmodern" to create contemporary documentary theatre.[12] Examples of these performances include Jorge Goldenberg's *Fotos de infancia* (*Photos of Infancy*), written in 2005, which displays the childhood photos of seven actors in a devised performance based on improvisations inspired by the images. Playwright Fernando Rubio has broached the relationship between memory and personal artifacts in his 2011 installation piece *Pueden dejar lo que quieran* (*You Can Leave What You Like*). In this project, thousands of varied garments have notecards affixed that share stories of the fictive characters who wore the clothes to tell the story of a person whose family died in a car accident and how he uses their clothing to retain memories of those he lost and build new connections to the outside world.

Martin's writing about documentary theatre serves as an interesting launching pad for a discussion about the creation of memory narratives grounded in reconstructing lived experiences of the postdictatorship generation. Documentary theatre proposes that everything presented is part of a person's archive; however, the documentary curates the archive, which raises the question of how such productions select materials for performance. For Martin, these acts of theatre making accentuate certain kinds of memories and submerge others, thereby having the power to change the way audiences think when watching performances. However, the act of curating subjective personal experiences, particularly personal testimonies related to the dictatorship, in contemporary documentary performances has drawn some concern from scholars uneasy about the ways such acts construct memory narratives. For instance, Beatriz Sarlo's *Tiempo pasado* (*Time Past*) serves as one of the most significant works of memory studies written since the nation's return to democracy. Sarlo argues that Argentine cultural production about the dictatorship and memory has undergone a "subjective turn" in which individual and personal narratives are granted legitimacy over other narrative forms that can help Argentines understand the past in terms of its own historical moment.[13] The danger of such actions, according to Sarlo, is that "memory colonizes the past and organizes it on the basis of concepts and emotions of the present."[14]

The philosopher and theorist takes on an acerbic tone in implying that first-person narratives are inherently unreliable, but through a close reading of the four plays addressed in this chapter, I intend to counter her essentialist position by noting how self-reflective personal testimonies combine with archival materials to create memory narratives whose ambitions reach beyond sharing personal experiences and instead speak to a larger cultural need to document the self, while recognizing the limits of representation. Moreover, I propose that many of these works, which were coproduced with European theatres and brought to the continent to stage at international festivals for predominantly Western audiences, positioned Argentina as a global leader in transitional justice practices. The plays demonstrate the ways Argentine citizens participate in new national strategies of commemoration and engagement with the past that would prevent the possibility of future disappearances. If the dramatic works in chapter 1 are to be read as resistance to transitional justice policies enacted by the Menem administration, the productions featured in this chapter reflect the artists' and their audience's favorable responses to the changes in executive, legislative, and judicial policy enacted under Néstor and Cristina Kirchner's presidencies.

The plays chronicled here use elements of documentary theatre making, even if the performances are not always "real," to address the ways Argentines are reconciling past and present through performance. This group of artists' efforts to prevent the memory voids of Argentina's past from continuing into the present are clearly evident in the four plays whose analyses follow: Damiana Poggi and Virginia Jáuregui's *170 explosiones por segundo*, Lola Arias's *Mi vida después*, Federico León's *Yo en el futuro*, and Mariano Pensotti's *El pasado es un animal grotesco*. The first two plays document the lived experiences of the postdictatorship generation and their efforts to understand the previous generation; the other two works draw from the techniques of documentary theatre performances to consider the construction of memory through fictive narratives.

Subjective Testimonies in Damiana Poggi and Virginia Jáuregui's *170 explosiones por segundo*

Introduced through mutual acquaintances, Damiana Poggi and Virginia Jáuregui did not immediately realize their joint connection to the dictatorship. The two actresses met as adults, and in the process of establishing their friendship, the duo realized that they shared many similarities. Most notably, both had fathers who had fought for the People's Revolutionary Army in resistance to the dictatorship and were subsequently detained. However, the budding friends concealed this information from each other for several months, until they had become closer. On realizing that they had shared many intimate details about their lives before revealing this essential part of their biographies, Poggi and Jáuregui decided to write about their experiences for the 2010 *Teatroxlaidentidad* festival.

In an interview with scholar Anna White-Nockleby, Poggi noted that the performers initially constructed their script following the typical didactic formula that traditionally signified a TxI production.[15] The duo performed an original draft of the script, titled *Bajo las nubes de polvo de la mañana es imposible visualizar un ciervo dorado* (*Under the Dust Clouds of Morning It Is Impossible to Visualize a Golden Deer*). However, as their play developed, the twenty-five-year-old writers moved away from creating a play representing an explicit political message with a binary relationship between good and evil to devise a more abstract script that engaged in the process of reconstructing childhood recollections using the hindsight of dictatorial awareness and the opacity of memory in the postdictatorship generation. As a result, their 2011 revision of *Bajo las nubes*, retitled *170 explosiones por segundo* (*170 Explosions per Second*) functions as an ideal segue from the memory narratives of advocacy and justice that existed under Menem's presidency to the theatrical explorations of documentary-inspired memory construction during the Kirchner administration.

With little more than the actors' bodies, *170 explosiones por segundo* attempts to reconstruct Poggi's and Jáuregui's childhood memories of their fathers to understand how their lives were shaped by a dictatorship that concluded before they were born. Director Andrés Binetti positions the actors at the center of the El Portón de Sánchez's stage, enabling his performers to enact the accounts of their upbringing without particular regard for elaborate scenography or blocking.[16] Aside from an onstage fan and a keyboard, no other properties or set pieces are used in the production. The actresses are joined by two other figures, a musician with no lines and a character listed as the Rapporteur, who attempts to make sense of the characters' memories. It is this organizational figure who begins the play with an address to the audience that emphasizes the theatre's lighting, positing that the theatre's illuminations direct the audience's attention no matter how much spectators might try to resist.[17]

Throughout the play, the Rapporteur continues to present himself at a remove from the performance, highlighting the efforts that the cast and crew make to build this production of recountal, raising skeptical questions about small details in Poggi's and Jáuregui's childhood remembrances so as to ensure greater accuracy, and emphasizing the hidden elements of the stage machinery as part of his explicit need to "disassemble and reassemble everything" to understand precisely how this theatrical construction of personal memories works.[18] In a theatrical production filled with ambiguity and reflexivity, this character attempts to anchor himself in a discursive strategy that resists engaging with what Michael Lazzara refers to as the "tenuousness and multiplicity of truth" that is part of contemporary documentary performance.[19]

While the rapporteur attempts to analyze and organize the narrative as a way of understanding the characters' experiences, Poggi and Jáuregui (fig. 3.1) have fully embraced metanarrative strategies that reveal the gaps and fissures in their process of recollecting the past. Poggi describes learning about her father's imprisonment as a child and expresses a desire to communicate her memories publicly without resorting to cliché. Her strategy involves "ruminating" on the experience so that her memories do not fall victim to homogenization or kitsch.[20] But as the performer shares her recollections with the audience, she reveals the challenge of making memories legible in a way that allows spectators to understand the past in a meaningful way by digressing from stating the facts of her father's disappearance to recounting her own subjective memories of growing up without a father. Poggi and Jáuregui begin to recall the exact circumstances of the moments when their mothers told them that their fathers were in jail. Both girls were told that they needed to remain silent about the information to avoid bringing shame to the family.[21]

From this shared admission of past experiences, the women transition through stream of consciousness to discussing their childhood cars, which leads to a further deviation away from the narrative of Poggi's father's detention so that the performers can banter about their similar childhoods and Jáuregui's recollections of Bariloche and other parts of southern Argentina. Poggi and Jáuregui's approach to the play evokes Proust's "involuntary memory," in which memory evades the consciousness's supervision

Figure 3.1. Virginia Jáuregui and Damiana Poggi share memories of their childhood on a largely empty stage in *170 explosiones por segundo*. COURTESY OF ALEJANDRA PÍA NICOLOSI.

in a way that blurs past experiences to provoke new perspectives.[22] The actresses may not be able to create a historically accurate representation of the facts of their fathers' disappearances, but the two women can construct a subjective memory of their pasts that can be archived and documented through the play's performance.

Yet this opening interaction also seems to essentialize the actors' experiences. White-Nockleby asserts that one of the play's strategies is to present the characters as a "doubling of the self" designed to create a communicative shorthand between the actresses.[23] But doing so creates the appearance that they have constructed similar narratives partially because of their lived experiences and because they have been conditioned to share their testimonies through forms of mass media that empty discourses of their complexities. The difficulties of creating distinctions between the characters' narratives of postdictatorship memory are further brought to bear when Jáuregui speaks of traveling from Buenos Aires to Bariloche as a child. Poggi listens to this experience, but when she interrupts Jáuregui to talk about what she remembers of the southern Argentina city, she immediately begins by listing familiar nouns that are merely popular locations, such as Bariloche's civic center, the boutique-laden Mitre Street, and the city's exclusive Llao Llao resort, before realizing that they are not actual memories, nor are they reflective of the character's childhood in any meaningful way. Her references replace narration with totems, which remind spectators that even personal memories are hypermediated and derived from a combination of lived experiences and cultural referents.

Nevertheless, efforts to recall specific moments of the actors' biographies speak to the subjective and fictitious process of constructing memory. In a later scene, Virginia Jáuregui recalls her father's wake, held when she was still an infant. She speaks in great detail about the circumstances of her father's 1985 death, which she describes as occurring just after the restoration of democracy, remembering that he proclaimed, "I'm so happy, I could die" before passing away a week later.[24] Additionally, Jáuregui shares details about the fellow People's Revolutionary Army (ERP) members who attended the vigil and subsequent funeral, the police presence, and her mother's demeanor, while noting that she was in a crib at the time. As *Página 12* reviewer Mariela Daniela Yaccar points out, Virginia presents these stories as though she consciously remembers them, even though she was an infant when her father died.[25] The actress's conflation of time and evocation of experiences that she could not possibly have recalled functions as an attempt to stretch her own memory, yet for the play's spectators, the tales call attention to memory's subjectivity, evoking what Paul Ricoeur refers to as the "imaginative character" of memory that is necessary for interpreting the past.[26] I would add that this need for expression is particularly crucial for generations born in the aftermath of genocide and mass trauma, whose histories are filled with gaps and lacunae.

As the play proceeds, both characters summon additional memories from their childhood while reflecting on how their efforts to avoid speaking about their fathers' histories have inflected those moments. Through the play's fragmentary process of sharing recollections, Poggi and Jáuregui build a personal archive grounded in the mundane realities of failed relationships, romantic pursuits that end because of a lack of understanding, and other smaller nuisances such as Virginia's inability to explain why she roots for a particular soccer team or Damiana's difficulty participating in sensory recall exercises in her Stanislavski-based acting classes. At stake for the actresses is a sense of ownership over the memories and identities necessary to make meaning of the past and communicate it effectively into the future.

Moreover, as *170 explosiones por segundo* moves toward its conclusion, Damiana Poggi does uncover one memory that prevents her past from becoming an irrevocable loss. Damiana reminisces about her father teaching her about the mechanics of a car's engine. For nearly the final quarter of the play, Poggi, Jáuregui, and the Rapporteur label, identify, and explain the varied parts and functions of a motor, from the cylinders to the crankshaft, and articulate how those parts communicate with the rest of the automobile.[27] Damiana recognizes that this memory, which she received in full from her father, can eventually be passed along to her offspring as advice given to them from their grandfather and also incorporated into this performance, in which it becomes part of the strategy for self-archiving that Poggi and Jáuregui employ.

Documenting the Postdictatorship Generation and the Malleable Archive in Lola Arias's *Mi vida después*

Lola Arias is one of Argentina's most acclaimed and internationally renowned theatre artists. Her work as a playwright, director, poet, songwriter, and deviser of several installations and performance pieces has been translated into several languages, and she has toured her creations throughout festivals in Europe and the Americas. Like Vivi Tellas, Arias has expressed a fascination with theatricalized strategies for archiving the self. Rather than simply staging everyday life, however, she has used her theatre to serve as a testing ground to push the boundaries between reality and fiction.

Paola Hernández writes of the complexities in Arias's work and how the artist's career has been built on staging reality within the framework of theatrical fiction, using traditional and unorthodox performance sites to question the relationship between documented facts and the notion of truth.[28] An example of this theatrical labor can be found in Arias's 2010 installation, *Mucamas* (*Maids*), a performance piece in which Arias invited individuals into hotel rooms where they considered a housekeeping staff's daily labors and personal rituals. Throughout the performance, the audience interacted with objects left in the rooms, listened to recordings on headphones and the room's television set, and examined dozens of images and texts that marked the realities of these often invisible workers. The piece was part of the *Ciudades Paralelas* (*Parallel Cities*) project, in which Arias and her colleague Stefan Kaegi created a series of interventions into the lives of day laborers to make spectators aware of their presence.

Arias followed up this project with a series of curated performances staged from 2012 to 2014 titled *Mis Documentos* (*My Documents*), in which the playwright invited artists and scholars to present a performative lecture about a personal experience that has stayed with them and informed their work. The varied talks range from discussions about the difficulties of obtaining a visa for international travel to the acquisition of rare books. In both of these projects, the playwright stretches the boundaries of documentary theatre outside of traditional theatrical spaces, while still creating engaging and entertaining spectacles.

Arias's most famous production, however, is her 2009 staging of the devised performance piece *Mi vida después* (*My Life After*). Initially conceived as part of Vivi Tellas's Biodramas project, the play developed into its own event removed from that series when Tellas resigned from the Teatro Sarmiento to pursue other creative opportunities. After running in Buenos Aires at the Sarmiento, the production toured extensively across Europe and the Americas, playing in Germany, Spain, Mexico, Brazil, Chile, France, the United Kingdom, Slovenia, the Czech Republic, Greece, and Hungary. Like many of Tellas's documentary-inspired Biodramas, *Mi vida después* presents the lived experiences of Argentines, but unlike many of the pieces staged as part of that series, the production used real

Figure 3.2. Cast members of Lola Arias's *Mi vida después* sort through clothing in a publicity photo taken before the company's international tour. PHOTO BY LORENA FERNÁNDEZ. COURTESY OF LOLA ARIAS.

citizens telling their stories onstage, rather than hiring actors to perform other people's narratives (fig. 3.2). Additionally, Arias's piece expanded on the Biodramas form by presenting a performance framed by multiple protagonists who share diverse viewpoints rather than featuring a singular protagonist or narrative.

Mi vida después depicts the remembrances of six actors born between the years 1972 and 1983 who reconstruct their parents' lives with the aid of various personal artifacts. The cast comprises individuals from a variety of backgrounds, including the descendants of parents who were detained or murdered by the Argentine military and others whose families were wholly unaffected. Additionally, the play features the stories of children whose parents supported the dictatorship's politics and others whose relatives violently resisted. The actors share their recollections of the mechanics, intellectuals, priests, and spies who raised them to determine how the retention of their parents' memories and personal belongings has informed their perceptions of past, present, and future so that they could take agency over their own archives.

Given the international acclaim and popularity of *Mi vida después*, several contemporary Argentine performance scholars have written about the work. The play has been read as an extension of documentary theatre techniques employed by Erwin Piscator and Peter Weiss, an example of the Argentine theatre's embrace of postmodernist techniques, a queer form of resistance to postdictatorship conversations centered on familial relationships, and a model of intergenerational transmissions of memory.[29] These analyses have ranged from theatrical reconstructions to explorations that use the play to elucidate theoretical concerns. Additionally, the works largely focus on spectator reception in Buenos Aires, if they give thought to audience at all. Although I admire all these essays and reference my colleagues throughout this section, my own contribution to critical discourse on Arias's play lies in providing a close reading of production, while giving significant consideration to the play's reception outside Buenos Aires, particularly in the European and American theatres, where I believe that the play has served as a performance that positions Argentina as a global leader in developing transitional justice strategies that respond to authoritarian political violence.

Scenically, *Mi vida después* employs a variety of personal objects that belonged to the actors' parents, including, but not limited to, family pictures, audio and video recordings, letters, toys, books, and a living turtle. In performance, several of these images are projected onto a large screen at the rear of the playing space. The projection screen enables the actors to manipulate the objects to alter the ways spectators see them. These personal possessions also allow the cast to construct a sense of familial space, mark history, narrate personal journeys, and commemorate significant events throughout each performance. Under Arias's direction at the Teatro Sarmiento, these objects are placed upstage along with a drum kit, in addition to a row of chairs and an electric guitar that sit stage left. The artifacts are unlit at the play's beginning, producing the effect of an empty stage until a mound of clothing pours down on the center of the theatre's proscenium. Emerging from the massive pile is actress Liza Casullo, who locates a pair of jeans and says:

When I was seven, I used to dress in my mother's clothes and walk around the house dressed like a miniature queen. Twenty years later, my mother's Lee jeans fit me precisely. I put on the pants and start to walk into the past.[30]

The actress proceeds to describe an imagined meeting with her parents in the 1970s in which they ride her father's motorcycle through the streets of Buenos Aires, before crossing to the electric guitar onstage and playing a solo while the other actors enter onstage and begin rummaging through the pile of clothes on the proscenium floor.

The opening scene highlights the performance's efforts to bridge the temporal distance between the performers and their parents through the use of personal items that bear the trace of the absent bodies who wore and marked that clothing. By creating this engagement among the performers, their possessions, and the audience, the production enables empathy, transforming the theatre into what cultural historian Alison Landsberg refers to as a "transferential space" in which memory narratives are passed along from performers to spectators under artificial parameters.[31] The actors embody their parents by wearing their clothing, which in some instances clearly draws from the styles of the 1970s. The result is that the spectator is theatrically transported to Argentina during the dictatorship.

Mi vida después continues to reconstruct experiences from the actors' memories in the play's next scene, titled "The Day I Was Born." In this section, actor Blas Arrese Igor draws a timeline on the stage floor marking the years of the performers' births. Each of the artists stands behind the year in which he or she was born, while giving voice to major political or cultural events that happened in the same year. For example, one ensemble member states, "Peron dies, and I am born after a fourteen-hour labor."[32] Rather than simply transmitting remembered experiences to the audience, the play establishes a relationship between the performers and the world at large, intersecting personal experiences with global history to bring awareness to the ways lived experience and archival knowledge blend together in the construction of memory. References to historical events occurring outside Argentina invite international audiences to make connections between their own biographies and these momentous events.

This process of fusing memory and history continues in the next scene, "Childhood Photos," where the relationship between past and present becomes more complex. Actress Vanina Falco presents a slide show of family photos projected against a screen at the back of the stage. Through these snapshots, she describes her recollections of growing up contextualized by the retrospective knowledge that her father kidnapped and appropriated her younger brother, whom she describes as the family member she loves most. Yet as Falco talks the audience through her pictures, it becomes apparent that the images do not reveal everything that the actress is imposing onto them. For example, in the first picture, Falco presents her grandfather, uncle, and father, who all served as police officers. She describes the men as having the attitudes, stern faces, and mustaches of police officers, yet to make the image read more clearly to the play's audience, another actor draws circles around the men, who all hold their hands on their hips, highlighting what the actress presents as her relatives' police attitudes. Additionally, as she describes the men's "police moustaches," the actor who is projecting the photographs draws mustaches onto the image in red marker so that the facial hair becomes more readily visible to the audience.[33] In the Teatro San Martín's recording of the production, this action draws laughter and brings a moment of levity to the performance, but the scene also communicates information about the actors' malleable relationship with archival documents.

This is brought to bear with the next image, in which Vanina's mother is bathing her baby boy. Falco gazes on the print and notes that at the age of three, she was confused about where her brother came from because she could not remember her mother being pregnant, while question marks are drawn onto the projected photograph. Now that the actress knows that the baby being bathed is not her biological brother, she has reconfigured her relationship with her mother in the picture.

Mi vida después's use of photographs cannot help but evoke connections to Marianne Hirsch's book *The Generation of Postmemory*, in which the scholar uses the term *postmemory* to designate the relationship that generations born after historical trauma feel with the victims of past atrocities. Hirsch posits that memories are transmitted through images and stories, and they can be horizontally communicated to anyone who seeks a connection to past events regardless of their connection to the particular moment in history.[34] Within this context, she argues that photographs play a vital role in postmemory because the images hold affective power, can offer direct access to the past, and communicate traumatic events.

Hirsch's ideas draw significant resistance in Argentina, however, where Beatriz Sarlo has denounced the term, referring to it as banal and arguing that the postmemory unnecessarily inflates the notion of memory, which to her mind is always "post."[35] Additionally, Sosa finds that the term has value but contends that the term is perhaps too attached to discourses of biological normativity that she sees limiting memory politics in Argentina.[36] While I find Sosa's argument persuasive, I contend that postmemory invests objects with value and meaning that are particularly necessary to communicate with international audiences, who may not have the requisite context to understand the historical trauma otherwise. Spectators can then inform that contextualization with their own lived experiences.

Arias's play moves beyond archival manipulation of photography to examine other objects, including toy racing cars, a saint figurine, and a family tree, in following scenes. In three monologues, Mariano Speratti, Blas Arrese Igor, and Pablo Lugones talk about personal possessions belonging to their parents and the ways that each interprets the object to better remember the past. Throughout these passages, the actors' objects are projected and displayed, so that spectators might see a reenactment of the method that Speratti's father used to hide weapons in cars, or trace the lineages of a family tree to draw connections between Pablo Lugones and his relatives who played a larger role in shaping Argentine culture. Such moments elucidate what Werth refers to as "the inheritance of memory."[37] Again, the use of projection allows for modification of the actors' personal items to disrupt the assumed relationship among documentary evidence, physical materials, and memory. These objects become malleable so that the performers can create prosthetic memories—"privately felt public memories that develop after an encounter with a mass cultural representation of the past, when new images and ideas come into contact with a person's own archive of experience"—that allow the actors onstage to take agency over the construction of how they remember their relatives and the ways others come to know them as well.[38]

Arias's project expands further with *Mi vida después*'s next two scenes, "Photos of My Youth" and "My Father and the Guerrilla." The former scene returns to Liza Casullo's childhood, as she speaks to the audience about the photos from her past. Her final image, however, is that of her mother, Ana Amado, who worked as a television newscaster in the early 1970s, before fleeing the country in exile. Casullo notes that her mother also was a member of the Montoneros and that she often had to balance the tensions between her political engagement and her job, which often led her to deliver censored news stories at the government's behest. Instead of transitioning into the next photograph, a news desk is brought onto the playing space, and Casullo puts on a dress that is strikingly similar to her mother's outfit in the photograph. The actress sits at the desk in a position that superimposes her body over the image of her mother, and she begins to recite the news. Midway through the newscast, Casullo lifts a reflective sheet over her face, and Amado's visage is reflected onto the actress's body. At this moment, the performer's enactment of memory evolves from constructing memory narratives based on recovered artifacts to embodying her absent mother to better empathize with her lived experience. Casullo has reconfigured her relationship to the photograph as an example of how memory narratives can be revised through what Marianne Hirsch refers to as the "imaginative investment, projection, and creation" of postmemory.[39] As the scene concludes, another pile of clothing falls onto Liza, as a reminder of the weight that archival materials hold over the interpretation of the past.

Similarly, "My Father and the Guerrilla" facilitates the performance of imagined figures from Argentina's past, projecting images of Carla Crespo's father onto the screen as the actress describes the intellectual and physical regimen that her father incorporated into his training as a member of ERP. As Crespo recites her father's daily itinerary, other actors enter the playing space and perform the roles of unnamed ERP members. The actors recite text from Marx, Che Guevara, and authors of liberation theology before exerting themselves in a regimen that includes dozens of push-ups, sit-ups, squats, and lunges.

Whereas *Mi vida después*'s first segment allows the actors to share their childhood photos and artifacts through monologic testimonies, the play's second movement creates further opportunities for the actors to take an active role in participating in each other's construction of memory narratives in ways that reinforce the importance of interpreting one's archival materials. This portion of the play begins with the actors changing out of their own clothing and into costumes meant to evoke their parents' attire. The items range from a priest's cassock to business attire to a racing suit. The wardrobe change represents an additional layer in the performance as the actors move beyond performing as themselves reminiscing about their parents to take on the task of performing portions of their relatives' lives. Pamela Brownell notes that the actors taking on these roles do not appear to be authentic representations of their ancestors, instead appearing as though they are re-creating imagined stories.[40]

Not all the performers' reenactments are emotionally traumatic. For instance, Mariano Speratti's and Pablo Lugones's performances recount having to walk on one's knees from a dormitory into a church chapel and shaving off a beard to avoid looking like a subversive. Other stories, however, take on more harrowing situations that rely on collaborative ensemble performance. In a scene titled "Exile," Liza Casullo imagines her parents' decision to flee Argentina in exile as though it were a film. The actress describes their reaction on receiving threats from Argentina's Anti-Communist Alliance, playing out the scene as an omniscient narrator who calls out stage directions. As Casullo describes dramatic action, two actors assume the roles of her parents, while other members of the ensemble record the performance with a video camera, projecting the reenactment on the upstage screen.

Casullo's direction is precise, calling for close-ups and fade-outs of the actors as dramatic action warrants, while Igor and Crespo savor their dialogue as if performing in film noir. As the actress's parents kiss just before departing for exile in different countries, Casullo directs the ensemble members playing her parents to run toward each other in slow motion before kissing for seven seconds. The scene provokes laughter, but it also adds another layer to the performance, as not only are the actors portraying their own lives and the lives of their parents, but now they must also fill in as ensemble members in each other's accounts of the past. In staging the play this way, Arias further blurs the lines among person, character, and actor or actress, but more significantly, she directs the production in a way that makes the act of constructing memory a collective process shared by the entire ensemble. The act of creating postmemory is not just in the hands of the actor who recounts his or her own stories, but in the hands of everyone who receives the narrative as well.

The communal act of remembering turns toward the traumatic in the next scene, "The Deaths of My Father." Actress Carla Crespo begins the scene noting, "I'd heard so many rumors about her father's death, that it is as if he had died many times or had never died. If my father's life were a movie, I'd like to be his stunt double."[41] With that prompt, Crespo assumes a double role as narrator and enactor of her father's potential deaths, accompanied by the other members of the ensemble, who play fellow members of the Revolutionary People's Army. The actors arrange plastic chairs as if in a car and move from staging a random car accident to a heroic infiltration mission performed as though it were occurring in an action movie. In this scene and "Exile," the use of cinematic staging and the presence of the video camera draw on what Landsberg refers to as the power of film to transport spectators across geographic or temporal boundaries.[42]

Yet the scene concludes by informing the audience that Crespo's father died as a result of being taken prisoner in a violent act in which the military also removed the guerrillas' hands to pull fingerprints that would help

Argentina's military find the resisters' family members and murder them too. Crespo and her mother were saved because the heat of the Argentine summer caused the hands to rot before the remains could be identified. The ensemble draws a mass grave to mark the resting place of the guerrillas, as Carla notes that she has had the remains of one burial site tested in hopes of identifying her father.[43] Collectively, the company shares in the act of disseminating a narrative about Crespo's father, but the troupe also takes on the added responsibility of sharing in her suffering to help her work through this upsetting memory.

Mi vida después continues to explore the permutations of memory in a scene titled "My Father's Many Faces." Vanina Falco returns to the center of the production and passes out blue suits to the members of the ensemble, who rush offstage to put them on. The performer remembers her father wearing a similar blue suit and recounts the multiple ways that she came to know her father. As she describes her father's many faces—faux medical salesman, intelligence officer, supportive parent, violent abuser, and purveyor of corny jokes—members of the ensemble emerge from offstage dressed in the blue suits that Falco remembers from her childhood. The audience further comes to understand that narrative construction is not composed of one memory, but rather is an amalgam of different ways of understanding the past. This section of the play concludes with all the actors seated in a row of chairs onstage, sharing dreams that they have had about their parents, extending memory beyond the archival and beyond lived experiences into the subconscious.

Arias's play then moves into series of scenes grounded in exploring not only how the construction of memory might grant an individual agency over the shaping of his or her past and present but also how it might lead to the creation of alliances that might transcend boundaries of class, geography, and politics in the future. The final segment of the play begins with a scene titled "Krapp's Last Tape," in which Mariano Speratti recalls that his oldest son is now three years old, roughly the same age that he was when his father was kidnapped. The actor then describes a tape recorder that he found, on which is a recording of his father's voice, before calling his heretofore unseen son, Moreno, to the stage. In the play's most openly sentimental moment, Mariano and son listen to the vocal recording as the archive works to build postmemory across three generations.

From the sentimentality of the previous scene, Arias's play moves into whimsicality with "My Father's Turtle," described in the chapter's opening paragraph. Paola Hernández writes that this exchange expands the documentary form by giving the medium an uncertainty that invites the possibility that history and the future may take other paths than those played out in this performance.[44] The random occurrence played out onstage speaks to the instability of memory. Whereas the actors and spectators can be mindful of the strategies for constructing memory and aware of the ways archival materials can be manipulated, it is impossible to know how this knowledge might alter the future.

Following the turtle's predictions for the future, the play provides a coda to Vanina Falco's relationship with her father. Vanina sits center stage, surrounded by her castmates. The actress informs the audience that her adopted brother filed a lawsuit against her father when he found out that he had been kidnapped. The trial was in its fifth year with no sign of resolution. Falco holds the trial records in her hand, which include her brother's forged identification certificates, legal depositions, and stenographer's transcripts, before imagining her father's testimony and confession, reenacted by members of the ensemble. As the scene continues, her fellow performers ask whether she will testify against her father (she cannot under Argentine law), the duration of her father's sentence should he be convicted (eighteen years), and how her brother has reacted to the news (he has since taken on his birth name and cut ties with all members of his adopted family except for Vanina).[45] Cecilia Sosa notes the actors' blocking evokes a nontraditional family album that hosts "unexpected affiliations emerging from loss," but while she reads this act as a queering of kinship models, I see the scene as reflective of shifts in memory narratives under the Kirchner administration in which all Argentines are invited to consider themselves brothers and sisters of the disappeared.[46]

Arias also provides actresses Carla Crespo and Liza Casullo with an opportunity to conclude their narratives about their fathers. In a scene titled "The Last Letter," the actress describes finding a letter that her father wrote to her mother just before his murder. As she concludes the letter, she notes that her father died when she was twenty-six, and that she is now twenty-seven and has outlived her deceased parent. Rather than portray the grief of that realization, the actress moves toward a drum kit at the back of the stage and plays an extended solo, using the instrument as another means of interpreting the archive and representing the self.

Following this performance, Casullo enters the stage in the scene "The Books of My Father" with copies of the nearly two dozen books that her father, Nicolás Casullo, wrote during his storied career as an intellectual. She notes one particular book titled *To Make Love in the Parks*, in which her father imagines an Argentine revolution. The book was banned during the dictatorship, but now she reads a particularly inflammatory passage aloud. As Liza dramatically interprets the text, the other cast members enter the playing space and begin running across the stage, throwing clothes at each other to enact the imagined revolution in the Argentine streets. In both scenes, the drum solo and the staged chaos allow Arias to shift the audience's focus away from the grief of mourning the disappeared and toward an understanding of how the actors have been shaped by their experiences to consider forms of expression beyond the use of words.

Mi vida después concludes with the ensemble-based scenes "Fast Forward/Autobiographies" and "The Day of My Death." In both scenes, actors speak directly to the audience, noting first the numerous personal and political events that have transpired since the start of the dictatorship. For example, one performer says, "1978. My mother starts dating a psychologist. The streets are full of people celebrating the World Cup."[47] "Day of My Death" allows the actors to foresee their futures, each imagining his or her own life and what Argentina might look like on the day of the actor's death. Some actors imagine Argentina mired in the same political struggles and conflicts that exist in the present; others imagine a more radical future in which Argentina has either become a global superpower or been devastated by the politics of neoliberalism.

Both scenes function as a reprise to "The Day I Was Born," in that the actors imagine that their biographies are part of a continuum that combines documented knowledge with lived experience, but rather than allow themselves to be bound to the past, these concluding moments enable the performers to imagine how the construction of memory might also inspire their visualizations of the future. Arias's production ultimately expands the traditional conceptions of documentary theatre by celebrating the subjective and interrogating the multiple ways that personal objects are constantly interpreted and reinterpreted in the construction of individual and collective memory narratives.

Although *Mi vida después* received positive reviews from the Argentine press, the play's critical reception from international reviewers underscores the ways the techniques of postmemory communicate meanings and values that allowed these commentators to read Arias's work as a signifier that the Kirchner administration's transitional justice policies were leading Argentina to successfully work past the emotional trauma of the dictatorship. For example, Chilean newspaper *El Mercurio* comments that the production reveals the success of Argentina's rebuilding process in the decades following the dictatorship, taking particular interest in how the juxtaposition of photos and onstage action contrasted past and present.[48] Similarly, Chara Loka's review of the production during its run in Athens, Greece, notes that the production's use of clothing, scratchy recordings, and other yellowed documents appear to evict the ghosts of the past through the production's playful engagement with memory, and Parisian reviewer Laura Plas writes that through the onstage garments, the production demonstrates that the generation of Argentines born after the dictatorship are no longer prisoners of the past.[49]

Although these readings of the play may seem reductive, the reviews do speak to Hirsch's description of the ways objects trigger affect shared across generations and between cultures.[50] The production of affect in turn produces empathetic observers, who note the ways Argentina is engaging in postdictatorship politics under the Kirchner administration. This emotional reaction is particularly noteworthy in contrast to the plays produced under the Menem administration, which seemed to implicate spectators for their complicity in the Process's oppression. Moreover, in a review of the production in Brazilian literary magazine *Questão de Crítica*, Daniele Avila Small mentions that the production could be instructive to Brazilian audiences, who are working through their own process of engaging with a traumatic national past.[51] Consequently, the production is not only producing empathy from European audiences but also potentially inspiring political action in other societies that have suffered from traumatic authoritarianism.

Memory, Representation, and Reenactment in Federico León's *Yo en el futuro*

Within the context of Argentina's postdictatorship, questions of reenactment and representation have preoccupied the nation's theatre artists, as seen throughout this project. But the late 1990s and early 2000s also saw the proliferation of documentaries created by filmmakers interested in questioning constructions of history, memory, and identity. The most cited example of these films is Albertina Carri's *Los Rubios* (*The Blondes*), filmed in 2003. The movie documents Carri's return to her childhood neighborhood and family home, where the filmmaker interviews former neighbors, long-distant family members, and others who might help uncover some unknown information about her parents and, by extension, herself. As interviewed subjects provide inaccurate and contradictory information or refuse to speak for the camera, the project questions whether documentary filmmaking can be capable of truthful storytelling. Additionally, Carri begins to depart from the genre's traditional format, experimenting with form and representation.

Los Rubios's most notable conceit is that Carri is played by herself and by actress Analiá Couceyro, who performs as an alter ego of the director-protagonist. Subsequently, critics have analyzed the film as part of what Jens Andermann calls autobiographical or autofictional essays about the sons and daughters of the disappeared searching for identity through the process of experimental filmmaking.[52] Other examples of such work are Andres Di Tella's *La television y yo* (*The Television and I*), María Inés Roqué's *Papá Iván*, Andre Habegger's *(H)istorias cotidianas* (*Quotidian Stories*), and Nicolás Privadera's *M*, all of which reflect on second-generation understandings of the dictatorship, its legacy, and intergenerational strategies for remembering.

Questions of remembrance took on particular importance during Cristina Kirchner's efforts to win reelection to office in Argentina's 2007 election. As part of her campaign, she urged Argentines to remember the strides that she and her husband made in shaping the nation's transitional justice policies, asserting that the public's need to participate in constructing memory narratives was as strong as ever. As part of this process, Andermann notes that Argentines were encouraged to take control of their own memories by documenting their biographical histories so that future generations might come to know their ancestors.[53] During this same time period, the Buenos Aires theatre featured several productions in which the collaborators explored personal histories, archival materials, and how the process of self-reflection transformed individual and collective memories. For these second-generation artists, taking control of their relationships to the past was part of an ongoing effort to experiment with theatrical strategies for exploring memory narratives' subjectivity.

For Federico León, who has had a distinguished career as a playwright, screenwriter, and director of stage and screen, the theatre is a space to create performance pieces that inquire into the strategies individuals use to perform their lives for the public while simultaneously being mindful of how spectators subsequently view those personas. One of the earliest examples from the artist's career is a performance piece titled *Museo Miguel Ángel Boezzio* (*The Miguel Ángel Boezzio Museum*), staged as part of

Viviana Tellas's Museums Project. The play, discussed at greater length in chapter 4, draws on the life of a Malvinas War veteran who shares his biography with an audience as a public lecture. León speaks to the actor through an earpiece that the soldier wears throughout the performance, unbeknownst to members of the audience until they walk into the lobby at the play's conclusion. Similarly, León's 2007 documentary film, *Estrellas* (*Stars*), evokes the tension between those who attempt to document themselves and the outsiders who gaze upon and interpret their objects and artifacts by depicting the lives of several people who live in Buenos Aires's notorious Villa 21 slum.[54] The movie's centerpiece is a film festival created by and staged for the residents of the neighborhood, in which the community's inhabitants present themselves to the viewers of León's film as they wish to be seen, rather than as their reputations color them.

Likewise, León's 2009 production, *Yo en el futuro* (*Me in the Future*), is deeply invested in the construction of self-reflective memory narratives informed by interaction with personal or familial possessions and the ways that such remembrances change over time. This short, forty-five-minute performance has drawn comparisons to Arias's *Mi vida después*, which was staged in the same year, given the abundance of multimedia in both works and the dual roles that each artist performs as playwright-director. Additionally, like Arias's production, the play toured extensively in Europe, playing in Germany, Belgium, Austria, France, Spain, and Italy, where numerous reviewers commented on the production's relationship to memory. But while Arias's project uses archival materials such as family photographs and other personal heirlooms, León constructs fictive home movies from the 1950s and 1970s that document the lives of imagined individuals whose efforts to reflect on the past unquestionably modify how the characters perceive themselves in the present and imagine themselves in the future. León describes giving the performance piece a "documentary look" to speak to how video footage registers and represents the past, while using live actors and the visuals of a proscenium stage to explore the tensions between what the video footage demonstrates to be true and what the living individual imagines.[55] As a result, this analysis of *Yo en el futuro* borrows heavily from discourses of memory and representation in documentary cinema.

León explores the construction of memory with an eye toward the spectator's gaze through *Yo en el futuro*. Rather than document living people, the playwright creates fictional characters that he can use to investigate his own ideas about the transmission and reception of memory and the self-reflective process of engaging with personal videos. In this way, he is borrowing from techniques in contemporary documentary filmmaking that cinema scholar Michael Renov describes as turning the genre into a type of performance "in which the representation of the historical world is inextricably bound up with self-inscription."[56] The play brings together a trio of septuagenarians who have filmed their lives since their preadolescent years in the 1950s. These friends gather to watch several home movies of themselves from the 1950s and 1970s, hiring actors in their preteen years and in their thirties to reenact scenes from the footage that they shot in those decades. Characters onstage interact with themselves on video through repeated gestures and live dubbing that blurs temporality. The play is composed almost entirely of stage directions, including fewer than thirty lines of spoken dialogue. The scarcity of language calls attention to the production's focus on the act of observing the past and constructing one's identity with the goal of self-reflexively interpreting historical moments for contemporary audiences. Questions of staging, reenactment, and representation are key for *Yo en el futuro*, and much of the performance is concerned with questions about remembrance that point to the difficulties of documenting oneself and making meaning of those materials.

León, who was mentored by the acclaimed avant-garde director Robert Wilson in 2002–3, often takes years between writing and staging productions, and his work on *Yo en el futuro* was no exception. The playwright and director received funding from the city of Buenos Aires in addition to several international theatre festivals to allow the play to gestate over a three-year period. To cast the show, León embarked on a lengthy audition process, spending five months looking for the nine actors who would embody the play's central trio at three disparate ages in addition to the performers who would represent them on film. Additionally, the surfeit of time allowed for the careful selection of a Buenos Aires venue for the inaugural production that could serve a dual purpose as a space for cinema and live theatre. León looked for similar spaces when touring the performance internationally too, acknowledging that it limited his ability to present the work as widely as he might have otherwise.[57]

Ultimately, León chose to stage the play in the Lugones Room of Buenos Aires's Teatro San Martín. Although the room primarily functions as a cinema, it also houses a small proscenium that the playwright felt would make the juxtaposition between theatre and film accessible to spectators. The theatre is modern, yet it harks back to a tradition dating from the

Perón administration when Argentine cinemas held live music or dance numbers before screening. Such acts would take place for ten to fifteen minutes before a film began, to give employment to struggling performers in the midst of economic recession. León's production exploits this stage configuration to evoke nostalgic connections between past and present from the play's opening moments that encourage the audience to consider their own memories and historical recollections.

The play begins as the audience enters the performance space and sees an aging woman playing the piano on stage.[58] The actress wears a costume that dates her character to the early twentieth century, and she plays through the seating of the spectators. As the pianist finishes her routine, an upstage curtain rises to reveal a projection screen displaying the silent images of two ten-year-old girls dressed in 1950s attire, referred to as Young Girl and Pretty Young Girl in the program, playing together in a child's bedroom. As the film appears on-screen, a child actress who looks and dresses like the Pretty Young Girl on screen enters the theatre's playing space along with a young boy also dressed in period costume. Simultaneously, an elderly couple in modern dress watch the child actors from the stage's periphery. The children in the film bear a physical resemblance to the children whom the spectators see live, but they are not identical. The projected images continue to play while the character referred to as Elderly Man speaks to the children who are onstage with him, letting them know that he is not visible in the projected images because he is filming the two girls.[59]

The children pass the camera between each other, each presenting the house from her own point of view, before Young Girl leaves the bedroom and films her friends and family watching a home movie on a projection screen in their 1950s living room. The film's shifting perspectives, transformed through the children's sharing of the camera, provides a slightly disorienting feeling as though the spectator is witnessing three fundamentally different takes on the same domestic space. It is a reminder of Emilio Bernini's assertion that in film and performance, the author provides the single or ultimate source of meaning through the visual frame he or she employs and through the structure of the work itself.[60] As León's staging begins to frame the production's concept, the spectators notice the child actors repeating subtle gestures that they see the children in the movie perform, beginning the process of interpretation. This use of repetition and the visible filmmaking apparatus detract from the passive quality of the cinematic image, creating an effect similar to Brecht's *Verfremdungseffekt* to invite the audience to think critically about the self-reflective nature of the performance and the ways León is beginning to manipulate his "archival" footage.

As the play continues, the family watches a film in which Young Boy stands next to an old man to whom he bears resemblance. The Elderly Man onstage dubs over the voice of the child on camera, announcing that he has persuaded his grandfather to shave his full-length beard. Again, León's direction disrupts the spectator's ability to engage with the film, as the onstage actor's dubbing reinscribes the interpretive relationship between movie and live performance. Nevertheless, as the performance's spectators watch the scene, they also become part of the family movie's intended audience, learning that the boy in the film has aged into the Elderly Man who is visible on the theatre's playing space.

During the filming of this introduction, the audience learns that Young Girl also taped the beard shaving and is now recording her family watching her footage of this momentous occasion. Young Girl zooms in on the old man's face as the family's screening begins to play in fast-forward. This change in focus again shifts the performance's emphasis from the relatively sparse narrative of the family video to an intensified awareness of the representational artifice of the production itself. León challenges the spectators' understandings of the characters' relationship to their home movies in a way that reflects what Stella Bruzzi sees as changes in contemporary documentary filmmaking, where performances are constructed and negotiated around the relationship between the director and her subject.[61] Young Girl's cinematography begins to move in fast-forward as well, so that *Yo en el futuro*'s live spectators begin to witness two different film recordings moving at high speed. When both projections return to normal speed, we see that the old man on the projection screen has trimmed his beard into a fashionable goatee. As Young Girl shifts her gaze from the newly shorn old man to his grandson, she zooms in on the boy's face as he imagines taking on his grandfather's visage in the future. The theatre audience recognizes that the Elderly Man onstage wears the same clothes and beard that the old man in the projection wore and comes to understand that the young boy in the film has indeed become the spitting image of his grandfather.

The projection screen in the theatre continues to display Young Girl's footage as she moves through the 1950s home. The production's projections nicely capture the aesthetics of home movies recorded during this period. The audience views the camera shifting lenses to move from wide frame to close-up, while the silence and black-and-white coloration also mark the passage of time. The camera jerks across space, and focus shifts in and out of clarity for the actors and spectators who view the action onscreen. The characters and spectators watch the nascent filmmaker shoot different mirrors to capture light's reflection bouncing off the glass, as well as a close-up of her own face. From this, the spectators learn that Young Girl grows up to become Elderly Woman, who will eventually marry Elderly Man.

The lens's constant shifting suggests what Laia Quílez Estevez refers to as a crisis of narrative agency in contemporary Argentine documentary films that communicates the impossibility of transmitting a cohesive understanding of the past.[62] Young Girl shoots additional images of her family members, who are now watching a cowboy movie on their projection screen, before returning to the bedroom, where she peers through a crack in the door to spy on Young Boy and Pretty Young Girl. As Young Girl zooms in on the couple with a close-up, the two children kiss, but the camera shakes and does not allow the audience a clear view. Shortly thereafter, Pretty Young Girl appears on camera, while Pretty Elderly Woman enters the theatre's playing space. The recording from the 1950s stops, and a child who bears a striking resemblance to Young Girl enters from offstage, bringing the play's first scene to an end.

Yo en el futuro's next scene, titled "The Young Adults of the '70s," focuses on the play's central triumvirate, now represented onstage by performers in their thirties, dressed in 1970s garb, who bear a striking resemblance to the children of the previous scene. These actors are listed as Young Man, Young Woman, and Pretty Young Woman. Elderly Man and Elderly Woman are positioned on the playing space along with Pretty Elderly Woman, who sits at the theatre's piano. The projection screen displays an image of the living room from the 1950s, in which Pretty Young Girl sits at the piano. The camera zooms out to reveal that the recording is actually taking place in the 1970s, as Young Girl is recording Pretty Young Woman sitting at an organ, while she and her friends watch a recording of herself as a child. Young Man is projecting this home movie from the 1950s on a reel-to-reel machine while smoking a cigarette (fig. 3.3). In performance, as Young Man onscreen takes a drag from his cigarette, he is joined by Elderly Man onstage, who then proceeds to pass the cigarette to Young Man's onstage doppelganger to have a smoke, who in turn passes the cigarette on to Young Boy. The onstage tableau speaks to Alison Landsberg's descriptions of the ways memories are transmitted both through recorded images and bodily memories that pass narratives across time.[63]

Figure 3.3. Cast members of Federico León's *Yo en el futuro* watch their past and future selves. COURTESY OF CHRISTOPH RAYNAUD DE LAGE.

Young Woman documents the friends' film viewing on a 1970s Super 8 camera that shoots footage in color, directing her lens back to the black-and-white recording from the 1950s, where we see Pretty Young Girl playing the piano as her family enters the living room. The audience cannot hear her music because of the 1950s camera's inability to record sound. The camera pans out, however, to reveal Pretty Young Woman playing the organ, whose audio we can hear as a result of 8 mm camera technologies of the 1970s. She plays the melody that the woman from the early 1900s played at the start of *Yo en el futuro*, and the production implies that Pretty Young Girl plays the same tune. In the performance space, Pretty Elderly Woman begins to play alongside the younger versions of herself using the theatre's piano. The layering of piano visuals and audio effectively portrays film's ability to construct memory narratives, as each iteration of Pretty Elderly Woman recalls the music's tune by watching their past selves on film. Each pianist's awareness of the camera recording her music suggests that Pretty Elderly Woman is actively constructing memory to be interpreted by her future self and those generations who will come after her.

The 8 mm camera's focus returns to the recording of the 1950s household, where family members gather around the projection screen to watch another film. The movie that the family watches is that of the piano-playing woman from the 1900s playing her piano as spectators enter a movie theatre. Organ music from Pretty Young Woman of the 1970s plays in the background, as the live audience now watches a recording in a recording in a recording, as temporality is blurred to the point of near confusion. When the footage of the piano player concludes, the projection screen from the 1950s living room cuts to the image of the old man shaving his beard, before the picture starts to move in fast-forward. The screen displays much of Young Girl's now-familiar recording of her friends from the 1950s, before slowing to a frame-by-frame shot of the kiss between Pretty Young Girl and Young Boy. What the audience could not see at normal speed is now made readily apparent.

As the projection screen freezes on the kiss that Young Boy gave to Pretty Young Girl in the 1950s, Elderly Man and Elderly Woman move toward the center of the playing space along with the actors who represent Young Man, Young Woman, Young Boy, and Pretty Young Girl. The elderly couple demonstrates what an onstage kiss should look like to their youthful reenactors, and the six characters proceed to exchange pecks on the lips with one another, as the actors try to discover the sensation of that first display of affection while becoming increasingly mindful of the experiential differences that occur in their repeated gestures. Echoing Diana Taylor's recognition that "a video of a performance is not a performance itself," a reenactment of a kiss is not a kiss itself.[64] Like all reenactments of history and memory, the rehearsal betrays the original act. The elderly couple's memory narrative of the kiss is displaced through cinematic manipulation and through the performance staged in the theatre. The exchange of familiarities continues until Pretty Elderly Woman enters the playing space and passionately kisses Elderly Man, creating tension among the play's three oldest characters. Simultaneously, Pretty Young Girl and Young Boy reenact the kiss that they see on-screen as Elderly Woman watches both sets of couples kiss. The Young Woman of the 1970s turns the Super 8 camera away from the image of Pretty Young Girl and Young Boy kissing and toward the bedroom. As she enters the bedroom, she sees Pretty Young Woman with Young Man as the scene concludes.

Yo en el futuro's final scene, "The Last Video," begins with Pretty Young Girl and Young Boy onstage in their street clothes while Young Girl films them. Elderly Woman grabs the camera from the children and presses play, and the images on the camera begin to project on-screen. Young Girl has filmed Pretty Elderly woman smoking nervously backstage, allowing the theatre's audience to access her emotions through a cinematic gesture that Murray Smith refers to as alignment, in which the audience gets access to the character's thoughts or perceptions, even if we cannot see from his or her point of view.[65] This alignment gives us insight into the character's understandings of how the production's manipulation of the archival footage has changed meaning. Young Girl frames the camera shot so that it is taken from Pretty Elderly Woman's point of view looking out onto the proscenium, where she can see the onstage action, as well as the audience in the theatre. Elderly Woman then sets the camera to record and begins filming live, capturing close-ups of the children's faces and turning the camera's gaze toward filming the play's spectators.[66] Elderly Woman searches for spectators who are resistant to being shot by a movie camera, capturing their faces on camera for all to see.

After several uncomfortable moments, in which one can hear the audiences' nervous whispers on the Teatro San Martín's recording of the production, Pretty Elderly Woman calls from offstage, and Young Girl grabs the camera away from Elderly Woman to begin filming backstage. Young Girl finds Pretty Elderly Woman kissing Elderly Man, in addition to capturing footage of Young Boy chasing after Pretty Young Girl before she stops filming. Onstage, Elderly Woman commands the images on the theatre's projection screen to rewind, showing the production in reverse until the screen displays images of the actors in their dressing rooms. Images accumulate without helping the spectator understand better. The actors are in their street clothes making casual conversation with each other, before the image on the theatre's projection screen cuts out again. When the image returns, the screen reveals the audience watching the play, before panning out to see the family from the 1950s watching the audience on their projection screen, before zooming out yet again to see Elderly Man and Elderly Woman watching both recordings on a modern television screen. The present becomes part of recorded time, before the screen projects a final viewing of *Yo en el futuro*, which concludes with a kiss between Young Girl and Young Boy as the play fades to blackout.

As the audience applauds at the end of the play, León continues to explore the construction of memory, bringing the cast out in multiple pairings during the curtain call to acknowledge the multiple ways that the play's spectators might link them together. He begins by inviting the actors out based on their age groups, before staging all the representations of each character onstage for the second bow. His final bow culminates with Elderly Woman and Beautiful Girl entering onstage together, as what León refers to as the excluded, before calling the three actors in their thirties onstage and then concluding with the couples who formed during the production—Elderly Man and the Beautiful Elderly Woman, as well as Young Boy and Young Girl. *Yo en el futuro* leaves its spectators with the sense that memories, like the images documented in film, are ephemeral, fleeting, and cannot be duplicated. They can only be interpreted and reinterpreted, but each new variation adds further layers of meaning that allow for a more fluid and ambiguous narrative to emerge out of the supposedly static archival footage.

Reviews of the production devote considerable attention to the ways that Leon's performance piece engaged in considerations of memory. Parisian reviewer Lorène de Bonnay writes about the piece's complex entanglement of theatre and film and how those interactions accurately reflected the difficulty of understanding past events through home movies.[67] Alternatively, Brussels-based theatre critic Michael Bellon discusses the intergenerational performance of character in the live performances and the ways older generations transmit memory, while mindful of younger generations' ability to absorb that information fully.[68] Finally, the review for German-language Austrian newspaper *Die Furche* posits that Leon's play uses the media of both theatre and cinema to blur the distinctions between past and present in a way that challenges the very nature of memory.[69]

What is most noteworthy, however, is that although several of the production's critics comment on the play's exploration of time and memory, none connected that discussion to the memory narratives of the Argentine dictatorship and the Process. Although that disconnect might be read to suggest that the performance does not adequately produce a memory narrative of postdictatorship self-reflection consistent with other works produced under the Kirchner administrations, I am mindful of Josette Feral's writings about performances of the Americas in international theatre festivals. In describing the ways Latin American countries represent themselves to the world, she notes that in nations where historical traumas and difficult social situations have lost some of their urgency, the theatrical productions staged for festivals lent themselves certain "formalism."[70] Critics' engagement with the play outside of the dictatorship bespeaks an international perspective that Néstor and Cristina Kirchner have facilitated transitional justice policies that indicate success in dealing with the dictatorship's aftermath.

Omniscient Narration and Memory Construction in
Mariano Pensotti's *El pasado es un animal grotesco*

Mariano Pensotti's career demonstrates a preoccupation with the distinctions between presenting and representing, as well as an investment in blurring the boundaries between fiction and reality. Like many of Buenos Aires's contemporary theatre artists, Pensotti has devised urban installation pieces and traditional play scripts to explore these ideas. One of the artist's earliest works, *La marea* (*The Tide*) (2005), presents nine different stories performed throughout public locations or nontraditional spaces made visible to the public throughout Buenos Aires. These scenes depict characters pretending that they are unobserved, revealing certain habits and personality traits through supertitles that give spectators access to the characters' thoughts. These ten-minute exhibitions start and stop at regular intervals and include scenarios such as a man lying on a street after a motorcycle crash, three performers sitting at a bar, and a couple breaking up through a kitchen's open window.

This fixation with making the thought processes of private or personal interactions publicly discernible continues with Pensotti's staging of *Interiores* (*Interiors*) in 2007. For this project, the deviser offers spectators access to six Buenos Aires apartments, where actors silently perform several scenarios. The audience members are invited to move through the playing space as if they are invisible, listening through headphones that communicate the interior thoughts or dialogues of several potential scenes, including a game of table tennis between friends, a teenager staring out from his apartment's terrace, and a man getting ready for a night on the town. Pensotti even turns his gaze on unknowing spectators in *A veces creo que te veo* (*Sometimes I Think I Can See You*) (2010), a performance piece in which hidden writers study citizens on their daily commutes in subway or train stations, typing their observations on projection screens that can be seen by the public. Argentine theatre scholar Andrés Gallina observes that these early performance installations make visible the ways private spaces can be intruded on and reconfigured to change the spectators' considerations of what is public.[71]

Pensotti's preoccupations with peering into private spaces to understand the innermost thoughts of characters expands to include considerations of memory in *El pasado es un animal grotesco* (*The Past Is a Grotesque Animal*) (2010), which premiered at Buenos Aires's Teatro Sarmiento, before touring internationally across the United States, Belgium, Germany, France, Canada, and Spain. Pensotti's play narrates the lives of four individuals between 1999 and 2009, as they evolve from the persons they imagine themselves to be in their midtwenties into the identities that the characters assume in middle age (fig. 3.4). Their lives do not intersect in any meaningful way, but the characters are thematically united through a series of critical choices that lead them into adulthood. Although the play can be read as an exploration into the "fluidity of identity," it may also be viewed as Pensotti's efforts to examine the construction of memory in Kirchner's postdictatorship Argentina.[72] In an interview with New York City–based blog *Culturebot*, the playwright notes that part of what prompted him to write the play was a feeling of how memories could be made meaningful for him and his peers, even though his generation did not have a collective experience that resonated quite as deeply as the dictatorship did for his parents' generation.[73]

The program presented alongside the play at the Teatro Sarmiento mentions Pensotti's inspiration from three separate sources: his remembrances of the sense of chaos he felt between the ages of twenty-five and thirty-five, a box of discarded and strange photos that he found in the dumpster of a photo lab near his home, and American independent rock band Of Montreal, which in 2008 released the album *Hissing Fauna, Are You the Destroyer?* The album's centerpiece was a sprawling twelve-minute pop song titled "The Past Is a Grotesque Animal," about the tensions between the life that the track's narrator wishes that he had and the actual reality in

Figure 3.4. María Inés Sancerni, Javier Lorenzo, Santiago Gobernori, and Pilar Gamboa (*left to right*) perform in Mariano Pensotti's *El pasado es un animal grotesco*. FILM STILL FROM RECORDED PRODUCTION STAGED AT ON THE BOARDS, SEATTLE, WASHINGTON.

which the character resides. The single resonated with the playwright and provided the name for his play.[74] Like the song, Pensotti's play explores how people categorize their lives into critical moments to examine how the organization of those instances creates incomplete memory narratives.

Mariana Tirantte's scenic design does notable work to highlight the passage of time and the fluidity of memory inherent in Pensotti's text.[75] The playing space consists of a rotating turntable partitioned into four distinct compartments. The stage rotates to make each section visible for a set period of time, although the production can moderate the speed at which the stage revolves between scenes. As sections of the turntable revolve away from the audience, members of the stage crew can rearrange or alter the furniture in the nonvisible sections to transport characters to new locations. While the *New York Times* and many other newspaper reviews note the use of the turntable as indicative of time's unceasing passage, it is also worth noting that the changing speeds and the play's ability to travel forward and backward in time can be read as representative of memory's fragmentation.[76] The audience is given access to short, yet critical moments in each character's life.

The four narratives in *El pasado es un animal grotesco* introduce spectators to the play's quartet of protagonists, as they exist on June 22, 1999. Mario is a failed musician who has decided to embark on a filmmaking career and who has begun dating a woman named Dana. Laura steals her father's savings to flee her family's home in the working-class Buenos Aires province town of Gerli and begin life as a Paris bohemian. Pablo works in marketing and lives a relatively normal life until he receives a severed hand in the mail. Vicky discovers a drawer of photographs, which reveal that her father has a second family hidden away in the Argentine countryside, including a daughter who is approximately the same age.

As the audience settles into the performance, Pensotti's staging reveals two conventions to which spectators must adjust. First, the four actors each serve as one of the play's protagonists, but they also play unrelated roles in the other characters' stories. Second, rather than introducing expository material through dialogue, Pensotti provides insight into the characters' motivations and psychology through the conceit of omniscient narrators, played at different times by each of the four performers. This use of narration continues throughout the play, as the actors rarely speak in character. In Pensotti's text, most of the characters' dialogue is delivered as improvisational chatter, simply recorded in the unpublished script as "talk," which is spoken at low volume so as not to overpower the narrators' words.[77] The use of an omniscient narrator gives Pensotti the freedom to explore his protagonists in the ways that conventional dramatic representations cannot. As Audrey Jaffe notes, narrators possess mobility and freedom "in relation to and at the expense of" fictional characters.[78]

The commentators introduce *El pasado*'s characters by revealing their subconscious tensions, fantasies, anxieties, aspirations, and skill sets. For example, Pablo is introduced with the information that he believes he looks like Mick Jagger, even if nobody else in the world sees the resemblance. Additionally, the narrators explain family backgrounds and other information about the characters' biographies, suggesting that knowledge of their personalities is incomplete without a sense of their personal histories. As the play progresses, the narrators use the benefit of hindsight to reveal that they know more about the characters than the individuals do about themselves at that moment in time. Most important, the narrator controls this performance of past experiences to interpret motivations for the play's audience.

The characters in *El pasado es un animal grotesco* proceed along the course of their lives. Mario begins a career writing bad screenplays; Laura moves to France and realizes that she lacks sufficient funding and adequate knowledge of French; Pablo grows increasingly paranoid about the hand that appeared on his doorstep; and Vicky tries to determine if and how she should approach her father with knowledge about his alternative family. The most striking aspect of these scenes is noting the change in year from 1999 to 2000. When this date change is announced, stagehands carry boxes labeled 1999 and place them to the left and right of the revolving turntable. Psychologist Diego Benegas posits that memory is stored to later serve as a catalyst for social forces to specifically combine elements of the past to create meaningful memory narratives.[79] The boxes serve as a symbolic archive that speaks to the fragmentary process of memory and the storage of memories to be accessed at a later date.

As time passes, Mario and Dana begin to grow apart because of an abortion that she had at her boyfriend's request; Laura finds her boyfriend, Esteban, cheating on her with their Parisian housemate before returning to Buenos Aires and accepting a job in the city's Tierra Santa religious theme park, playing the role of Mary Magdalene; Pablo's obsession with the severed hand grows into sexual attraction to the limb and a romantic relationship with an amputee; and Vicky begins to spy on her father's second family. When the play's calendar changes from 2000 to 2001, the destruction of New York City's World Trade Center and Argentina's economic crisis are marked. However, *El pasado es un animal grotesco* does not make these days extraordinary occasions. Life goes on for the characters, who attend parties and pitch their screenplays to unreceptive producers. In 2005, the production also evokes recollections of the massive transit workers' strike that shut down Buenos Aires's subway system. Pensotti suggests that these references to historical events enable him to think about how contemporary global history gets diminished in individuals' autobiographical memories.[80] However, I read these moments as illustrative of the ways memory construction makes links between individual experiences and historical referents. The depiction of the recent past creates a memory narrative that remembers these traumatic events to establish an emotional connection with the play's spectators.

An additional shift occurs in a 2001 scene when Pablo visits a coroner to ask if they regularly receive deliveries of severed appendages in hopes of determining if he was sent a detached hand by mistake. This scene indicates the first of few instances in which a character narrates his or her own thoughts without the assistance of a narrator. Pablo's description of this encounter, delivered without the ability to see into the future or evoke the past, is difficult to follow, a stream-of-consciousness patter that is emotionally volatile and revelatory of the character's vulnerabilities in a way that the narrator is not. Similar instances occur in subsequent scenes, when Laura narrates her own state of mind after suffering a miscarriage and when Vicky learns of her mother's death. Later, the narrator's absence is felt in a scene when Laura meets a romantic interest. The narrator is present throughout the scene, but when Laura's suitor whispers in the character's ear, the narrator states that she does not know what he is saying. In all these cases, the audience notices that the narrator's inability to provide contextual information underscores how much the spectators have come to rely on this figure to interpret memories that have been archived as seminal occasions in the characters' lives. The scene calls attention to the difficult task of constructing memory narratives without an organizing presence.[81]

Over the course of the decade, the play's characters continue to adapt to both major and mundane changes in their lives. Characters move in and out of relationships, experiencing suicide attempts, career changes, and shifting political mindsets. Rather than enabling the audience to understand these developments as the natural progression of a coming-of-age narrative, Pensotti inserts reminders into text and performance that suggest the ways this account of adulthood is made legible through a curatorial process enacted by a narrator who labors to draw connections between past and present. However, I share in the opinion of Jennifer Parker-Starbuck and Sarah Bay-Cheng, whose review of the play for *Performance Research* notes that the production marks the impossibility of fully remembering, as the script's fragmentary structure makes the spectator's understanding of any moment temporary and incomplete.[82]

Performance's explicit role in this process of constructing memory narratives gets explored in greater depth as the play draws to its conclusion. Each of the play's characters engages in considerations of cultural production and the construction of memory. One of the earliest examples of this assessment occurs when Pablo visits a dinosaur park with his girlfriend. The couple look at an assemblage of bones as the narrator describes Pablo's thoughts about the history of dinosaurs and the beginnings of civilization, before undercutting both the park and Pablo's contemplations as imaginings of "a reconstructed past."[83] Simultaneously, Laura creates a photography book depicting the poverty that she saw growing up and as a political organizer working in support of Bolivian president Evo Morales. As she compiles the photographs, the narrator notes that Laura's photos communicate "what is, what could have been, and what was."[84]

The process of archiving the self through the theatre becomes self-reflexive through the characters of Vicky, Mario, and Laura. Vicky begins to date an actor who has devised a performance in which he acts out the daily occurrences of his life. The character lives a normal life during the day, but at night, he and a group of actors perform these actions onstage at a small theatre. The character's catchphrase is "A life becomes fiction," which he shouts during the performance and over the course of his quotidian activities.[85] Meanwhile, Laura fails to find publishers who are interested in her photography book, but a friend asks if he can use her biography to develop a theatrical production that "uses real people's lives to create a performance." As she begins collecting ephemera from her past that she can pass along to the director, including old voice recordings, the narrator notes that "she can barely recognize herself in these artifacts." Later, she attends a rehearsal of the play, and while observing the dramatic action, the narrator says, "She can't recognize herself in anything she sees at all. She looks at the acts; the situations; and the dialogue, finding it all grotesque and meaningless. She thinks, 'Maybe this is what my life looks like from the outside.'"[86]

Pensotti also explores the relationship among theatre, history, and memory through Mario. Believing that the only way he will become an honest filmmaker is by taking inspiration from documentary, he shoots a film where he records strangers on the street and imagines stories about them. The narrator tells us that Mario tries to get inside people's minds and imagine their lives, turning the private into a public exhibition. The film becomes a critical success, earning Mario accolades and invitations to show his work at international festivals across the globe, before he is offered a second film to be shot in Japan using Japanese actors. For this project, Mario decides to develop a film based on his life, but *El pasado es un animal grotesco* concludes by noting that shooting the film makes the director feel "as though everything was strange and alien to him."[87]

The totality of these moments lends recognition to the impracticality of constructing memory narratives through cultural production. As Pensotti stages these scenes juxtaposed against stagehands placing boxes with dates marking the passage of time onstage, the performance suggests that, contrary to popular assumption, the process of self-documentation does not bestow an individual with greater agency for controlling one's narrative. Instead, this process simply provides future generations with more documentation that they can impose meaning onto. *El pasado es un animal grotesco* poses questions about agency and subjectivity, asking questions about the social scripts that organize our experiences, the ways individuals present their life's events for public consumption, and how those accounts are received. Ultimately, the play challenges audiences to consider the relationship between memory and time, in addition to reminding spectators that the process of self-archiving is simply another construct of memory and is capable of making the lived experience feel strange no matter how familiar the story might seem.

International critical reaction to the play notes Pensotti's exploration of memory with admiration. The *New York Times* acknowledges that the play addresses the ways individual lives become fictions as they "become our pasts," ending up as alien, yet inescapable.[88] While the *Times* appraisal generalizes the play's meaning outside of a specific historical context, Charles McNulty's review of the play for the *Los Angeles Times* notes that the play's numerous historical references are inescapable but nevertheless play a minor role in the construction of memory.[89] However, Parisian *Théâtre du blog* writer Véronique Hotte attempts to link the play to the dictatorship, noting that the play is proof of Argentina's recovery from the dictatorship and indicative of the nation's return to order, given how familiar the characters and circumstances are from her Parisian perspective.[90] In all these instances, however, the play is seen as a challenge to constructing biography from memory.

The plays in this chapter explore the relationship among the archive, individual memories, and the process of documenting the self during a period in which Néstor and Cristina Kirchner used archival materials and memory narratives to recenter the dictatorship and transitional justice policies as part of understanding the dictatorship. As a result of advances that human rights activists were making in enacting transitional justice practices grounded in symbolic representation, restitution, and the judiciary, the theatrical productions staged during this period appear less explicitly political than the works discussed in the previous two chapters. However, the plays were instrumental in communicating the ways a postdictatorship generation coming into adulthood with the growing power of the Internet and other digital technologies at their disposal began to document and curate their lived realities for others to see, sometimes even in the present time. Moreover, the works produced by Poggi, Jáuregui, Arias, Léon, and Pensotti demonstrate that even when seemingly removed from Argentina's dictatorial past, theatrical productions can play a meaningful role in the process of memorialization.

4

Performing Public Memorialization
of the Malvinas War

WHEN DRIVING INTO BUENOS Aires from Ezeiza International Airport, or boating in from Uruguay, road signs featuring a map of two tiny and otherwise unrecognizable islands greet incoming travelers with the phrase "The Malvinas belong to Argentina."[1] This South Atlantic Ocean archipelago comprises forty-seven hundred square feet and a population of fewer than three thousand residents, yet no international affairs matter has dominated the nation's public discourse over the twentieth and twenty-first centuries more than Argentina's relationship with this body of land. The islands have captured the country's political and artistic imagination, as evidenced by David J. Keeling's assertion that more films, plays, novels, and other forms of cultural production have been written about the Malvinas than any other territory in South America or any other temporal period in Argentina's history.[2] Although the Malvinas were geopolitically settled as a British territory in 1833, Argentine political figures have frequently created memory narratives linking the colony to the state as a matter of historical precedent. Moreover, in recent years, Britain and Argentina have escalated their political rhetoric about the islands in speeches addressed to both domestic and international audiences, proving that the Malvinas' sovereignty remains an important component of Cristina Fernández de Kirchner's foreign policy agenda.[3]

The final years of Argentina's dictatorship brought hyperinflation and growing popular unrest. By the early 1980s, the embattled military leaders sought a political measure that would turn the country's attention away from economic problems. Under the leadership of General Leopoldo Galtieri, the government began to speak about reclaiming the islands from the British as a means of mobilizing long-standing feelings of patriotism and cultural identification with the Malvinas. The dictatorship's efforts proved successful, as massive crowds demonstrated on the streets of Buenos Aires, chanting their support for the islands' reclamation regardless of whether they supported the political actions of the nation's leadership in totality.

Argentine cultural theorist Beatriz Sarlo noted the tensions that arose among leftists who felt as though the recovery of the Malvinas was a necessary measure of resistance to a legacy of British imperialism in South America, while they also questioned whether the current political administration held the moral authority to pursue an invasive military conflict.[4] Nevertheless, with near unanimous popular support, the dictatorship ordered a deployment of troops to invade the islands on April 2, 1982. After a seventy-four-day conflict that saw more than six hundred Argentine soldiers killed and several thousands more captured or injured, Britain's Royal Navy and Royal Air Force overwhelmed Argentina's outmanned military and coerced a cease-fire in June of that year.

The South American nation's defeat in the Malvinas War decimated public morale and is widely regarded as the dictatorship's death knell.[5] From this loss, however, two major questions have emerged for the democracies that have governed Argentina in the three decades since the announced truce. First, how would the state move forward in considering the Malvinas as part of its foreign policy strategy? And second, how would political leaders reframe the military conflict within a memory narrative of nationalism that made the war politically useful and commemorated the soldiers who served, without bestowing praise on the oppressive military officers who also led Argentina's dictatorship? These questions proved to be intertwined in ongoing efforts to understand national politics and attitudes toward the islands.

In the years following the Malvinas War, Argentina continued to stake a claim to the disputed territory. Democratic administrations proposed diplomatic communications with Great Britain to gain sovereignty over the islands, while consistently positioning themselves as rightful inheritors of the Malvinas and its resources through rhetoric designed to incite popular sentiment. Argentina's primary legal claims to the Malvinas lie in assertions that when the nation declared its independence, it was entitled to the same borders that it possessed as a Spanish colony, as well as arguments based on geographic proximity to the archipelago in comparison with Great Britain. In 1994, Argentina added a provision to its national constitution declaring the islands as a legitimate and "integral part of the national territory."[6]

Under the Kirchner administrations, Argentine foreign policy toward the Malvinas has taken an increasingly combative position. Klaus Dodds notes that Néstor and Cristina Kirchner's presidencies have developed several performative facets of their Malvinas foreign policy discourse, including public displays of cooption among fellow Latin American nations and the construction of memory narratives grounded in Argentine sovereignty.[7] The Argentine leaders developed closer ties with Raúl Castro, Nicolás Maduro, Evo Morales, Dilma Rousseff, and other Latin American leaders who have been outspoken in their resistance to colonialism's legacy in the Southern Hemisphere and in their support for Argentine sovereignty over the Malvinas. Internationally, Cristina Fernández de Kirchner and Argentine minister of foreign affairs Héctor Timerman have lobbied the United Nations, Organization of American States, and G20 to negotiate the governance of the island, framing Great Britain as a political antagonist.[8]

Argentina has also supported its claim to the islands by creating and performing a series of memory narratives that encourage bonds between the nation and the Malvinas. James Billig writes about the performances of quotidian practices that embody a form of national identity that he refers to as "banal nationalism."[9] These activities include the development of and participation in material culture, such as purchasing flags and stamps as a show of patriotism; practiced forms of embodiment, including publicly staged songs and pledges; and internalized social discourses, such as referring to the islands as "ours" or participating in political conversations within informal social circles. Performance scholar Amelia Beatriz Garcia notes that Argentine political legislators dating back to the Perón administration have passed a series of initiatives designed to educate the nation's citizens with a particular way of understanding the country's relationship with the Malvinas.[10] The territory is presented in national weather reports, maps produced by the state, and signs that citizens regularly encounter in everyday life. Schoolchildren take special history classes on the Argentina-Malvinas relationship and devote the weeks surrounding the war's anniversary to learning lessons structured around the islands in classes ranging from art to literature to physical education.[11]

Under Cristina Fernández de Kirchner's administration, the president has actively forged relationships with empathetic movie stars and musicians, including Sean Penn and Morrissey, whom she has encouraged to speak out about Argentina's right to the Malvinas. She also has developed an aggressive Twitter persona, using the social media feed to directly transmit political messages about the islands to her millions of followers, while critiquing journalists who present information that runs counter to her preferred narratives.

In addition to these daily enactments of nationalism, Argentina's political leaders have regularly used the war's April 2 anniversary as an opportunity for shaping memory narratives about the Malvinas through frames of remembrance and reenactment. In 1998, the Argentine National Congress enacted a law declaring that the soldiers who were killed on the islands were national heroes. Two years later, Argentina initiated the Day of the Veterans and the Fallen in the Malvinas War, a national holiday that has appropriated war memories as part of a nationalist discourse. Television shows across Argentina's networks present newscasts and reports that speak to the importance of the Malvinas to Argentina's national identity, and politicians across the country deliver speeches on behalf the nation's veterans. The thirtieth anniversary of the war, celebrated in 2012, was particularly noteworthy for the strident rhetoric of Cristina Fernández de Kirchner's speech delivered at a memorial in Tierra del Fuego, which called for the commemoration of veterans as a way of keeping national memories of the conflict linked to narratives of honoring fallen servicemen.

As with the government's interaction alongside human rights organizations, leftist activists, such as Argentine theorist Hugo Vezzetti, have levied criticisms that the Kirchners have appropriated the past as it relates to the Malvinas in a way that problematically sacralizes the soldiers who participated in the war to advance the administration's political agendas.[12] Additionally, Benwell and Dodds cite polling data suggesting that the Malvinas holds less policy importance for the postwar generation of Argentines, whose connections to the island are born out of a loosely held feeling of national pride and cultural identity.[13] Nevertheless, young Argentines do hold emotional ties to the island. In this chapter, I introduce and analyze several plays written during and after the thirtieth anniversary of the Malvinas War at a historical moment when Cristina Kirchner had become particularly vocal about the need to memorialize the veterans who fought as part of her strategy for reasserting the islands' importance in national discourse. Although these plays and playwrights would not be considered among Buenos Aires's finest, the works represented do contribute to a critical understanding of a seminal historic anniversary.

Staging Malvinas in Contemporary Argentine Theatre

Significant critical analyses have been written about the Malvinas Islands' presence in films and novels; however, little consideration has been given to the ways the Buenos Aires theatre has explored this terrain.[14] Rather than unequivocally affirming the memory narratives of memorialization favored by hegemonic discourses on the Malvinas, cultural producers have presented a multifaceted exploration of the international conflict that has challenged prevailing assumptions about the motives that drove Argentina into warfare and the values imposed on the men who participated in battle when they returned home. Extending Julieta Vitullo's comments regarding literature and art to the Malvinas, the theatre has played an essential role in helping Argentines understand the nation's "profound unease" toward the islands in the years leading up to, during, and following the war.[15] The performances centered on the British-Argentine conflict have taken many forms, reflecting on the sources of Argentina's long-standing international tensions: the conflict's effect on soldiers in combat, as well as on the families who awaited their return to Argentina, and the ramifications of battle for those who bear the mental, emotional, and physical scars. In many instances, the theatre has constructed representations of the Malvinas that allowed audiences who did not serve or who were born after the war to understand the complexities of war.

In the theatre, four major approaches to writing about the Malvinas have emerged over the past decades: allegory, farce, war narratives, and postwar explorations of memory and trauma. As discussed in chapter 1, Argentine playwrights have regularly used allegory as a means of couching political messages. Within the context of the Malvinas War, Jorge Dubatti notes that works such as Mauricio Kartun's 1987 *Pericones*, named after the Argentine national dance, encourage politicized readings that communicate information about the conflict.[16] In his play, Kartun invites spectators to consider the process of nation building as it relates to the islands through a plot about a frigate ship sailing from Europe to Argentina in 1889. As the characters in this work encounter threats from pirates and each other, the main character's unnecessary death can be read as a commentary on the pointless casualties that occurred for the sake of national unity during the Malvinas conflict. Other allegorical works include Jorge Leyes's *Bar Ada* (*Ada's Bar*) (1997), in which the relationship between a veteran and the obese owner of a local tavern makes visible the difference between the adulation that servicemen received at war and the neglect and indifference that awaited soldiers on their return to Argentina. Even Claudio Tolcachir's 2010 staging of Arthur Miller's *All My Sons* was read as a commentary on the Argentine military-industrial complex's culpability for underequipping the more than six hundred soldiers who died during the Malvinas War. In each of these instances, the theatre becomes a site of resistance to hegemonic discourses about the war that frame the event as a patriotic act, by avoiding what Ana Elena Puga refers to as "the lure of false memory."[17]

Similarly, a series of farces has emerged out of the Malvinas conflict, ridiculing the assumptions that led Argentina and Great Britain into war with one another, while pointing out the logical deficiencies in governmental and popular support for the war. Roberto Ibañez's *Fireworks* (2011) employs musical numbers and broad comic staging in a performance about Britain's need to conquer all unexplored and uninhabited terrain, in addition to commenting on the youthful naïveté of the young men who were sent to war on behalf of Argentina and the gullible public who cheered them into battle. Likewise, Alejandro Acobino's 2003 play *Continente Viril* (*Virile Continent*), staged by comedic acting troupe Los Macocos, uses the play's Antarctic setting to provoke uneasy laughter from the relationship between a climatologist and a former soldier whose desire to uphold nationalist discourses about Argentina's territories prevents the scientist from disclosing uncomfortable truths about the state's southernmost territory. Recently, acclaimed Argentine dramatist Rafael Spregelburd has even appropriated British farce, creating a loose adaptation of Steven Berkoff's *Sink the Belgrano*, in which a fictitious British prime minister named Maggot Scratcher authorizes a massive military campaign against Argentina, dreamed up by neoliberalist economic advisors to cover up economic woes and popular unrest in her own country.

The most regularly told stories, however, are war narratives that speak to the battle experiences of the ground forces who fought during the Malvinas War and postconflict reflections on the war that address the tensions that exist for soldiers who were marginalized as part of the effort to reframe the military engagement from political failure to nationalist symbol of colonialist resistance. The former category includes plays such as Augustín Palermo's *Queen Malvinas* (2012), in which two Argentine soldiers bond over their love of the eponymous British rock band. The young men build what they hope will be a lasting friendship, until the realities of war set in and the soldiers find themselves cold, undernourished, and ill prepared for the notorious Battle of Mount Longdon, which saw thirty-one Argentines killed and more than a hundred wounded. Diego Quiroz's *Los tururú* (*The Rejected*) (2012) highlights several deserted soldiers whose need to negotiate with both British and Argentine troops to ensure their survival leads to betrayals and double crossings in a tragic story adapted from Rodolfo Fogwill's acclaimed Malvinas novel *Los pichiciegos* (*The Armadillos*) and Erich Maria Remarque's *All Quiet on the Western Front*.

On the other hand, plays about the postwar experience have captured the realities of Malvinas veterans, who departed for war praised as heroes that were part of a lineage of Argentine independence dating back to Generals Manuel Belgrano and José de San Martín in the early nineteenth century, but who returned from battle to public indifference, inadequate physical and mental health services, minuscule pensions, and meager job prospects.[18] Among the earliest of these works was Federico León's *Museo Miguel Ángel Boezzio* (*The Miguel Ángel Boezzio Museum*), staged as part of Vivi Tellas's museums project in 1998. The play stars the titular Malvinas War veteran in a staged press conference as he presents the artifacts of his life to an audience that is unaware of the fact that the performance is mediated by León, who speaks to the performer through an earpiece. The veteran and amateur actor tells of life events ranging from mundane recollections of his high school graduation and current occupation to tragic accounts of surgeries needed to correct war injuries and a heartbreaking remembrance of his ex-girlfriend committing suicide when military officials falsely informed her that Boezzio had died at war. The production draws attention to the process of curating history and reframes spectator perceptions of veterans who have suffered mental disorders and domestic tragedy on their reintegration into Argentine life.[19]

Vicente Zito Lema's *GUrKA* (1988) also speaks to the lived experiences of Malvinas veterans, in this case seeking mental treatment at the José T. Borda Psychiatric Hospital, through a one-person show in which the author-performer depicts multiple characters. More recently, Lola Arias created the video installation *Veteranos* (*Veterans*) in 2014, inviting several Malvinas soldiers to each stage a particular memory of the war that has remained with them, using only the everyday objects in their immediate vicinity. Arias returned to the Malvinas War again in 2016 with her staging of *Minefield*, a devised documentary theatre piece drawing on the war memories and performances of both British and Argentine veterans. The play opened at the London International Theatre Festival, before moving on to the Royal Court Theatre, a run in Buenos Aires, and productions in Chile, France, and Germany in 2017. These performances reflect on of the ways memories become fictionalized to process the trauma of war.

Fictional accounts of the postwar have also found audiences. Alejandro Tantanian offers a postmodern account of postwar integration through his 2011 adaptation of Carlos Gamero's *Las islas* (*The Islands*), in which a former Malvinas soldier with brain shrapnel is asked to use his computer-hacking skills to find the witnesses of a major crime. In the process, the play's protagonist must reconcile his own memories of criminality and violence committed during military conflict. Additionally, Fabian Díaz staged *Los hombres vuelven al monte* (*The Men Return to the Mountain*) in 2015, which imagines the dual narratives of a war veteran, who returns from the Malvinas to become a small-town bandit, and his son, who longs for a bond with a father he does not know.

Las islas and *Los hombres vuelven al monte* are part of recent theatre seasons that have seen a proliferation of plays about the Malvinas, reflecting the increased attention that Cristina Kirchner is giving the islands as she emphasizes their sovereignty as a primary foreign policy goal in her remaining years as president.[20] The plays addressed in the bulk of this chapter are all works written after Cristina Kirchner's shift to a more aggressive position on the Malvinas in 2012. Some of the selected productions draw from the narratives typically associated with hegemonic memories about the Malvinas, while others put forward new critiques about the war and its continued impact on Argentine politics. None of the plays take the position that Argentina should not have gone to war with Britain or that Argentina should not have sovereignty over the Malvinas, but they do raise questions about why the nation has invested so much cultural capital in this particular territory.

Julio Cardoso's *Islas de la memoria* (*Islands of Memory*) provides a state-supported historical contextualization of Argentina's relationship with the Malvinas that underscores why the minuscule islands have played such an outsize role in the nation's cultural identity, in addition to giving voice to the men who fought and died at war. Patricio Abadi's *Isla flotante* (*Floating Island*) engages in a realistic depiction of the relationship between a soldier and his mother the night before he departs for military duty, highlighting the attitudes of the young men who could only imagine armed conflict. Mariana Mazover's *Piedras dentro de la piedra* (*Stones inside of Stone*) offers an antiheroic account of military deserters, and Lisandro Fiks's *1982*

Obertura solemne (*1982 Solemn Overture*) considers artistic representations of the Malvinas and polarizing public narratives about the war in the generation following this conflict.

Julieta Vitullo posits that in recent years, the Malvinas have been positioned as a symbolic "no man's land," where the islands remain an unquestioned part of the dictatorship's legacy, while the Kirchner administration has tried to co-opt the war as a symbol of democratic resistance to colonialism.[21] The following plays mark a continued effort to explore and map the memory narratives that have emerged from this contested territory.

Contextual Reframing in Julio Cardoso's *Islas de la memoria*

Julio Cardoso's preoccupation with the Malvinas plays a central role in his work as a writer and director. As creator of the island-based documentaries *Locos de la bandera* (2004) (*Crazies of the Flag*) and *Malvinas, viajes del bicentenio* (2011) (*Malvinas, Journeys of the Bicentennial*), he has shown a deep personal investment in the islands and how they are represented to the Argentine public. As of result of this interest, Cardoso has found himself a frequent collaborator with the scholars and artists in residence at the Malvinas Observatory at the National University of Lanus, an academic think tank composed of scholars, cultural producers, war veterans, and relatives of deceased soldiers who produce research about the islands, hold interdisciplinary seminars, and create artistic projects designed to develop knowledge about Argentina's relationship to the lands in accordance with National Education Law No. 26,606.[22] In a discussion of artistic representations of the Malvinas, Cardoso and his colleagues began to consider how the organization might develop a theatrical performance that highlighted the islands' history and military testimonies in a way that might resonate with Argentina's theatre-going audiences across all ages.

With this mandate, Cardoso cast a group of young actors, ranging from ages eighteen to twenty-five, to create a script that would memorialize the soldiers who fought and died during the war while also providing historical contextualization about Argentina's claims to the territory. His ensemble received dramaturgical information from scholars at the Malvinas Observatory before workshopping scenes at the Recoleta Cultural Center in 2008. Through this experimentation, the ensemble developed a conceit in which the troupe acted as itinerant performers, relying on a design concept dependent on quick costume changes, masks, and trunks filled with hand props. The company aspired to create an aesthetic reminiscent of the Río de la Plata's folk theatre, which blended popular song, dance, short scenes, and direct address in a production that rapidly shifted emotional tones between sentimentality and satire.[23]

After years of intermittent development, Cardoso's *Islas de la memoria* premiered at Buenos Aires's Teatro Cervantes in the spring of 2012, then began a national tour that included student performances followed by a series of stagings in Europe. The production traces the history of Argentina's conflict with Great Britain over the sovereignty of the Malvinas Islands from the sixteenth century to the end of the armed conflict between the two nations in June 1982, drawing from historical documents, military testimonies, and letters written to and from soldiers at war. Cardoso's work can be situated as a negotiation between historical tragedy and farce that memorializes the Malvinas and caricatures the global entities that have resisted the state's claim to the islands.

Leonardo Borré's scenic design places the audience in tennis court seating, while also enabling members of the ensemble to walk onto the theatre's seating platforms to communicate directly with spectators.[24] Once the theatre opens, the audience enters the performance space to the sounds of an Argentine cumbia playing over the Teatro Cervantes's speakers, as two actors on stage throw flyers at the spectators that provide factual information about the Malvinas. In the theatre's seating sections, two other performers approach audience members to present the images of Andrés and Nacho, soldiers who died during the war. The immediate experience for spectators entering the performance space is overwhelming, particularly as they are made to study the photographs of the two war casualties. The photographs of these two soldiers, along with the utterance of their names, encourage theatregoers to resist the tendency to see the victims of the Malvinas conflict as a homogenous entity. As spectators look at the pictures, the actors state that they are going to "tell their story and others like them," offering the visitors several individualized narratives to consider over the course of the evening.[25]

The preshow concludes with the actors gathered together in singing a memorial to the men who died. On the melody's conclusion one performer, who functions as a master of ceremonies, announces that the play will draw inspiration from Argentina's classic literature to entertain audiences. The use of cumbia creates what Svetlana Boym describes as a "romantic nostalgia" about folk culture that attempts to situate the work outside of present-day discourses about the Malvinas as an effort to claim historical authority.[26] Likewise, the presence of a narrator, a role that alternates among the members of the ensemble through the course of the play, creates the construct of an authorial voice.

Through the play's next scenes, Cardoso and the *Islas de la memoria* ensemble seek to provide a chronological context for the Malvinas conflict through short, comically exaggerated vignettes. For instance, an actor who recites dialogue delivered by British ambassador Malcolm Robertson adopts an ostentatious vocal affectation as he describes the Malvinas as a "vital strategic value for the British" that they cannot part with, even while acknowledging that the islands hold no cultural value for the United Kingdom.[27]

Later in the play, actors wear pirate masks and speak with a brogue in a section of the play that links the British invasion of the Malvinas to the nation's long lineage of colonizing and plundering, and in yet another onstage moment, the ensemble displays a series of placards spanning the vastness of the performance space to mark the decades in which Great Britain refused to negotiate with Argentina about the Malvinas Islands' sovereignty. In contrast, scenes of Argentine resistance, such as Argentina's defeat of the British invasion of 1805 and *Islas de la memoria*'s depiction of Antonio Rivero's armed rebellion against the British in 1833, are played in a realistic style and narrated with heroic language that presents the nation's continued experience of oppression and injustice. Federico Lorenz notes that Argentina's nineteenth-century resistance to British colonization is often juxtaposed with the Malvinas War of 1982 in contemporary literary, historical, and political narratives.[28] In most instances, including the production, this trope enables the production to downplay the political and cultural differences between the most recent Argentine conflict with Britain to assert all of the battles as equally essential to the construction of national identity and the patria.

Throughout these initial efforts to provide historical contextualization, actors carry dilapidated history books from which they read to communicate shifts in geographic and political perspective. If the book presents a British viewpoint of the Falklands, the text's front cover is emblazoned with a British flag, whereas if the history is told from an Argentine point of view, the book's cover denotes that information with the national flag. On multiple occasions, the production's use of quick-change costumes and stage properties creates what Andrew Sofer refers to as "spatial trajectories" and "temporal narratives" that transport the audience along on the play's four-hundred-year journey.[29] Cardoso and company stage the play in a way that inscribes national history with the memory narratives preferred by the Kirchner administration and other political regimes throughout Argentina's past.

When *Islas de la memoria* turns its attention to the years immediately before the start of the Falklands War, however, the frictions between historical interpretation and deferential commemoration of the war and its veterans become particularly visible. The production largely erases the dictatorship from national history. As the actors display a placard marking the calendar's turn to 1976, the production does not address the coup that brought the dictatorship to power, but instead plays an audio recording of a news report stating that military officials had convinced British prime minister Harold Wilson that Argentina was preparing to invade the islands. The recording continues to play excerpts of intelligence bulletins noting the escalating antagonism between Great Britain and Argentina, before concluding with a recording of Margaret Thatcher announcing that the Argentines had invaded and captured the Malvinas.

As the scene ends, an actor transitions into the next section of the play by observing that the streets of Buenos Aires were "filled with people." Then each actor describes how the masses waved flags on the streets in support of the men and women. The only implicit statement that connects the war to the dictatorship is an acknowledgment that men and women who had only "three days prior run away from soldiers wielding batons and tear gas" were now marching in lockstep alongside them, speaking as if they had known each other for years.[30] The play does not reference then-president Galtieri or the dictatorship, and it certainly does not speak about the violence and oppression inflicted on thousands of Argentines.

In an interview in Buenos Aires newspaper *Página 12*, journalist Hilda Cabrera asks Cardoso if it had been hard for him to separate the dictatorship from the Malvinas War, and the playwright responds by saying that if he were to reference state terrorism, he would be committing "an injustice to the soldiers who died and the survivors who carried the weight of war with dignity."[31] However, I propose that the dictatorship's absence speaks to Paul Harvey Williams's assertion that the process of memorialization is most successful as a vehicle for political appropriation when it is made to appear apolitical. Williams posits that memorials create "reverent remembrances" that enclose an event in the past so that regimes in the present can impose meaning on them. Through this act of omission, Cardoso makes explicit his intent to create a memory narrative of nationalist commemoration at the expense of a richer analytical engagement with the conflict.[32] In this sense, the play is typical of other educational measures related to the Malvinas conflict.[33]

Once the play turns to the actual conflict between Argentina and Great Britain, Cardoso and his ensemble transition between scenes of historical reenactment and epistolary accounts of the war told from the perspectives of the soldiers who fought and the families who waited for them in Argentina. During the initial stages of conceptualizing the show at the Malvinas Observatory, the organization provided Cardoso with hundreds of letters written to and from soldiers. The second half of *Islas de la memoria* begins with one of these letters as it recounts the experience of Andrés, the young man whose picture was presented to the audience at the start of the play. The character's missive recounts a feeling of peacefulness on the islands prior to the arrival of British bomber jets. He concludes by asking his mother to send a camera so that he can document what he is doing in hopes that the images will instill in her a sense of pride. Soon other letters are read by the ensemble in an overlapping montage in which soldiers ask their families to send small items such as chocolates, notebooks, and a silver cross, as well as kisses from loved ones.

As the actors read the notes aloud, they also move about the space handing out envelopes doctored to appear as if soldiers had sent them from the islands decades beforehand. When the spectators open these packages, they find replicas of notes written by Argentine soldiers. The distribution of these dispatches creates memory narratives of remembrance that are derived from what Alison Landsberg refers to as "experientially oriented encounters" that produce empathy.[34]

In contrast to Cardoso's efforts to elicit empathy for Argentine soldiers, the dissemination of letters is followed by a scene reenacting Margaret Thatcher's decision to sink the *General Belgrano*, an Argentine battleship that carried over a thousand troops and whose destruction led to the death of more than three hundred Argentine soldiers and two civilians. For the performance of this scene, Cardoso had two actors wearing masks of Thatcher and Ronald Reagan enact the global leaders as pirates. The two political allies stand over a map of the Malvinas Islands, stomping on the map and convening with each other over the fate of the nation and the territory with amoral glee (fig. 4.1). In impersonating Thatcher giving the orders to "sink the Belgrano," Lucía Adúriz bellows across the stage with particular venom.[35] Unlike the previous scene, here the playwright is not interested in creating empathy for these characters; rather, the actors perform the two figures as caricatures that "dehumanize and demonize" Reagan and Thatcher, divesting them of their complexity to frame the politicians as immoral and destructive as opposed to the peace-bringing Argentine soldiers.[36]

Following this imagining of Thatcher's war room, Cardoso continues to humanize the Argentine soldiers, reenacting letters and scenes that document a man who falls in love with a woman native to the Malvinas, soldiers taking heroic measures to save the lives of their fellow countrymen, and messages of support from anonymous Argentines to the men who fight for national pride. The production also continues to advance the epistolary narratives of Nacho, Andrés, and several other soldiers, until the audience learns of their deaths as the play moves toward its conclusion. In many of these narratives, Cardoso's playwriting constructs an Argentine hero who performs courageous acts born out of youthful naïveté and a love of country while in the midst of otherwise routine activity. Vezzetti suggests that this particular manufacturing of valor is typical of state-produced

Figure 4.1. Lucía Adúriz and Cristina Suárez perform as Margaret Thatcher and Ronald Reagan in Julio Cardoso's *Islas de la memoria*. COURTESY OF JULIO CARDOSO.

discourses on the Malvinas, which demonstrate a particular reverence for the bravery, heroism, and death of individuals.[37]

Islas de la memoria concludes with a scene that reaffirms Argentina's national pride, even in the midst of military defeat. In the final moments of the play, the actors stage a scene in which a group of Argentine war prisoners find themselves detained in the ballroom of a massive ship that is returning the troops home from war, when they discover that a piano remains in the space. Three soldiers, one of whom happens to be an extraordinary musician, risk discipline from the British guards to access the piano. When the soldiers do successfully reach the instrument, the musician plays a stirring rendition of Argentina's national anthem, which leads all two thousand of his fellow prisoners of war to rise and sing in unison. The British knock the young pianist off his stool with a rifle butt to the back, but the servicemen continue to sing the anthem as a testament to their love for country and resilient spirit in the face of adversity.

In remarks delivered on the thirtieth anniversary of the Malvinas War, Cristina Fernández de Kirchner reaffirmed her belief that Argentina should continue to pursue sovereignty of the Malvinas for several reasons, including the need to honor the brave men who fought at war and gave their lives.[38] Although *Islas de la memoria* does not explicitly declare a political position about the islands, the play participates in an act of memorialization that reinforces the administration's political messaging.

Victoria Basham writes that war must be remade and retold to remove the politics and viscera of battle and make the narrative acceptable for nationalistic memorialization.[39] Julio Cardoso's *Islas de la memoria* creates sentimental bonds among the play's spectators that facilitate memory narratives of commemoration, but at the expense of historical accuracy. The play erases the dictatorship's affiliation with the war and emphasizes the humanity of the Argentines to the detriment of the other global players involved in the Malvinas conflict, but in doing so, he connects the war's history to both Argentina's national past and the sociocultural and political concerns of the Kirchner presidency.

Narratives of War and Childhood in Patricio Abadi's *Isla flotante*

Historically, childhood has been reconfigured across geographic and temporal boundaries.[40] This inherently temporary period is constructed based on a society's collective beliefs about what a child should be in opposition to the social and biological markers that define adulthood. Victoria Basham writes that childhood has been positioned as a process of "being unfinished" that lingers through adulthood, categorizing this youthful stage of life as necessarily being marked by irrationality and disorder, in contrast to the logical and methodological mindset that governs adulthood. Basham continues by positing, "Whereas adults are drivers of agency, children are vehicles for structure."[41]

Throughout preparations for the Malvinas War, military and political figures referred to the troops drafted and selected for battle as children. President Leopoldo Galtieri frequently referred to the troops as "boys of war," using the designation to highlight the military's vigorous energy and symbolically evoke the armed forces as Argentina's sons and daughters.[42] After suffering a humiliating defeat at the hands of the British, Argentine troops continued to be addressed as the sons of war. The term no longer retained its warmth and regard, however; rather, the phrase was repositioned as a justification for defeat, denoting the large percentage of Argentine troops who were conscripted just out of secondary school when they were eighteen years old and who were in many instances naïve enough to believe that they could defeat the British with their lack of training and equipment. The boys of war became Argentina's orphans, victims whom postwar administrations could strip of their representational power to transform the young adults into martyrs whose death and mistreatment could be redressed only through political action that would rightfully restore sovereignty over the Malvinas.

Brenda Werth mentions several films that position the soldiers who went to war as youth, citing Bebe Kamin's 1984 film *Los chicos de guerra* (*The Boys of War*) as a prime example, and one could also include Miguel Pereira's *La deuda interna* (*The Domestic Debt*) (1988).[43] Both films frame the soldiers who fought in the war as childlike figures from largely rural backgrounds who imagine the prospect of war with patriotic enthusiasm but whose actual experiences end in tragedy or disillusionment. More recent films such as *Iluminados por el fuego* (*Illuminated by Fire*) (2005) and *Desobediencia debita* (*Debts of Disobedience*) (2008) also present youthful soldiers, but their innocence proves to be an asset, as it leads to heroic acts such as pursuing medical treatment for a wounded British pilot or taking extraordinary measures to save men in danger in spite of incompetent superior officers.

Patricio Abadi is also interested in exploring the transitional space between childhood and adulthood as it relates to the soldiers who fought in the Malvinas War. Rather than direct his attention to a totalizing exploration of the soldiers who fought in battle, the playwright focuses his energy on a singular young man, growing up in a neighborhood just outside Buenos Aires. *Isla flotante* shares the story of Ramón, an eighteen-year-old enjoying a final evening with his mother before departing for battle. Abadi's play, which he directed in its initial performance at Buenos Aires's Onirico Espacio de Arte, is set on the evening of March 27, 1981, less than a week before Argentina will invade the Malvinas. Scenographer Ariel Vaccaro's design for the production accurately captures the 1980s dining room with remarkable exactness, furnishing the setting with numerous pieces of décor that establish the period.[44] Ramón will depart the next morning for Rio Gallegos before becoming part of a troop that will mount Argentina's invasion on the islands. In an interview with Argentine journalist Paola Boente, the playwright notes that he wanted to focus his play on the evening before departure to reveal the soldier's acceptance of adulthood prior to entering combat, as well as to make the spectators palpably feel the tension that existed within families who did not know whether they would see their children return home from war.[45]

As *Isla flotante* begins, Abadi establishes a relationship between mother and son, suggesting that the play will proceed in the tradition of the "boys of war" narratives. The playwright names his protagonist Ramón, but in the performance's playbill and script, he is listed only as the Son.[46] The opening scene of the play situates the boy and his mother within a working-class milieu. Ramón has recently graduated from secondary school, and his mother is a widowed maid to a family with spoiled children. Typically, according to Julieta Vitullo, this narrative of poverty is used as a justification for victimizing the soldiers who fought in the Malvinas, suggesting that the boys were conscripted because they did not have the economic capital to defer or because joining the army would provide a household with some measure of financial stability.[47]

In addition to highlighting the family's economic position, the play's text also creates scenarios that call attention to Ramón's youthfulness: his mother knits him scarves and launders his clothes, she worries that he has been spending too much time at a local bar with his friends, and when he injures his ankle playing soccer the afternoon before his departure, his mother openly questions whether a boy who would decide to physically exert himself the day before enlisting is equipped for military service (fig. 4.2). In each of these scenarios, Abadi acknowledges political discourses

Figure 4.2. Alicia Palmes and Nicolás Mizrahi portray a mother and son partaking of their last meal together before he departs for the Malvinas War in Patricio Abadi's *Isla flotante*. COURTESY OF PAULA DAIANA MARRÓN.

that frame the character as typical of the drafted Malvinas soldiers who were incapable of making rational or adult choices and subsequently allowed the military to lead them into a war they could not win.

Yet, as trauma scholar Jenny Edkins contends, the prospect of war unsettles the routines and relationships of social life.[48] *Isla flotante* counters this reductive reading of Ramón as childish by presenting several instances in which the character demonstrates a rational and ordered agency that resists narratives of victimhood. The play's protagonist makes arrangements with a neighbor to ensure that somebody can provide his mother with regular assistance. He repeatedly offers emotional support to his mother and, in a late night phone call, his aunt, who worries about his well-being. Even as he is being chided for spending too much time at the local tavern, he assures his mother that he is being a responsible friend. Ramón is taking control of his destiny and the destinies of others in ways that suggest he is capable of determining what courses of action are most sensible at home and on the battlefield.

Abadi's script turns toward the melodramatic at the midway point of the play, when Anabela, Ramón's literature teacher, comes to wish the soldier off under the guise of a patriotic initiative from the secondary school. The educator has been conducting an affair with her student and has come to persuade Ramón to desert the army and run away with her to a house in Mar del Plata, to avoid the likelihood that the war "will be a slaughter."[49] For over a third of the play, Anabela and Ramón discuss this plan, and although the play problematically conflates adulthood with "a reinforcement of the superiority of masculine characteristics such as rationality, resolve, and strength," the character once again asserts his adulthood through a firm declaration that he understands the risks of battle and that he will depart for Rio Gallegos, not as what political scientists Victoria Basham and Nate Vaughn-Williams would refer to as a passive actor, but as a figure who rejected childish irrationality in his own best interest and the best interests of Argentina.[50] Moreover, the admission of an extramarital affair grounds the character with a flaw that discourages the play's spectators from imagining Ramón as one of the nation's mythologized national heroes.

As the play concludes with dawn breaking the morning that Ramón is to report for duty, he and his mother share a final cup of coffee before parting ways. His mother asks if he will come back to her when the war ends. "The Son shrugs. The Mother cries." The two characters hug as the lights fade to black.[51] The play concludes on a somber note, reminding audiences that even as Ramón's decision to go to war undermines the discourse of the unprepared child, the act of war itself is chaotic, irrational, and yes, often childish.

Benwell and Dodds assert that geopolitical tensions affect soldiers and their families in a variety of different ways.[52] The Argentines who fought against Great Britain in the Malvinas were tactically underequipped and lacked the leadership and physical training necessary to excel at warfare, but rather than reinscribe a narrative of victimhood in which eager young soldiers were coerced into war out of love for country, *Isla flotante* imagines a scenario in which the soldiers who participated in the war understood the odds that were against them and took agency for their decision to serve, even if under conscription. The play rejects memory narratives of martyrdom and suffering that have been imposed on Argentine soldiers under administrations from Raul Alfonsín to Cristina Fernández de Kirchner, and in doing so, it encourages spectators to consider alternative possibilities for Argentina's military defeat, including a lack of investment from the state that now seeks to commemorate their memory. Abadi's production uses a micronarrative of the past to challenge contemporary political discourses and provoke a new direction in Argentina's memory politics.

Staging Desertion and Abandonment in Mariana Mazover's *Piedras dentro de la piedra*

Although the Malvinas War played a seminal role in bringing Argentina's dictatorship to a conclusion, it is worth remembering that the nation went into battle with near unanimous popular encouragement from both supporters and opponents of military rule. Overlooked in Argentine citizens' desire to wage war against the British and regain sovereignty over the islands was the treatment of soldiers in battle. Whereas Galtieri and other political leaders referred to the men who fought the war as heroes, senior officers treated conscripted men in particular as though they were incompetent and unnecessary to the war effort. Marcos Novaro and Vicente Palermo note in their history of the dictatorship that military leaders simply transferred the oppressive and violent methodologies inflicted on the citizens during the Process to the soldiers who were drafted into combat. The authors document conscripts departing from their homes to isolated bases in remote parts of southern Argentina, where the trainees engaged in exhausting training exercises and military drills before returning to their barracks and were forcefully discouraged from communicating with their relatives and loved ones. Additionally, draftees suspected of insubordination faced torture or death at the hands of army and naval officers.[53] In sum, as noted by several authors writing about this period, the military employed the same tactics against its own troops as it did against the leftists whom they hoped to eradicate as part of the Process of National Reorganization.[54] Despite publicly disseminating memory narratives of national identity and patriotism that dated back to Argentina's independence as a way of provoking public sentiment, the military demeaned and mistreated its draftees.

Because of the military's mistreatment of its soldiers and the significant differences in training and equipment Argentine soldiers received in comparison to British troops, many conscripted and enlisted servicemen sought opportunities to abandon their posts on arriving in the Malvinas. Although it is impossible to estimate how many ground troops deserted the Argentine Army, their numbers were large enough that they spawned a vast body of literature imagining their experiences on the island. Julieta Vitullo writes about a handful of Malvinas novels featuring characters that have gone AWOL, including Marcelo Eckhardt's 1993 text *El desertor* (*The Deserter*).

Yet the most famous tale of abscondment is also perhaps the most important and influential book ever written about the Malvinas: Rodolfo Fogwill's 1983 novel *Los pichiciegos*, named after the tiny burrowing armadillos found on the Argentine pampas.[55] The novel concerns a group of Argentine soldiers who, after landing on the Malvinas and recognizing the futility of the war and the ineptitude of the men who lead them, decide that spending the remainder of the war hiding in a bunker is better than the fate of death that potentially awaits them. Once the soldiers desert their fellow troops, however, they realize that they cannot leave the confined space of the island, and both British and Argentine soldiers seek to gain from their capture and recovery. Consequently, to survive, the characters must burrow deep into the earth, gather food by any means necessary, and form their own hierarchies of community as best they can.[56]

Fogwill's text, allegedly written over a two-week period in the final days of the Malvinas conflict, is generally regarded as the first fictional work written about Argentina's war with Great Britain. It was a rejoinder to the Argentine public's fervor for war, and presently the text can be read as a critique of those who use the memories of fallen soldiers as a strategy for arousing nationalist sentiment. As such, *Los pichiciegos* serves as the inspiration for Mariana Mazover's 2012 play *Piedras dentro de la piedra* (*Stones Inside of Stone*), staged at Buenos Aires's Teatro La Carpintería.

Inspired by Fogwill's 2010 death, Mariana Mazover gathered a cast of six actors to imagine a loose adaptation of this seminal novel. The company began with a dramaturgical exploration of Malvinas War history before turning its attention toward literary texts written about war experiences, including Joseph Heller's *Catch-22*, Kurt Vonnegut's *Slaughterhouse-Five*, and Sun Tzu's *The Art of War*.[57] Through this acquisition process of research and dramaturgical documentation, the ensemble formulated several questions to explore in devising the play. In an interview with a Buenos Aires theatre website, Mazover says that the company wanted to know how the nature of war frays the soldiers' morale, how patriotism and national identity are constituted at war, and whether it is possible to be labeled as a deserter or traitor in a war with no honor.[58] With these themes in mind, the actors began to use Fogwill's novel as touchstone for determining the plot of their creation, improvising from the novel to shape the play for production. Mazover also cites the influence of acclaimed dramatist Ricardo Monti, who served as her writing adviser during the course of rehearsal and revision.[59]

Although inspired by *Los pichiciegos, Piedras dentro de la piedra* is not a faithful adaptation of Fogwill's text. To begin with, Mazover's group of soldiers includes two women, even though females did not fight for Argentina in the Malvinas War and could not participate in the nation's military until 1997.[60] The playwright suggests that her reasons for adding female characters were to include a romantic entanglement, so as to consider how war destroys traditional conceptions of love, while also making the play feel more contemporary, reflecting the current state of female participation in the nation's armed forces.[61] Aside from the introduction of female characters into the context of the Malvinas War, the play takes a more realistic look at the deserters over the course of one twenty-four-hour period in their bunker, rather than the multiday and sometimes surreal examination of AWOL troops found in Fogwill's novel. Additionally, the play is an ensemble-based narrative, rather than being told from one person's point of view. Mazover changes characters' names from Fogwill's text, and there is little of the novel's explicit criticism of the British and Argentine military. Moreover, soldiers in *Piedras dentro de la piedra* do not commit treasonous acts such as exchanging information to the British for food; instead, the servicemen trade away accumulated supplies such as batteries. These alterations enable Mazover to turn her gaze away from a critique of the Argentine and British militaries to better direct her attention on the former soldiers and the labors that they take to survive. Consequently, the play challenges memory narratives that seek to canonize the war's veterans and calls attention to the fact that the war effort saw its young as disposable, an idea that continues to be felt in present-day Argentina because of neoliberalism's continued reverberations.

Cecilia Zuvialde's scenic design captures the bunker's isolation through the utilization of several pillows, wooden pallets, and elements of set dressing that fill the theatre's playing space (fig. 4.3). The decor evokes the appearance of a sandbag-filled bunker buried deep in the ground to highlight the sense of remove between the soldiers and the outside world.[62] This evocation of a Malvinas bunker draws the audience into the performance as Mazover's play begins and the lights rise to find Enríque, an Argentine soldier timidly standing guard over the facility's entrance, shivering in fear as he holds a rifle in his hand.[63] As other deserters enter the playing space, the former servicemen and women begin bickering over cigarettes, teabags, and chocolate stolen from fellow escapees.

The characters' behavior draws laughter in performance, partly because Mazover's script marks a departure from the reverent depictions of

Figure 4.3. Mariano Falcón, Sebastián Romero, Alejandra Carpineti, Alejandro Lifschitz, and Laura Lértora (*left to right*) await their fate in a Malvinas bunker in Mariana Mazover's *Piedras dentro de la piedra*. COURTESY OF MARIANA MAZOVER.

Malvinas fighters traditionally seen in war-related fictions. Whereas most narratives, including the plays referenced earlier in the chapter, depict brave and noble military figures, the characters in *Piedras dentro de la piedra* are initially presented as amoral, serving their own self-interests rather than acting on behalf of a collective good. As the play progresses, characters will continue to act in ways central to their own self-interest, dividing the personal belongings of a character believed to be dead and risking revealing the group's location to recover a personal artifact. Martín Kohan writes that such character depictions in fictional works undercut the narratives of valor used to honor Malvinas veterans.[64]

As the remaining deserters enter the bunker, their collective incompatibility becomes particularly legible. The initial group of soldiers who abandon their posts to live in the bunker represent a diverse array of backgrounds, including Mabel, a thirty-one-year-old sergeant who defected from the army when her beloved died in her arms; Enríque, a twenty-one-year-old who is tactically astute but cannot execute in battle; Oscar, who

comes from a generation of military men that trace back to battle in the
Napoleonic Wars; Gandini, a discipline-oriented sergeant who is the oldest
deserter at age thirty-two; and Marcellino, who enlisted in the war of his
own accord, leaving his career as a cattle transporter so that he could be the
only citizen who donated his personal vehicles to the war cause. The ages of
these characters are noteworthy because they undermine the narrative that
all the Malvinas soldiers were just boys. The soldiers were initially linked
to each other through the hierarchies of combat and military rank, but
they must now reevaluate their chain of command based on the skill sets
needed to survive in the bunkers. Additionally, the soldiers in Mazover's
play are from several remote cities across Argentina's most remote and
poorest provinces, including Cuyo, Chubut, Corrientes, Santiago del Estero
and Suipacha. The soldiers' varied backgrounds and regional differences
further exacerbate the tensions within the confined space of the bunker,
but in performance, these divergent backgrounds can be read as what Ehrmantraut suggests is a reflection of the difficulties veterans would have
organizing and advocating for themselves in the postwar.[65]

As *Piedras dentro de la piedra* continues, the characters work to balance
their personal desires with the development of the tenuous community
that they have built together. Within the confines of the bunker, they learn
basic rules of decency toward one another, including a respect for personal
property. At times, the former soldiers display remarkable generosity, such
as when Oscar and Gandini share the oranges and cans of potato salad
that they obtained by trading with British soldiers. Yet the deserters are
still capable of turning on each other, as demonstrated in a scene where
soldiers inside the bunker deny Marcellino entry for fear that he has given
away their hiding spot.

The group faces a particularly heated moment when their bunker is
discovered by Olga, an Argentine soldier who found the group based on information from a now-deceased inhabitant. The newly arrived escapee has
arrived at the bunker with a gunshot wound in her shoulder. Some worry
that the wound will turn gangrenous and infect their living space, while
others fear that she will give away their location to British or Argentine
soldiers or will be a drain on already limited food and resources without
being capable of foraging for the group. After a lengthy debate about the
former soldiers' core values and obligations to each other, the group decides
to take Olga in, but what is telling about the exchange is that, unlike in
other Malvinas narratives, the deserters make the brave decision without

evoking narratives of national identity, honor, heroism, or the need to take care of a fellow citizen. As writers have also noted about *Los pichiciegos*, the play fundamentally disregards philosophical concepts in the face of the soldiers' efforts to survive another day with minimal subsistence and the ever-present threat of death.[66]

The play's central conflict emerges as the deserters come to understand the precariousness of their living situation in the bunker. They conduct an inventory and learn that their ration supply is limited and cannot sustain the inhabitants for more than another day or two. Shortly thereafter, they hear a detonated mine from inside the bunker. The former soldiers know that armed forces are near, but they cannot determine whether it is the British or the Argentines who are drawing closer, reduced to far-away observations through a makeshift periscope and hearsay acquired on their scavenger hunts. Either way, the former servicemen face a risk: the possibility of execution at the hands of their fellow countrymen or being captured and held as prisoners of war by the British. Adding to their tensions, the bunker's inhabitants see the signs of melting snow and an emerging spring. Temperature change brings the threat that the meltwater will seep through the cracks in their bunker and flood it, destroying their supplies and potentially killing them. The idea of community begins to disintegrate under the possibility of extinction.

The play moves toward its bittersweet resolution when the ex-soldiers realize that their very survival depends on splitting up the temporary community that they have created to find individual safety. After much debate about the best course of action, Mabel and Gandini agree to surrender to British soldiers in hopes that they might take mercy on the deserters for giving themselves up. Marcellino elects to get in his truck and drive to the nearest Argentine outpost, hoping that his fellow troops will welcome him back because of the value that his truck will bring to military endeavors. Olga and Oscar decide that they will try to sneak into a nearby town and blend in with citizens as a German couple. Only Enríque chooses to remain in the bunker, preferring to accept the fate that he has been given rather than venture into the unknown. *Piedras dentro de la piedra* concludes with Enríque positioned in precisely the same place where he began, shivering alone in the bunker, holding a rifle for protection.

Unlike *Los pichiciegos*, Mazover's play leaves open the possibility that the deserters will survive the war and find new lives for themselves. In doing so, she undercuts the irony found in Fogwill's novel, which suggests that the deserters will be commemorated through the narratives of valor and bravery in death. Nevertheless, Mazover is successful in resisting the memory narratives frequently presented about the heroes who fought against Great Britain in the Malvinas War.

The theatre can illustrate already established memory narratives, depicting its characters as representatives of certain hegemonic discourses, but as Martin Müller claims, performance can challenge audiences and assert subjective viewpoints that can transform how they know and understand the world.[67] Both Rodolfo Fogwill and Mariana Mazover note how political figures have framed the Malvinas veterans as Argentine heroes to pursue specific policy goals, and both writers created characters who work to resist that typecasting. *Piedras dentro de la piedra* presents soldiers whose desire for survival leads them to take actions that fall outside the traditional tropes of war literature and challenges spectators to reconsider why political figures continue to use the memorialization of the war's veterans as a nationalist symbol.

Postmemories of Malvinas in Lisandro Fiks's *1982 Obertura solemne*

Nations use anniversaries as junctures to circulate memory narratives about historical events that serve political objectives in the present.[68] The thirtieth anniversary of the Malvinas War in 2012 functioned as a particularly important opportunity for Argentine politicians, the media, and the public to repeat and reinscribe ideas about the war that served the nation's foreign policy agenda. Christina Kirchner's 2012 speech commemorating this anniversary of Argentina's invasion of the Malvinas, delivered at the Malvinas War Memorial in Tierra del Fuego, has been seen by many as one of the major speeches of her political career.[69] In it, she made a concerted effort to separate the war's noble aspirations of colonial resistance from the legacy of oppression affiliated with the dictatorship that had initiated the conflict. Kirchner spoke emphatically about the "misery, pain, and shame" of the Process, while also making explicit that although the war might have been started under authoritarian rule, the conflict drew support from millions of public citizens and self-sacrificing soldiers who were advocating for the Argentine values of "memory, truth, and justice."[70]

The Argentine president's speech was one of many that she has delivered since her second election in 2011 that upholds hegemonic constructs of national identity and valor on the shifting foundations of the Malvinas

War's legacy. Yet Cristina Fernández de Kirchner's totalizing memory narrative does not wholly coincide with the recollections of several soldiers who fought against British troops. As a historian, Federico Lorenz considers how their remembrances of battle and reasons for engaging in conflict can coexist with the president's accounts of the war. Lorenz is particularly invested in exploring how Fernández de Kirchner's reframing of the Malvinas conflict elides the dictatorship's attempt to frame the war as part of its efforts to eliminate subversives, while also wondering about how active and retired members of the military who "still uphold the role of the armed forces during the last dictatorship" respond to the president's messaging.[71]

Playwright Lisandro Fiks is also interested in using his dramaturgy to explore how the war is remembered by those who served as opposed to those who did not and how different political opinions shape those recollections. Fiks probes these difficult queries in his 2012 play *1982 Obertura solemne* (*1982 Solemn Overture*). The play, codirected by the playwright and Diego Quiroz in its premiere at Espacio Polonia and running intermittently in Buenos Aires through May 2017, depicts a composer named Martín who wants to create an overture to commemorate Argentina's participation in the Malvinas War. He hopes that this composition will carry as much cultural significance as Tchaikovsky's 1812 Overture, which marked the Russian Army's valiant defeat at the hands of Napoleon Bonaparte during the French invasion. When a Malvinas War veteran comes to his home, the duo initiate a dialogue that covers war, politics, art, and who shapes the narratives of how they are publicly received.

The play begins with a conversation introducing Martín and his girlfriend, Victoria. The couple interact in the apartment that they have built together, furnished by scenic designer Ana Bellone as an elegant home filled with paintings, clay vases, and a bookshelf that prominently displays several political texts, including Marx's *Capital* and Walter Benjamin's *Critique of Violence*.[72] The duo discuss Martín's overture, and Victoria chides her boyfriend for allowing the project to keep him from participating in several recent demonstrations. Martín lacks his partner's political fervor and encourages her to go to these protests on her own so that he can finish composing. Their argument becomes increasingly heated until Victoria's brother, Federico, enters the playing space. The trio planned to celebrate Federico's birthday, but on his taxicab ride to their home, the guest of honor learned that his driver was a Malvinas veteran and invited him into the house to speak with Martín, whose only knowledge about the war has been accumulated through mass media.

The opening scene raises initial questions about the ways art can contribute to political conversations. Although Victoria is skeptical of Martín's work, he believes that the overture will inspire Argentines to remember the honorable men who died in battle in what he calls "our war."[73] The reference to the war as "ours" is particularly noteworthy, as it raises questions about Martín's belief regarding ownership of the Malvinas conflict. He implies that the war is part of the shared cultural heritage of all Argentines, but as he describes the ways he is depicting the conflict in his opus, he reveals an understanding of the conflict that is particularly driven by narratives of youthful resistance in spite of poor military leadership and lack of preparation. This Malvinas narrative, which is familiar to many Argentine audiences, serves as a reminder of the ways Argentina's cultural elites "arbitrarily select elements" of the war narrative with what Federico Lorenz refers to as "the aim of perpetuating a vision of history, which was also a model of virtue."[74]

When taxi driver Leonardo enters Martín and Victoria's apartment, he immediately challenges their perceptions of Malvinas veterans. Victoria, a zealous graduate student in sociology at the University of Buenos Aires, begins asking the driver about his politics to make small talk. Initially, Leonardo defers to her, but over the course of the conversation, he mentions that he primarily receives his political insight from listening to talk radio, citing Buenos Aires radio station Radio 10 and popular daytime talk-show hosts Oscar González Oro and Baby Etchecopar. The references to these hosts are immediately familiar to Argentine audiences, who know the controversial radio station and its ubiquitous demagogues as purveyors of conservative tabloid fodder that leftists derisively refer to as *facho*, or fascist. The conversation catches Victoria, Federico, and Martín off guard, in part because mass media narratives surrounding the war have presented soldiers as allied with Argentina's democratization, yet as Paola Ehrmantraut reminds readers in her essay on Malvinas War memorials, the soldiers are not monolithic, and some continue to uphold the dictatorship's virtues.[75] When Victoria responds to Leonardo's revelation by suggesting that the driver would be better served by reading the essays of liberal Peronist Arturo Jauretche, the two begin heatedly debating Argentine politics, and the play establishes itself as a comic political exchange.

Federico and Martín become mediators in the partisan crossfire between liberal Victoria and conservative Leonardo, each intervening in his own way (fig. 4.4). Whereas Federico tries to get the two characters to reach some tentative points of agreement, Martín attempts to return the conversation to his overture. When the characters temporarily change discussion topics, Martín asks Leonardo to talk about his war experiences, and once again the dialogue fundamentally transforms the composer's perceptions about the men who fought in combat against Great Britain. The taxi driver provides a chronicle of his wartime experiences that includes fond remembrances of Lieutenant Commander Alfredo Astiz, recollections of fighting valiantly alongside his senior officers on the front lines of battle, being captured and coerced into clearing land mines with other prisoners of war, and witnessing the British military kill surrendering soldiers with point-blank gunshots to the head. Leonardo continues to describe the war by making reference to British troops sinking the *General Belgrano* when it was outside the Malvinas exclusion zone that delineated the boundaries for combat. The veteran concludes by lamenting how he and his fellow soldiers went to war "to bring joy to the Argentine people," but on returning, he faced indifference and diminished employment prospects.[76]

Figure 4.4. Lisandro Fiks, Darío Dukáh, Christian Alvarez, and Roxana Artal (*left to right*) begin a heated political debate in Fiks's *1982 Obertura solemne*. PHOTO BY ANNA BELLONE. COURTESY OF LISANDRO FIKS.

Leonardo's discourse in this lengthy exchange is essential to understanding the play. At several moments, the taxi driver presents information that runs counter to the Malvinas narratives typically presented. His report about fighting alongside fellow officers subverts narratives that suggest that the troops who died at war were victims of poor military management. These passages evoke Rosana Guber's essay about Argentina's reasons for ignoring or obfuscating British military crimes, such as the abuse and execution of war prisoners and the sinking of the *General Belgrano*, in its war narratives despite the likelihood that such revelations would further unite Argentines in their efforts to see the Malvinas Islands returned to national sovereignty.[77] Moreover, although Leonardo's chronicles of war deviate from politically minded memory narratives of the Kirchner administration, historical evidence suggests that the veteran's positions reflect the actual beliefs of many ex-soldiers. Federico Lorenz's oral history of former Malvinas combatants suggests that former servicemen have resisted the narrative that incompetent military leadership undermined the war effort, finding that several of his interviewed subjects believe that such discourses turn them into helpless victims and citing one conscript who claims that by degrading the officers, these politicized narratives undermine the courage demonstrated by all veterans.[78]

In spite of Leonardo's personal testimonies of war, Martín cannot reconcile what he has been told against his understanding that has been informed by reading war novels and watching documentaries about the Malvinas. Fiks's play shifts into a richer discussion about mass media representations of the war. As the composer asks Leonardo what he thinks about war films, citing *Iluminados por el fuego* specifically, the veteran notes the movie's multiple inaccuracies while continuing to speak of his own lived experience. That Martín, Victoria, and Federico cannot believe the soldier's statements speaks to Ehrmantraut's notion that the military found itself embodying an outmoded discourse of combative nationalism in the early years of democracy, which led human rights groups and other purveyors of memory to develop narratives about the soldiers who fought at war that were truer of postwar political realities.[79]

Through this moment in *1982 Obertura solemne*, the play seems to favor Leonardo's descriptions of his war experiences as being more accurate than Victoria's political beliefs, Martín's understandings of the war through film and literature, or Federico's vacillation between the other characters' perspectives. The play begins to turn the audience's sympathies away from the former soldier, however, after it is revealed that Federico and Martín took efforts to avoid being drafted into service. The Malvinas veteran loses his temper, affirming his love of Argentina and hatred of those who oppose it, before accusing the other two men of being people who "love to play the victim" like his countrymen who opposed the state's efforts to eradicate the subversion that was "tearing the country apart" and "preventing the nation from growing as it deserves" in the years leading up to and during the dictatorship.[80]

Although Fiks's play implied Leonardo's conservative beliefs at earlier points with his references to Argentine Radio 10 and Alfredo Astiz, this moment reveals the character as a sympathizer for the dictatorship, fundamentally undermining war narratives that seek to define the soldiers who fought at war as noble men. Such confessions blur the distinctions between the military's authoritarian torturers and the Malvinas war heroes that democratic administrations dating back to Alfonsín have tried to uphold. In performance, Leonardo's declaration elicited a gasp from several spectators, yet again the historical record makes clear that several of the soldiers who fought in the Malvinas conflict also participated in the Process of National Reorganization. Lorenz and Guber note that several military leaders saw both the eradication of Argentine subversives and the Malvinas conflict as wars fought on behalf of Argentina's Process.[81] The taxi driver's reference to Alfredo Astiz proves particularly telling, as the former Naval commander whom Leonardo describes as a hero was one of the first officers to be convicted of human rights abuses once the Kirchner administration began to retry officers for crimes related to the dictatorship.

Leonardo's stating of his dictatorial sympathies shifts the audience's understandings of his character and aligns the spectators with Victoria, Martín, and Federico, particularly as the argument between the four actors continues and the Malvinas veteran appears to defend the military techniques of Adolf Hitler. This repositioning of the spectators continues in the play's most melodramatic turn, when it is revealed that Leonardo did not actually serve in the Malvinas War. He defends himself by noting that the narrative he created was no less artificial than the war account that Martín hopes to share through the creation of his Malvinas overture. In all instances, the characters have become so entrenched in disseminating their own particular ideologies about Argentina's war with Great Britain that they are imbuing their conversations about the Malvinas with what Carol Martin calls a heavily curated process of "selection, editing and organizing" that feels real to each of the characters yet is not entirely accurate.[82]

As the play moves toward its conclusion, the characters decide to separate, and Fiks feigns once more at allowing Leonardo to depart as a villain, when Veronica makes a derisive comment about the former soldier's ability to be a good father to his children. The veteran turns toward the sociology student with intent to harm, and when Federico intervenes, the taxi driver grabs him by the neck and holds a knife to his throat. During this scuffle, Veronica is able to knock out Leonardo with a rolling pin, and in another melodramatic scenario, the characters contemplate killing him, but he then recovers consciousness and is escorted out of Martín and Veronica's apartment. Although the play devolves into histrionics at the expense of a more complex resolution, the denouement still provides insight into the state of Malvinas politics. Fiks's play speaks to the way Malvinas War memory narratives have become so ingrained among liberal and conservative ideologues that there can be no reconciling the two points of view. Moreover, the three characters' willingness to consider killing the war veteran and then burning and disposing of his body for a brief moment when they think he is dead is a subtle yet meaningful allusion to the ways that ex-Malvinas soldiers and their lived experiences have been discarded when they do not adhere to specific political discourses.

In an interview conducted with Argentine newspaper *Clarín*, Fiks acknowledges that the memory narratives surrounding the Malvinas still contain rifts that have not been addressed or acknowledged. For him, the theatre can contribute to Argentines' collective consciousness about the war to make the fissures visible to a public who might not know otherwise.[83] Fiks's *1982 Obertura solemne* may not offer any solutions to the tensions among competing Malvinas narratives, but in the wake of political efforts to erase some of those discourses altogether, the mere presence of resistant perspectives can recontextualize the war and give it meaning that expands beyond contemporary political agendas. The Malvinas War remains a contested part of Argentina's history, and discussions about contrasting viewpoints can create spaces for both memorialization and critical engagement, but *1982 Obertura solemne*'s conclusion suggests that Argentina is not presently prepared for such discussions.

Nationalist reframings of war often try to depict an imagined past that justifies present interests. Although the Kirchner administrations have constructed a memory narrative of the Malvinas that situates the armed conflict as a necessary response to centuries of colonialist overreach, as opposed to a dictatorship's last-ditch efforts to mobilize popular support, the theatre has functioned as a site of resistance that has helped provide a richer understanding of the islands' historical ties to Argentina. Additionally, the theatre has created a multilayered representation of the men who fought over the islands to counter discourses that seek to marginalize the men's agency and the Argentine public's investment in success. As the postwar generation's perspectives about the Malvinas and their relationship to the state continue to develop in the wake of Cristina Fernández de Kirchner's presidency, performance once again provides awareness of the political apparatus's construction of memory narratives.

Conclusion:
The Next Stages of Theatrical Production, Postdictatorship Memory, and Transitional Justice

IN THE FINAL YEARS of Cristina Fernández de Kirchner's presidency, Argentina continued to serve as a global trailblazer in transitional justice practices. In March 2013, an Argentine federal court in Buenos Aires began a judicial inquiry into the totality of kidnappings, murders, and other criminal acts staged in Argentina, Bolivia, Chile, Peru, and Paraguay as part of Operation Condor—a clandestine campaign allegedly coordinated by several Latin American countries during the 1970s and 1980s to marginalize subversives who opposed military rule. The trial sought to explore the full extent of collaborations among these Southern Cone republics and their collusion to cover up hundreds of violent and politically motivated misdeeds. These proceedings examined thousands of pages of documents and called nearly four hundred witnesses to the stand to offer testimony in an investigation that ran for more than three years.

On May 27, 2016, fourteen former Argentine and Uruguayan military officers, including Reynaldo Bignone, were convicted of working together in international criminal activity. Although many of the defendants are dead or imprisoned, Argentine officials hope that the measures will produce further information about political atrocities across the continent. Transitional justice scholar Francesca Lessa notes that the trial was an unprecedented transnational experiment that may advance transitional justice practices from being limited to proceedings enacted in individual nation states to larger collaborative efforts across the continent.[1] Simultaneously, dozens of other trials are currently ongoing across Argentina in which individual mid-level and low-level officers stand accused of kidnapping, torture, and other Process-related crimes.

Moreover, Argentina's impact on transitional justice practices during the Kirchner administrations also shaped political actions in other nations across the Americas. In December 2014, Brazil's national Truth Commission completed its investigation into human rights abuses during its own dictatorship. Citing the influence of Argentina's Truth Commission, the Brazilian panel of seven interviewed hundreds of individuals and researched archival death certificates and morgue records to explore the government's crackdown on students, labor unions, indigenous tribes, and other entities who resisted military rule. The commission also proposed the repeal of amnesty laws so that the nation could prosecute the perpetrators of political violence.[2] Although neither embattled Brazilian president Dilma Rousseff nor her successor, Michel Temer, has acted on these edicts, the two-thousand-page document that the committee produced signaled a profound change in Brazil's transitional justice policy as the country makes its first steps toward redressing its past and preventing similar authoritarianism in the future.

Similarly, in April 2017, the Colombian government announced the formation of a truth commission with the FARC guerrilla movement to investigate culpability for the political atrocities that have occurred across that nation over the past fifty years. The truth-finding council is expected to call thousands of citizens to testify about human rights violations, and Argentina's National Commission on the Disappearance of Persons has been cited as a model for what the council might look like and how it might function. Although the status of this commission remains in question until Colombia's Constitutional Court can rule on its legality, it is important to note that Argentina serves as a model for a legislative and judicial path toward peace.

Additionally, Argentina continued to contest British sovereignty over the Malvinas Islands. Cristina Fernández de Kirchner made the islands her primary foreign policy priority in the final year of her presidency, marking June 10, 2015, as a Day of Affirmation of Argentine Rights over the Malvinas Islands. In a speech delivered that day, the president declared that British rule was anachronistic, colonialist, and illegitimate, while advocating for continued dialogue with British prime minister David Cameron to negotiate a peaceful recovery of the islands. In response, the British government began tapping the islands' oil, and the British Parliament approved the expenditure of £180 million to enhance the Malvinas military defenses. Although a 2013 referendum confirmed that 99.8 percent of the contested territory's residents would prefer to remain under British rule, Argentine popular support for regaining control of the lands remains extraordinarily strong, and the president used the primacy of this issue to boost her approval rating.

Yet in spite of Argentina's ongoing transitional justice efforts and the country's influence on practices abroad, the nation's citizens remain skeptical about their government's ability to maintain human rights and act within the rule of law. An April 2015 poll revealed that nearly 75 percent of Argentines believed that the nation's politicians were not law-abiding and that the government would act in its own self-interest during times of political duress.[3] These numbers are not just indictments of the Kirchner administration, as they mirror data from a similar poll taken in 2004, before charges of corruption began to beset Cristina's presidency. Skepticism toward the government's ability to fully advocate for victims of dictatorial violence grew in June 2006, when bricklayer Jorge Julio López disappeared hours before he was scheduled to give testimony about Miguel Etchecolatz, one of the first defendants tried for crimes related to the dictatorship following the overturning of Argentina's impunity laws. López was regarded as a key witness in the trial when he was kidnapped on his walk to the courthouse.

Argentines have also grown wary of the government's ability to successfully investigate violent acts where it finds itself implicated. For example, government prosecutor Alberto Nisman was found dead from a gunshot wound in his apartment on January 18, 2015—days before he was scheduled to give testimony to Argentina's Congress concerning a report in which he accused Cristina Fernández de Kirchner and her foreign minister, Héctor Timerman, of conspiring to protect Iran from culpability for the 1994 bombing of the Argentine Israelite Mutual Association building, which killed eighty-five people and injured hundreds more. Argentine intelligence officers continue to investigate the prosecutor's death, but it remains unknown whether Nisman died of suicide or murder.

At present, however, change is on the horizon for Argentina and for the country's transitional justice policies. As is often the case, financial concerns and a recent presidential election have driven Argentina's politics in a new direction. Under the Kirchner administrations, Argentina made significant economic gains. According to information from the Socioeconomic Database for Latin American and the Caribbean, poverty levels decreased 70 percent.[4] Additionally, the International Monetary Fund notes that the nation's unemployment rate fell from 17.2 to 6.9 percent. However, the nation's economy had stalled in recent years, leading to slow growth, inflation levels approaching 25 percent, a financial crisis stemming from refusal to comply with a 2012 ruling that Argentina needed to repay its U.S. creditors, and an emergent black market for U.S. dollars. With Cristina Fernández de Kirchner term-limited out of office, her handpicked successor, Daniel Scioli, failed to galvanize Argentine voters and defend the fiscal accomplishments of the Kirchner administration.

In opposition, businessman and Buenos Aires mayor Mauricio Macri presented himself as a technocratic and fiscally minded agent of change who would propose market-friendly measures to encourage foreign lending and investment without undermining the nation's social services. This reform-oriented economic messaging enabled the opposition-party candidate to undercut Argentina's strong Peronist base and win an upset election over Scioli by the narrow margin of 51.44 percent to 48.56 percent. On assuming the presidency in December 2015, Macri began filling his cabinet with former executives of major corporations, including Shell, JP Morgan, General Motors, and Telecom Argentina. Moreover, he has initiated policy changes designed to curb inflation and prevent capital flight, including lifting the currency controls put in place by the Kirchner administration. Yet as the president has enacted new policies, he has been mindful that the Peronist party controls the nation's legislature, governors, and trade unions. Additionally, Cristina Fernández de Kirchner still functions as her party's de facto leader and currently seeks a seat on the Argentine Senate.

Before leaving office, Cristina Kirchner continued to advocate on behalf of the *desaparecidos* and the activists who fought for their memory. She delivered a final address to human rights supporters in the closing week of her term, noting her and her husband's long commitment to working on behalf of Argentina's disappeared and the presidential couple's shared history of creating commemorative spaces, removing legal barriers, and opening judicial proceedings against officers and others who had committed wrongdoings during the dictatorship. As the outgoing president stood alongside members of the Grandmothers of the Plaza de Mayo, the Association of the Mothers of the Plaza de Mayo, and H.I.J.O.S., she communicated an intergenerational need to continue searching for answers, while suggesting that the Macri administration would look the other way. Although Macri was not particularly vocal about human rights, transitional justice policies, and memory politics in the run-up to his election, executive and judicial policy changes in the early years of his presidency unnerved human rights activists.

Shortly after Macri's election, conservative newspaper *La Nación* published an anonymously written op-ed, which saw the presidential election as a favorable moment to "bury the desire for revenge once and forever" and called for renewed amnesty and impunity for soldiers convicted of crimes connected to the dictatorship.[5] Additionally, governmental entities that had previously been empowered to gather evidence for human rights trials were closed as cost-saving measures. As a result, several trials and court proceedings have been delayed, and there is some concern that they will cease altogether.[6] Macri's austerity policies are also affecting memory spaces, as the president has changed the leadership structure for Argentina's National Memory Archive.

More disturbing for proponents of continued transitional justice measures was an interview with Buzzfeed in August 2016 in which the president questioned the long-accepted estimate of thirty thousand *desaparecidos* detained or murdered by the dictatorship.[7] Such statements are seen as part of a growing trend of dictatorship denialism pervading Argentina. Additionally, in May 2017, the Argentine Supreme Court ruled that Argentina's 2x1 law applied to Luis Muiña, a man convicted of Process-related crimes. The decree, which was law in Argentina from 1994 to 2001, states that detained prisoners who had not yet been convicted of crimes could receive credit for two days of custody for every day served. As a result, the prison terms of many military leaders who were detained for lengthy periods before receiving guilty verdicts may end early. Although justices appointed by Macri cast the decisive votes, political leaders of all affiliations, including the president, have condemned the ruling, and the National Congress is working to close this loophole.

Nevertheless, human rights activists have made some gains in the Macri presidency. In March 2016, U.S. president Barack Obama visited Buenos Aires's Parque de la Memoria on the fortieth anniversary of the dictatorship and announced the declassification of more than four thousand U.S. government documents related to the Process. However, a seeming lack of interest in pursuing perpetrators of dictatorship-era violence, in addition to a number of perceived aggressions toward memory activists, has unnerved many of the nation's largest human rights organizations, including the Mothers and Grandmothers of the Plaza de Mayo and H.I.J.O.S.

Unexplored Aspects of Argentine Theatre, Dictatorship, and Transitional Justice

Argentina's postdictatorship transitional justice policies have profoundly affected the nation's politics and public life. Alfonsín's election and the restoration of democracy created the promise of justice and discipline enacted on the perpetrators of dictatorial violence. Although the National Commission on the Disappearance of Persons and the publication of *Nunca Más* made the Process's brutality legible, the passage of the Full Stop and Due Obedience Laws, alongside Menem's pardons, enabled those responsible for political violence to enjoy impunity. Transitional justice policies grounded in memory narratives of reconciliation failed to account for former political prisoners and the disappeared families' need for recompense. Even the overturning of amnesty laws and efforts to restore confidence in the government through reconciliatory gestures during the Kirchner administration did not wholly satisfy human rights activists, who recognized that Argentina's wounds could not be mended solely through government-enacted transitional justice measures. Trials, reparations, and other political actions cannot wholly explain the conditions that made dictatorship possible, nor can they entirely ensure that such situations will never arise again. As Argentine sociologist Héctor Schmuncler writes, political justice must be understood in relation to its effects on individuals and social institutions.[8] The narratives that these entities produce ultimately determine the legitimacy of governmental action.

This book has explored state-enacted transitional justice strategies and justifications for authorizing such procedures in relationship to publicly generated memory following Argentina's dictatorship. I have argued that cultural production creates memory narratives and that such discourses are necessary to determine how a society understands historical events and pressure political agents to enact transitional justice policies. Argentina's collective memory of the Process has long been divided between those who desire to leave this critical moment in the nation's history behind them and those who insist that memory has what Paul Ricoeur refers to as a "moral priority" to do justice toward history's victims by reminding future generations of national trauma.[9] The transmission of both aspects of collective memory across the nation's populace would not have been possible without cultural agents who offered an alternative perspective to the Argentine government's official narratives on the dictatorship. Exploration of Buenos

Aires's vibrant theatre through this lens makes visible the ways that performance has catalyzed resistance to memory narratives of forgetting and made legible the difficulties of engaging with the nation's legacy of violence.

The postdictatorship's plays and performances introduced acts of political resistance that produced a richer engagement with transitional justice policies, as evidenced by nearly four decades of dramatic material and the growth of Argentina's theatregoing audiences during the majority of these years. The nation's history of repression becomes perceptible to spectators and the potential for social change has grown as a result of theatrical works that produce complex memory narratives that either resist or reinforce political efforts to redress the nation's violence toward the *desaparecidos* and their families.

Argentina continues to house vibrant theatre communities that produce challenging plays that reach a large portion of the nation's theatre-going population. Although the works featured in this study have drawn on a distinguished and critically significant group of artists whose productions have toured the globe, other major playwrights have also influenced the Buenos Aires theatre to think beyond domestic realism and deserve critical examination. These theatre makers include Claudio Tolcachir, Rafael Spregelburd, Lucía Laragione, Cristina Escofet, Alejandro Tantanian, Romina Paula, Santiago Loza, Matías Feldman, Marcelo Mininno, and dozens of other playwrights, directors, and devisers who are producing exciting work in Buenos Aires's independent theatres—taking part in critiques of neoliberalism, exploring the psychology of Argentine families, and calling attention to marginalized figures whose stories deserve to be told. Their work has been increasingly circulating in festival circuits across Europe and the United States and is starting to appear in journals such as *Latin American Theatre Review, Gestos,* and *Karpa.* Theatre studies still has ample room to consider these artists within the context of present-day Argentina and in relation to world drama.

Buenos Aires's theatre has also drawn attention to many aspects of the postdictatorship, creating memory narratives about Argentina's varied transitional justice strategies. Nevertheless, several aspects of the democratic transition remain underexplored by the theatre and other cultural producers. For instance, several of the plays featured in this study allude to political efforts to move the nation toward a state of remembering Argentina's *desaparecidos.* The theatre has not provided perspective on those thousands of Argentines who advocate on behalf of memory narratives of closure and forgiveness. Similarly, although several of the Malvinas plays depict soldiers who question military orders, abdicate their responsibilities, and commit acts of desertion in response to the dictatorship's failed military strategy, the theatre could better explore depictions of military figures who opposed the Process and the internal conflict between duty to country and defending personally held beliefs about the state's treatment of its citizens. This frame of reference may hold particular value for spectators who also share a sense of uncertainty and shame about not having resisted the political calls for monitoring neighbors and reporting on fellow citizens with allegedly subversive behaviors. While recent theatre projects reassess the archive and engage in documentation of the self, artists may consider the ways that revealing too much of themselves online and in performance spaces may lead to increased governmental surveillance.

As the theatre continues to focus on the postdictatorship experiences of the *desaparecidos*' children, playwrights have dramatized young adults who examined their parents' involvement in political organizations such as the Montoneros. While characters such as María in *Instrucciones para un coleccionista de mariposas* occasionally question why their mothers and fathers participated in leftist political activities as a way of lamenting their lived experiences growing up alone, the theatre still fails to account for children of the disappeared who genuinely opposed their parents' political involvement. In this sense, the theatre lags behind Argentina's independent filmmakers, who are calling attention to this lacunae in memory discourse in films such as Luis César D'Angiolillo's *Potestad* (*Power*), María Inés Roqué's *Papá Iván*, and Albertina Carri's *Los Rubios* (*The Blondes*). Moreover, several plays out of the *Teatroxlaidentidad* festival present characterizations of children raised by appropriators who embrace their guardians' beliefs about leftists and the dictatorship's merits. Exploring these experiences might challenge human rights activists' narratives that viewpoints on violence and politics are reproduced through child-rearing practices.

However, perhaps the greatest challenge for theatre artists in Buenos Aires is to advocate for transitional justice policies that move beyond a human rights agenda grounded in the positionality of the biological family. Elizabeth Jelin suggests that such action might "open up and invite the wider participation of citizens in the political debate on 'settling accounts with the past.'"[10] While Cecilia Sosa's monograph *Queering Acts of Mourning in the Aftermath of Argentina's Dictatorship* points to numerous performance, films, and literary works that "queer" the hierarchical "biological normativity" that informs postdictatorship human rights activism in Argentina, these artistic creations have not meaningfully changed the emphasis on kinship ties in the nation's political discourse.[11]

For example, when Argentina passed legislation legalizing same-sex marriage, as well as a subsequent measure that required public health-care plans to include hormonal therapy and gender-reassignment surgery for any citizen over the age of eighteen, several conservative organizations and individuals led by Buenos Aires archbishop Jorge Bergoglio—later appointed Pope Francis—argued that the law would fundamentally disrupt the natural identity of the family, historically seen as mother, father, and children.[12] However, the advocates for these causes appropriated the language of kinship and biology to highlight how conservatives have consistently upheld the importance of the "traditional" family as essential to the development of a strong Argentina, echoing the discourse of gender and patriarchy appropriated by the military during the dictatorship. This restrictive framing of family dynamics limits the ability of the nation's human rights activists and politicians to engage in strategies that might make unrepresented bodies more visibly recognized.

Although a study of Argentine theatre performed by working artists outside Buenos Aires is beyond the scope of this book, it is important to note that the theatre thrives as a site of political activism in a number of other cities in Argentina, including Santa Fe, Mendoza, Tucumán, and Córdoba. Many of these cities have their own theatre funding mechanisms, and they produce quality work created by trained theatre professionals of high caliber at performance spaces that are impressive architectural structures with extraordinary technical capabilities. Similarly, an examination of Argentina's vibrant community theatre organizations could produce a rich tapestry of knowledge about the ways specific communities have engaged in the process of creating memory narratives that provide local specificity for reconciling the state's transitional justice policies with remembrances of the disappeared.

At this moment of potential upheaval and change from transitional justice policies of truth and reparation to those again tied to the process of impunity, the theatre remains a catalyst for creating memory narratives that challenge the official political perspectives of the Argentine government. Recent years have seen the emergence of plays that explore the full legacy of Carlos Menem's presidency and the ongoing aftermath of his disastrous economic policies. For example, Marcos Perearnau's *Menem*

Actor (2012) explores the former president's political duplicity and the ways the notoriously smooth-talking politician manipulated multiple political constituencies to sell the public on pegging the Argentine peso to the U.S. dollar and privatizing the nation's utilities as a way of prompting economic growth. Although the play takes a seriocomic tone that mocks Menem's reliance on tarot card–wielding psychics and his use of plastic surgery, while depicting the internal drama of his family as melodrama, the play is among the first to seriously examine the administration and explore the causes of Argentina's swift financial rise and fall during the 1990s.

Additionally, Argentine theatre artists are developing the techniques that they used to create postdictatorship memory narratives in response to the dictatorship and taking their dramaturgical methods to other countries. In 2012, Lola Arias staged *El año en que nací* (*The Year I Was Born*), which clearly draws influence from *Mi vida después*. The playwright and director collaborated with a group of Chilean actors to create a theatre piece that shares the experiences of young men and women who speak of their childhood under Pinochet's dictatorship. As in her earlier work, the production incorporates personal artifacts belonging to the characters and their relatives, live music, and historical documents and photographs that are projected and manipulated onstage. In a 2013 interview, Arias mentions she has been invited to create variations in Brazil and Peru and has spoken to theatre artists in Hungary and the Czech Republic.[13] The production has toured across Latin America, Europe, and the United States and is serving as a model for how the theatre can inform memory narratives about transitional justice processes with transnational impact. Arias is one of many Argentine artists whose work now tours internationally where she can find adequate funding to share her productions with wide-ranging and diverse audiences.

Civil society and cultural production have often driven human rights efforts in postdictatorship Argentina, placing pressure on the government through publicly visible and performative actions, including massive-scale protests and collaboration with the theatre. Since the dictatorship's end, Buenos Aires's theatre artists have criticized Argentina's impunity-driven transitional justice policies and have spoken out against the Process's sociocultural and political effects on the nation's citizens. The plays and performances discussed in this text have participated in shaping Argentina's memory discourse by challenging the statements of political figures who resisted redress, while also proposing strategies for reparation and

commemoration narratives that assist in providing solace for those directly and indirectly affected by the political oppression of the 1970s and
1980s. Theatrical creators and playwrights collaborated with human rights
activists to explore the multiple levels of accountability that the nation's
citizens share for allowing political violence to occur. Moreover, the scripts
and productions examined have helped propel the nation's theatre into new
genres and aesthetics that have reasserted the theatre's vibrancy and relevance to *porteño* audiences. As the theatre creates new memory narratives
that emerge from the needs of Argentina's postdictatorship generations,
performance offers the promise of shaping future efforts to enact justice
across Argentina by resisting official discourse and inciting spectators to
action.

Notes

Bibliography

Index

Notes

Introduction: Shaping Memory and Performance in Postdictatorship Argentina

1. The most complete theatre listings for Argentine performances are found on the *Alternativa Teatral* website, accessed January 31, 2016, www.alternativateatral .com.

2. Jean Graham-Jones, "Rethinking Buenos Aires Theatre in the Wake of 2001 and Emerging Structures of Resistance and Resilience," *Theatre Journal* 66.1 (March 2014): 39.

3. Mercedes Menendez, "Entrevista con Daniel Fanego: 'No hago tele porque no me llaman,'" *Tiempo Argentino*, September 8, 2010, accessed May 12, 2015, http://tiempo.infonews.com/nota/115249/no-hago-tele-porque-no-me-llaman.

4. Eugenio Barba, *Beyond the Floating Islands*, trans. Judy Barba, Richard Fowler, Jerrold C. Rodesch, and Saul Shapiro (New York: PAJ Publications, 1986), 26.

5. For research on Teatro Abierto, see Miguel Angel Giella, *Teatro Abierto 1981* (Buenos Aires: Corregidor, 1992), 1: 13–62; Jean Graham-Jones, *Exorcising History: Argentine Theatre under Dictatorship* (Lewisburg, PA: Bucknell University Press, 2000), 89–122; Beatriz Trastoy, "Teatro Abierto 1981: Un fenómeno social and cultural," in *Historia del Teatro Argentino en Buenos Aires*, vol. 5, ed. Osvaldo Pellettieri (Buenos Aires: Galerna, 2001), 104–11.

6. Tina M. Campt, *Other Germans: Black Germans and the Politics of Race, Gender, and Memory in the Third Reich* (Ann Arbor: University of Michigan Press, 2005), 86–87.

7. Brandon Hamber and Richard A. Wilson, "Symbolic Closure through Memory, Reparation, and Revenge in Post-Conflict Societies," in *The Role of Memory in Ethnic Conflict*, ed. Ed Cairns and Michéal D. Roe (New York: Palgrave Macmillan, 2003), 165.

8. Francesca Lessa, *Memory and Transitional Justice in Argentina and Uruguay* (London: Palgrave Macmillan, 2013), 31.

9. Laurel E. Fletcher and Harvey Weinstein, "Violence and Social Repair: Rethinking the Conditions of Justice to Reconciliation," *Human Rights Quarterly* 24 (2002): 574.

10. Ellen Lutz, "Transitional Justice: Lessons Learned and the Road Ahead," in *Transitional Justice in the Twenty-First Century: Beyond Truth and Justice*, ed. Naomi Roht-Arriaza and Javier Marriezcurrena (London: Cambridge UP, 2006), 33.

11. Marina Walker, "Framing the Falklands/Malvinas War: National Interest in the *London Times*, *La Nación* (Argentina), and *El Murcurio* (Chile)," *Universum* 19.1 (Fall 2004), 219.

12. CONADEP (National Commission on the Disappearance of Persons), *Nunca Más* (Buenos Aires: Eudeba, 1984), 381.

13. Priscilla Hayner, "Fifteen Truth Commissions, 1974–1994: A Comparative Study," *Human Rights Quarterly* 16.4 (November 1994): 597–655.

14. Inés Gonzáles-Bombal, *El diálogo politico: La transición que no fue* (Buenos Aires: Centro de Estudios de Estado y Sociedad, 1991), 23.

15. Brenda Werth, *Theatre, Performance, and Memory Politics in Argentina* (New York: Palgrave Macmillan, 2010), 48.

16. See Laura Tedesco, *Democracy in Argentina: Hope and Disillusion* (London: Frank Cass, 1999), 126, for information about Alfonsín's appropriation of the Malvinas soldiers as a justification for negotiating with the *Carapintadas*; see also Federico Poore, "CFK Inaugurates Malvinas Museum," *Buenos Aires Herald*, June 11, 2014, accessed November 23, 2015, http://www.buenosairesherald.com/article/161783/cfk-inaugurates-malvinas-museum-.

17. See Gabriela Cerruti, "La historia de memoria. Entre la fetichización y el duelo," *Puentes* 1.3 (Fall 2001): 20–22; Elizabeth Jelin, *State Repression and the Labors of Memory* (Minneapolis: University of Minnesota Press, 2003); Daniel Lvovich and Jaqueline Bisquert, *La cambiate memoria de la dictadura. Discursos públicos, movimentos sociales y legitimidad democrática* (Los Polverinos, Argentina: Universidad Nacional de General Sarmiento, 2008).

18. See Henry L. Roediger III and James V. Wersch, "Creating a New Discipline of Memory Studies," *Memory Studies* 1 (January 2008), 9–22; Jeffrey K. Olick, Vered Vinitzky-Serouissi, and Daniel Levy, introduction to *The Collective Memory Reader* (Oxford: Oxford University Press, 2011), 3–62.

19. See Felipe Agüero and Eric Hershberg, "La Fuerzas Armadas y la memorias de la represión en el Cono Sur," in *Memorias militares sobre la represión en el Cono Sur*, ed. Eric Hershberg and Felipe Agüero (Madrid: Siglo XXI, 2005), 1–34; Jelin, *State Repression and the Labors of Memory*; Susana Kaiser, "To

Punish or Forgive? Young Citizens Attitudes of Impunity and Accountability in Contemporary Argentina," *Journal of Human Rights* 4.2 (2005): 171–96; Michael J. Lazzara, *Chile in Transition: The Poetics and Politics of Memory* (Gainesville: University of Florida Press, 2006); Steve J. Stern, *Remembering Pinochet's Chile: On the Eve of London 1998* (Durham, NC: Duke University Press, 2008).

20. Lazzara, *Chile in Transition*, 2.

21. Maurice Halbwachs, *On Collective Memory* (Chicago: University of Chicago Press, 1992), 13.

22. Jelin, *State Repression and the Labors of Memory*, 25.

23. Ibid., 18.

24. Ibid., 33–34.

25. Andreas Huyssen, *Present Pasts: Urban Palimpsests and the Politics of Memory* (Palo Alto, CA: Stanford University Press, 2003), 22.

26. See Jon Elster, *Retribution and Reparation in the Transition to Democracy* (London: Cambridge University Press, 2006) for further discussion of the distinctions between immediate and second-wave transitional justice.

1. Resisting the Menem Administration's Narratives of Reconciliation and Forgetting

1. Carlos Menem, "Discurso de asunción del Presidente Carlos Saul Menem ante la Asamblea Legislatava al asumir como presidente de la nación," political speech, Buenos Aires, Argentina, July 8, 1989.

2. Clara Nieto, *Master of War: Latin American and US Aggression from the Cuban Revolution through the Clinton Years* (New York: Seven Stories Press, 2001), 275–76.

3. See Leigh Payne's discussion of vital lies in *Unsettling Accounts: Neither Truth nor Reconciliation in Confessions of State Violence* (Durham, NC: Duke University Press, 2009).

4. Maria Pozzoni and Carla Sangrilli, "Algunas percepciones sobre el desencanto politico en la Argentina reciente," in *Memorias de la Argentina contemporánea, 1946–2002*, ed. Marcela Ferrari, Lila Ricci, and María Estella Spinelli (Buenos Aires: Eudem, 2007), 189.

5. For further discussion of the *escraches*, including firsthand accounts, performative analysis, and additional historical and political context, see Susan Kaiser, "*Escraches*: Demonstrations, Communication, and Political Memory in Post-dictatorial Argentina," *Media, Culture, and Society* 24.4 (July 2002): 499–516; Diana Taylor, "You Are Here: The DNA of Performance," *TDR* 46.1 (Spring 2002): 149–69.

6. Horacio Verbitsky, *El Vuelo* (Buenos Aires: Planeta, 1995), 3.

7. Marguerite Feitlowitz, *A Lexicon of Terror* (New York: Oxford University Press, 2006), 193.

8. Graham-Jones, *Exorcising History*, 158.

9. Osvaldo Pellettieri, ed., *Teatro Argentino y crisis, 2001–2003* (Buenos Aires: Eudeba, 2004), 14, 20.

10. Sharon Magnarelli, "The 1984 Theatre Season in Buenos Aires," *Latin American Theatre Review* 19.1 (Fall 1985): 89.

11. Jorge Dubatti, "El teatro en la dictadura: A 30 años de Golpe militar," *Picadero* 16 (2006): 19.

12. See Jorge Dubatti, "El canon de multiplicidad," in *El teatro labertino: Ensayos sobre teatro argentino*, ed. Jorge Dubatti (Buenos Aires: Atuel, 1999), 111–22; Graham-Jones, *Exorcising History*; Osvaldo Pellettieri, *Teatro Argentino del 2000* (Buenos Aires: Galerna, 2000).

13. Jorge Dubatti, "El teatro argentino en la post-dictadura, 1983–2010: Época de oro, Destotalización, y Subjetividad." *Stichomythia* 11–12 (2011): 74.

14. Laura Cerrato, "Lo postmoderno en la literatura de habla inglesa," in *Doce vueltas a la literatura*, ed. Laura Cerrato (Buenos Aires: Botella al mar, 1992), 161.

15. Martín Rodriguez, "La puesta en escena emergente y su futuro," in *Teatro Argentino del 2000*, ed. Osvaldo Pellettieri (Buenos Aires: Galerna, 2000), 177.

16. Hayden White, *Metahistory: The Historical Imagination in Nineteenth-Century Europe* (Baltimore: Johns Hopkins University Press, 1973), 20.

17. Werth, *Theatre, Performance, and Memory Politics*, 129.

18. Jonathan Kalb, *The Theatre of Heiner Müller* (London: Cambridge University Press, 1998), 109.

19. Lola Proaño-Gomez, "Posmodernidad y metáfora visual: *Máquina Hamlet*," *Gestos* 14.27 (April 1999), 77.

20. Matthew Isaac Cohen, "Puppetry and the Destruction of the Object," *Performance Research* 12.4 (2007): 124.

21. Amy Strahler, "A Theatre of Dangerous Illusions: *Máquina Hamlet* at BAM," *Latin American Theatre Review* 34.2 (Spring 2001): 204.

22. Bruce Weber, "To Be or Not to Be Something," *New York Times*, October 20, 2000, accessed June 1, 2013, http://theater2.nytimes.com/mem/theater/treview.html?res=9905E3DE133EF933A15753C1A9669C8B63.

23. Brian Walsh, "The Rest Is Violence: Müller Contra Shakespeare," *Performing Arts Journal* 23.3 (September 2001): 27.

24. Heiner Müller, *Máquina Hamlet*, trans. Gabriella Massuh and Dieter Welke, Center for Documentation of Theatre and Dance, Teatro San Martín, Buenos Aires.

25. Unless otherwise noted, all descriptions of staged action come from Heiner Müller, *Maquina Hamlet*, directed by El Periférico do Objetos, recorded October 15, 1995, Center for Documentation of Theatre and Dance, Teatro San Martín, Buenos Aires, VHS.

26. Müller, *Máquina Hamlet*, trans. Massuh and Welke, 3.

27. Diana Taylor, *Disappearing Acts: Spectacles of Gender and Nationalism in Argentina's "Dirty War"* (Durham, NC: Duke University Press, 1997), 6.

28. Lesley Gill, *The School of the Americas: Military Training and Political Violence in the Americas* (Durham, NC: Duke University Press, 2004), 20.

29. Müller, *Máquina Hamlet*, trans. Massuh and Welke, 10.

30. Ibid.

31. Ibid, 12.

32. Proaño-Gomez, "Posmodernidad y metáfora visual," 81.

33. Strahler, "Theatre of Dangerous Illusions," 204; Pat Donnelly, "Deconstructing the Bard: *Máquina Hamlet* Is a Dark, Prophetic Mix of Poetry and Politics," *Montreal Gazette*; May 28, 1999, D8; Diana Taylor, "Transculturating Transculturation," *Performing Arts Journal* 13.2 (1991): 90; Josette Ferál, "There Are at Least Three Americas," in *The Intercultural Performance Reader*, ed. Patrice Pavis (New York: Routledge, 1996), 56–57.

34. Kalb, *Theatre of Heiner Müller*, 16.

35. Ana Elena Puga, "The Abstract Allegory of Griselda Gambaro's *Stripped* (El despojamiento)," *Theatre Journal* 56.3 (October 2004): 427.

36. See Graham-Jones, *Exorcising History*, 20–54, for a discussion of allegory in Argentine theatre of the dictatorship.

37. It has been said that Javier Daulte renamed the suspect of his play Suarez Zabala, changing one letter in the character's surname to evade charges of libel. However, some believe this explanation to be apocryphal and say that the slight variation in name is simply due to a misspelling.

38. Unless otherwise noted, all descriptions of staged action come from Javier Daulte, *Martha Stutz*, directed by Diego Kogan, recorded May 23, 1997, Center for Documentation of Theatre and Dance, Teatro San Martín, Buenos Aires, VHS.

39. Sharon Magnarelli, "Telling Stories: *Martha Stutz* by Javier Daulte," *Latin American Theatre Review* 35.1 (Fall 2001): 11.

40. Javier Daulte, *Martha Stutz* (Buenos Aires: Ediciones último reino, 1997), 13.

41. Magnarelli, "Telling Stories," 6.

42. Daulte, *Martha Stutz* (1997), 14.

43. Shortly after confirmation as president, Menem increased the number of judges on Argentina's Supreme Court from five to nine justices and appointed four new members during a secretive parliamentary session.

44. Program for Javier Daulte's *Martha Stutz* at the Teatro San Martín, playbill, May 23, 1997, Buenos Aires: Center for the Documentation of Theatre and Dance, Teatro San Martín.

45. Beatriz Trastoy, "*Martha Stutz* de Javier Daulte: el teatro a través del espejo," in *Tradición, modernidad y posmodernidad*, ed. Osvaldo Pellettieri (Buenos Aires: Galerna, 1999), 288.

46. Brenda Werth, "Performing the Family Portrait in Marcelo Bertuccio's *Señora, esposa, niña y joven desde lejos*," *Latin American Theatre Review* 40.2 (Spring 2007): 23.

47. Beatriz Trastoy, *Teatro autobiográfico: Los unipersonales de los 80 y 90 en la escena argentina* (Buenos Aires: Nueva generación, 2002), 9.

48. Inger Agger and Søren Buus Jensen, *Trauma and Healing under State Terrorism* (London: Zed Books, 1996), 148.

49. Eric Santner, *Stranded Objects: Mourning, Memory, and Film in Postwar Germany* (Ithaca, NY: Cornell University Press, 1993), 37.

50. Unless otherwise noted, all descriptions of staged action come from Marcelo Bertuccio, *Señora, esposa, niña y joven desde lejos*, directed by Cristian Drut, recorded February 1, 1998, personal collection, DVD.

51. Alejandro Cruz, "El horror que navega en un recuerdo difuso," *La Nación*, February 6, 1998, accessed June 22, 2014, http://www2.lanacion.com.ar/nota.asp?nota_id=87227.

52. Marcelo Bertuccio, "Señora, esposa, niña y joven desde lejos," in *Teatro de la disintegración*, ed. Martín Rodriguez (Buenos Aires: Eudeba, 1999), 98–99.

53. Werth, "Performing the Family Portrait," 25.

54. Elizabeth Tabak de Bianchedi, Marcelo Bianchedi, Marian Braun, et al., "La política de la memoria: El movimiento de derechos humanos y la construcción democrática en la Argentina," in *Restitución de niños, Abuelas de Plaza de Mayo*, ed. Elizabeth Tabak de Bianchedi (Buenos Aires: Eudeba, 1997), 228.

55. Bertuccio, "Señora, esposa, niña y joven desde lejos," 99.

56. Ibid., 105.

57. Ivana Costa, "La palabra también es una desaparecida," *Clarín*, February 6, 1998, accessed June 22, 2014, http://edant.clarin.com/diario/1998/03/12/c-01401d.htm.

58. Bertuccio, "Senora, esposa, niña y joven desde lejos," 111.

59. Ibid., 105.

60. Michael Taussig, *Defacement: Public Secrecy and the Labor of the Negative* (Palo Alto: Stanford UP, 1995), 2.

61. Judith Filc, *Entre el parentesco y la política: Familia y dictadura 1976–1983* (Buenos Aires: Biblos, 1997), 83.

62. Marcelo Bertuccio, "Senora, esposa, niña y joven desde lejos," 111.

63. Ibid.

64. Lora Chernel, "Sophiensälle: Argentinien eingeladen, Arbieten die fehlenden Männer," *Wiener Zeitung*, June 6, 2000, 12.

65. Frido Hütter, "Die Tragödie der Verschwundenen," *Berliner Zeitung*, June 15, 2000, B5.

66. Federico Irazábal, "Manteniendo viva la memoria," *Cámara negra* (January 1998): 32.

67. Pellettieri, *Teatro Argentino y crisis*, 20.

68. Luis Cano, *Los Murmullos* (Buenos Aires: Editorial nueva generación, 2003), 51.

69. Ibid., 63–67.

70. Silvina Diaz, "El teatro 'posmoderno' en Buenos Aires: Una repuesta a la globalización cultural," *Dramateatro Revista Digital* 6 (September–December 2005), accessed October 21, 2014, http://dramateatro.fundacite.arg.gov.ve/ensayos/n_0016/silvina_diaz.htm.

71. Unless otherwise noted, all descriptions of staged action come from Luis Cano, *Los murmullos*, directed by Emilio García Wehbi, recorded May 2, 2002, Center for Documentation of Theatre and Dance, Teatro San Martín, Buenos Aires, DVD.

72. Alejandra Rodríguez, Leila Ocampo, and Mariana Milanesi, "Murmullos de ausencia," in *Teatro, cine, narrativa: Imagenes del nuevo siglo*, ed. Marta Lena Paz (Buenos Aires: University of Buenos Aires Press, 2003), 340.

73. Cano, *Los murmullos*, 31.

74. Ibid., 35.

75. Ibid., 37.

76. Taylor, *Disappearing Acts*, 222.

77. Cano, *Los murmullos*, 40.

78. Julia Elena Sagaseta, "*Los murmullos* de Luis Cano: Interrelación artística y compromiso," in *Teatro, cine, narrativa: Imagenes del nuevo siglo*, ed. Marta Lena Paz (Buenos Aires: University of Buenos Aires Press, 2003), 169.

79. See Jean Graham-Jones, *Evita Inevitably: Performing Argentina's Female Icons Before and After Eva Perón* (Ann Arbor: University of Michigan Press, 2014) for an extended conversation about the imagery and iconography of Evita Perón.

80. Cano, *Los murmullos*, 44.

81. Feitlowitz, *Lexicon of Terror*, 51.

82. Cano, *Los murmullos*, 47.

83. Ibid., 48.

84. Ibid., 48–49.

85. Alejandro Cruz, "Un espectáculo que no llega a conmover," *La Nación*, May 3, 2002, accessed June 1, 2014, http://www.lanacion.com.ar/393449-un-espectaculo-que-no-llega-a-conmover.

86. Lorena Verzero, "La desmesura, o qué hacer con tanto pasado," *Teatro XXI* 15 (Spring 2002): 61.

87. Antonius C. G. M. Robben, "State Terror in the Netherworld: Disappearance and Reburial in Argentina," in *Death Squad: The Anthropology of State Terror*, ed. Jeffrey A. Sluka (Philadelphia: University of Pennsylvania Press, 2000), 116.

2. *Teatroxlaidentidad:* The Right to Memory and Identity

1. See Naomi Roht-Arriza, *Transitional Justice in the Age of Human Rights* (Philadelphia: University of Pennsylvania Press, 2006) and Elin Skaar, *Judicial Independence and Human Rights in Latin America* (London: Palgrave Macmillan, 2011) for further information about European trials of Argentine military officers.

2. Equipo Argentino de Anthropología Forense (EAAF), "Sección Especial—Derecho a la Verdad," in *Informe Anual 2002* (Buenos Aires: EAAF, 2002), 130–35.

3. Inter-American Commission on Human Rights, "Report 21/00," *Case 12.059: Carmen Aguiar de Lapacó*, February 29, 2000, paragraph 17.1.

4. Francesca Lessa, *Memory and Transitional Justice in Argentina and Uruguay* (New York: Palgrave Macmillan, 2013), 64.

5. Leonardo Filippini, "Criminal Prosecution in the Search for Justice," in *Making Justice: Further Discussions on the Prosecution of Crimes against Humanity in Argentina*, ed. Centro de Estudios Legales y Sociales (CELS) (Buenos Aires: CELS, 2011), 14.

6. Diana Taylor, *The Archive and the Repertoire: Performing Cultural Memory in the Americas* (Durham, NC: Duke University Press, 2003), 19.

7. See Rita Arditti's *Searching for Life: The Grandmothers of the Plaza de Mayo and the Disappeared Children of Argentina* (Berkeley: University of California Press, 1999) for a thorough history of the organization and how it distinguishes itself from the Mothers of the Plaza de Mayo.

8. When the Grandmothers formed in 1977, they initially took the name Abuelas Argentinas con nietitos desaparecidos (Argentine Grandmothers with Disappeared Children).

9. Arditti, *Searching for Life*, 74.

10. Michelle D. Bonner, "Defining Rights in Democratization: The Argentine Government and Human Rights Legislation, 1983–2003," *Latin American Politics and Society* 47.4 (Winter 2005): 62.

11. María Teresa Sánchez, "Intervención en la mesa el derecho a la identidad," in *Juventud e identidad: III Congresso Internacional* (Buenos Aires: Abuelas de Plaza de Mayo, 1997), 38.

12. Taylor, *Archive and the Repertoire*, 20.

13. Werth, *Theatre, Performance, and Memory Politics*, 180.

14. Daniel Fanego, "Las Abuelas nos abrieron el alma," *Página 12*, March 26, 2001, accessed May 12, 2015, http://www.pagina12.com.ar/2001/suple/Teatro/pag02.htm.

15. Werth, *Theatre, Performance, and Memory Politics*, 182.

16. Asociación de Abuelas de la Plaza de Mayo, *La historia de Abuelas: 30 años de busqueda* (Buenos Aires: Ministerio de Relaciones Exteriores de Italia, 2007), 149.

17. See Werth, *Theatre, Performance, and Memory Politics*; Kerry Bystrom, "The Public Private Sphere: Family Narrative and Democracy in Argentina and South Africa," *Social Dynamics* 36.1 (March 2010): 139–52.

18. For additional information about the *Teatro Abierto* festival, see Jean Graham-Jones, *Exorcising History*, and Miguel Angel Giella's multiple essays and reviews published in *Latin American Theatre Review* from 1981 to 1984.

19. Graham-Jones, *Exorcising History*, 90–91.

20. María de los Ángeles Sanz, "Tras la senda de una identidad," *Teatro XXI* 11 (2000): 52.

21. Fanego, "Las Abuelas nos abrieron el alma."

22. Grisby Ogas Puga, "Teatroxlaidentidad: Un teatro busca en su identidad," *Latin American Theatre Review* 37.1 (Fall 2003): 141; Sanz, "Tras la sendo de identidad," 51.

23. Ibid., 153.

24. Graham-Jones, "Rethinking Buenos Aires Theatre, 51.

25. See Monica Botta, "El derecho a la identidad y su correlato escénico en *A propósito de la duda*, de Patricia Zangaro," *Latin American Theatre Review* 45.2 (Fall 2010): 71–92; María Luisa Diz, "Los modos de representación de la apropiación de menores y la restitución de la identidad durante el proceso de institucionalización de *Teatro x la identidad*," *Kamchatka* 3 (Fall 2014): 27–45; and Werth, *Theatre, Performance, and Memory Politics*.

26. Araceli Mariel Arreche, "Teatro e Identidad—Violencia política y representación estética: Teatro x la Identidad, 2001–2010," *Stychomythia* 11–12 (2011): 112.

27. Beatriz Sarlo, *Tiempo pasado: Cultura de la memoria y giro subjetivo* (Buenos Aires: Siglo XX, 2005), 57.

28. Ibid., 102.

29. Botta, "El derecho a la identidad," 83.

30. Bertolt Brecht, *Brecht on Film and Radio*, trans. and ed. Marc Silberman (London: Methuen, 2001), 116.

31. Unless otherwise noted, all descriptions of staged action come from Patricia Zangaro, *A propósito de la duda*, directed by Daniel Fanego, recorded June 5, 2000, Archivo Digital, Centro Cultural Recoleta, Buenos Aires, DVD.

32. Patricia Zangaro, "A propósito de la duda," in *Teatroxlaidentidad: Obras de teatro del Ciclo 2001*, ed. Hermina Petruzzi (Buenos Aires: Eudeba, 2001), 156.

33. Luciana Peker, "La deuda eternal," *Página 12*, May 10, 2013, accessed May 9, 2015, http://www.pagina12.com.ar/diario/suplementos/las12/13-8009 -2013-05-10.html.

34. Zangaro, "A propósito de la duda," 158–59.

35. Patricia Devesa, "Aportes a la historia del teatro argentino: Teatro x la Identidad," in *El teatro de grupos, compañías y otras formaciones (1983–2002), Micropoéticas II*, ed. Jorge Dubatti (Buenos Aires: Ediciones del Instituto Movilizador de Fondos Cooperativos, 2003), 390.

36. Ari Edward Gandsman, "Retributive Justice, Public Intimacies, and the Micropolitics of the Restitution of Kidnapped Children of the Disappeared in Argentina," *International Journal of Transitional Justice* 6.3 (November 2012): 441.

37. Zangaro, "A propósito de la duda," 160.

38. Ibid.

39. Ibid.

40. Tzvetan Todorov, *The Morals of History*, trans. Alyson Waters (Minneapolis: University of Minnesota Press, 1995), 39.

41. Sydney Shoemaker, *Self-Knowledge and Self-Identity* (Ithaca, NY: Cornell University Press, 1963), 284.

42. Bystrom, "Public Private Sphere," 141.

43. Taylor, *Archive and the Repertoire*, 19.

44. Unless otherwise noted, all descriptions of staged action come from Héctor Levy-Daniel, *El archivista*, directed by Marcelo Mangone, recorded April 2, 2001, personal collection of Héctor Levy-Daniel, DVD.

45. Paola Hernández, "Memoria Incompletas: El espacio del escenario argentino de la posdictadura," *Symposium* 61.4 (Winter 2008): 268.

46. Héctor Levy-Daniel, "El archivista," in *Teatroxlaidentidad*, ed. Hermina Petruzzi (Buenos Aires: Colihue, 2009), 21.

47. Halbwachs, *On Collective Memory*, 38.

48. Luis Roniger and Mario Sznajder, "The Problem of Memory and Oblivion in Redemocratized Argentina and Uruguay," *History and Memory* 10.1 (Spring 1998): 142.

49. Louis Bickford, "Human Rights Archives and Research on Historical Memory: Argentina, Chile, and Uruguay," *Latin American Research Review* 35.2 (Winter 2000): 162.

50. Michel Foucault, *Discipline and Punish: The Birth of the Prison*, trans. Alan Sheridan (New York: Vintage Books, 1995), 220.

51. Ari Edward Gandsman, "Do You Know Who You Are? Radical Existential Doubt and Scientific Certainty in the Search for the Kidnapped Children of the Disappeared in Argentina," *Ethos* 37.4 (December 2009): 448.

52. Taylor, *Disappearing Acts*, 187.

53. Bickford, "Human Rights Archives and Research," 172.

54. Emilio Crenzel, "Between the Voices of the State and the Human Rights Movement: Never Again and the Memories of the Disappeared in Argentina," *Journal of Social History* 44.4 (Summer 2011): 1068.

55. Arditti, *Searching for Life*, 156.

56. Héctor Levy-Daniel, "Teatro. Sentido y política," *La Revista del CCC* 7, September 12, 2009, accessed May 15, 2015, http://www.centrocultural.coop/revista/articulo/138/teatro_sentido_y_politica.

57. A notable difference from the 2001 proceedings was that for the 2002 festival, authors had to submit their plays under a pseudonym. Neither the Grandmothers nor the festival's selection committee provided any justification as to why they made that change.

58. Mariana Eva Perez, "Una carta a mi hermano," *Mensuario de las Madres de la Plaza de Mayo* 12 (June–July 2001): 7–8.

59. Unless otherwise noted, all descriptions of staged action come from Mariana Eva Perez, *Instrucciones para un coleccionista de mariposas*, in *Teatro x la Idendidad*, directed by Leonor Manso, recorded July 29, 2002, Ministerio de Educación, Cicencia y Technología, Buenos Aires, 2004, DVD.

60. Mariana Eva Perez, "Instrucciones para un coleccionista de mariposas," *Kamchatka* 3 (Fall 2014): 5.

61. Alison Landsberg, *Prosthetic Memory: The Transformation of American Remembrance in the Age of Mass Culture* (New York: Columbia University Press, 2004), 19.

62. Perez, "Una carta a mi hermano," 7.

63. Arditti, *Searching for Life*, 37–40.

64. Paul Ricoeur, *Memory, History, and Forgetting* (Chicago: University of Chicago Press, 2004), 521.

65. Perez, "Instrucciones," 6.

66. Ana Laura Pauchulo, "Retelling the Stories of the Madres and Abuelas de Plaza de Mayo in Argentina," *Canadian Woman Studies* 27.1 (Fall 2009): 31.

67. Gandsman, "Retributive Justice," 427.

68. Perez, "Una carta a mi hermano," 8.

69. Ogas Puga, "Teatroxlaidentidad: Un teatro busca en su identidad," 146.

70. Diz, "Los modos de representación," 29.

71. Ibid., 32.

3. Reparation, Commemoration, and Memory Construction in the Postdictatorship Generation

1. Unless otherwise noted, all descriptions of staged action come from Lola Arias, *Mi vida después*, directed by Lola Arias, recorded March 26, 2009, Center for Documentation of Theatre and Dance, Teatro San Martín, Buenos Aires, DVD.

2. Lessa, *Memory and Transitional Justice*, 71.

3. Néstor Kirchner, "Address to the United Nations General Assembly," political speech, September 25, 2003, New York.

4. In 1986, the Mothers of the Plaza de Mayo split into two groups: the Founding Line of the Mothers of the Plaza de Mayo and the Mothers of the Plaza de Mayo Association. The former has supported governmental memorialization initiatives, whereas the latter has rejected them in pursuit of advancing a more revolutionary politics of culpability.

5. "Diputados declaró 'politica del Estado' a los juicios por los crímines de lesa humanidad," *Página 12*, May 12, 2010, accessed May 22, 2015, http://www.pagina12.com.ar/diario/ultimas/20-145567-2010-05-12.html.

6. Raúl Kollmann, "La cultura de los derechos humanos," *Página 12*, July 8, 2012, accessed December 19, 2014, http://www.pagina12.com.ar/diario/elpais/1-198206-2012-07-08.html.

7. Lessa, *Memory and Transitional Justice*, 71–72.

8. See chapter 6 of Huyssen, *Present Pasts*, for a detailed analysis of the numerous debates over the memory politics of the *Parque de Memoria* and ESMA.

9. Gabriel Gatti, *El detenido-desaparecido* (Montevideo, Uruguay: Ediciones Trilce, 2008), 25.

10. Oscar Cornago, "Biodrama: Sobre el teatro de la vida y la vida del teatro," *Latin American Theatre Review* 39.1 (Fall 2005): 17.

11. Alan Pauls, "Kidnapping Reality: An Interview with Vivi Tellas," trans. Sarah J. Townsend in *Dramaturgies of the Real on the World Stage*, ed. Carol Martin (New York: Palgrave Macmillan, 2010), 247.

12. Carol Martin, "Bodies of Evidence," *TDR: The Drama Review* 50.3 (December 2006): 9.

13. Sarlo, *Tiempo pasado*, 57.

14. Ibid., 92.

15. Anna White-Nockleby, "Staging Recollections," *Drama in Argentina*, May 1, 2011, accessed September 12, 2012, https://dramainargentina.wordpress.com/.

16. Unless otherwise noted, all descriptions of stage action come from Damiana Poggi and Virginia Jáuregui, 170 explosiones por segundo, directed by Andrés Binetti, attended October 27, 2011, El Portón de Sánchez.

17. Damiana Poggi and Virginia Jáuregui, *170 explosiones por segundo*, unpublished manuscript, 2011, 1, personal collection.

18. Ibid.

19. Michael Lazzara, "(Post-)Memory, Subjectivity, and the Performance of Failure in Recent Documentary Films," *Latin American Perspectives* 36.5 (September 2009): 149.

20. Poggi and Jáuregui, *170 explosiones por segundo*, 1.

21. Ibid.

22. A. E. Bernstein, "The Contributions of Marcel Proust to Psychoanalysis," *Journal of the American Academy of Psychoanalysis and Dynamic Psychology* 33.1 (March 2005): 137.

23. Anna White-Nockleby, "Fragmentos del pasado: *Lo documental* en el teatro de una nueva generación," paper presented at the IV Seminario Internacional Políticas de la Memoria, Buenos Aires, Argentina, September 28–October 1, 2011.

24. Poggi and Jáuregui, *170 explosiones por segundo*, 3.

25. To parse the timeline of the imprisonment of Jáuregui's father, his release from jail, Virginia's birth, and her father's subsequent death from a heart attack, see Mariela Daniela Yaccar, "El pasado desde el presente," *Página 12*, September 6, 2010, accessed July 17, 2011, http://www.pagina12.com.ar/diario/suplementos/espectaculos/subnotas/19188-5279-2005-04-23.html.

26. Ricoeur, *Memory, History, and Forgetting*, 85.

27. Poggi and Jáuregui, *170 explosiones por segundo*, 8–11.

28. Paola Hernández, "Biográfias escénicas: *Mi vida después* de Lola Arias," *Latin American Theatre Review* 45.1 (Fall 2011): 117.

29. See Pamela Brownell, "El teatro antes del futuro: Sobre *Mi vida después de Lola Arias*," *Telondefondo* 10 (December 2009): 1–13; Hernández, "Biográfias escénicas"; Cecilia Sosa, *Queering Acts of Mourning in the Aftermath of Argentina's Dictatorship: The Performances of Blood* (London: Tamesis, 2014); and Werth, *Theatre, Performance, and Memory Politics*.

30. Lola Arias, *Mi vida después*, unpublished manuscript, March 12, 2012, personal collection, 1.

31. Landsberg, *Prosthetic Memory*, 135–36.

32. Arias, *Mi vida después*, 1.

33. Ibid., 2.

34. Marianne Hirsch, *The Generation of Postmemory* (New York: Columbia University Press, 2012), 148–49.

35. Sarlo, *Tiempo pasado*, 138.

36. Sosa, *Queering Acts of Mourning*, 118.

37. Werth, *Theatre, Performance, and Memory Politics*, 174.

38. Landsberg, *Prosthetic Memory*, 19.

39. Hirsch, *Generation of Postmemory*, 5.

40. Brownell, "El teatro antes del futuro," 4.

41. Arias, *Mi vida después*, 13.

42. Landsberg, *Prosthetic Memory*, 24.

43. Cecilia Sosa notes that Crespo did find her father's remains through DNA testing and that later performances of *Mi vida después* changed the scene's resolution to account for that recovery. See Sosa, *Queering Acts of Mourning*, 113.

44. Hernández, "Biográfias escénicas," 124.

45. Falco's performance in *Mi vida después* was so powerful that a federal judge overturned the law that children could not testify against their biological parents so that the actress could offer testimony in a court of law. In 2010, the actress's father was sentenced to eighteen years in an Argentine prison. See Valeria Perasso, "Si la sangre fuera un mandato yo estaría condenada," *BBC Mundo*, March 25, 2010, accessed February 11, 2015, http://www.bbc.com/mundo/lg/america_latina/2010/02/100126_mandamientos_honraras_padres_mz.shtml.

46. Sosa, *Queering Acts of Mourning*, 162.

47. Arias, *Mi vida después*, 23.

48. Claudio Vasquez, "Lola Arias estrena versión chilena de obra sobre la dictadura argentina," *El Mercurio*, January 11, 2011, accessed November 23, 2015, http://www.bbc.com/mundo/lg/america_latina/2010/02/100126_mandamientos_honraras_padres_mz.shtml.

49. Chara Loka, "Lola Arias's *Mi vida después* at the Onassis Cultural Center in Athens," *City Box*, November 14, 2014, accessed November 23, 2015, http://cityboxathista.blogspot.com/2014/11/latin-america-mi-vida-despues-lola.html; Laura Plas, "Et la mort, et l'humour et l'amour des pères," *Les Trois Coups*, December 19, 2011, accessed November 15, 2015, http://www.lestroiscoups.com/article-mi-vida-despues-de-lola-arias-critique-de-laura-plas-theatre-des-abbesses-a-paris-93339415.html.

50. Hirsch, *Generation of Postmemory*, 206.

51. Daniele Avila Small, "Actos físicos de la memoria, descripciones en la historia," *Questáo de Crítica*, June 30, 2011, accessed November 22, 2015, http://www.questaodecritica.com.br/2011/06/actos-fisicos-de-la-memoria-reinscripciones-en-la-historia/.

52. Jens Andermann, *New Argentine Cinema* (London: I. B. Tauris, 2012), 107.

53. Jens Andermann, "Showcasing Dictatorship: Memory and the Museum in Argentina and Chile," *Journal of Educational Media, Memory, and Society* 4.2 (September 2012): 84.

54. See Jens Andermann's analysis of Leon's *Estrellas* in *New Argentine Cinema*, 93–129.

55. Federico León, e-mail message to author, July 16, 2013.

56. Michael Renov, *The Subject of Documentary* (Minneapolis: University of Minnesota Press, 2004), 176.

57. Richard Maxwell, "Interview with Federico León," *Bomb Magazine* 123 (Spring 2013), accessed January 14, 2015, http://bombmagazine.org/article/7095/ federico-le-n.

58. Unless otherwise noted, all descriptions of staged action come from Federico León, *Yo en el futuro*, directed by Federico León, recorded August 15, 2009, Center for Documentation of Theatre and Dance, Teatro San Martín, Buenos Aires, DVD.

59. Federico León, *Yo en el futuro*, unpublished manuscript, 2009, Center for the Documentation of Theatre and Dance, Teatro San Martín, Buenos Aires.

60. Emilio Bernini, "Un estado (contemporáneo) del documental. Sobre algunos films argentines recientes," *Kilómetro* 111.5 (2004): 41–2.

61. Stella Bruzzi, *The New Documentary* (New York: London, 2006), 186–87.

62. Laia Quílez Estevez, "Autobiografía y ficción en el documental contemporáneo argentino," *El cine argentino de hoy, Entre el arte y la política*, ed. Viviana Rangil (Buenos Aires: Biblos, 2007), 76.

63. Landsberg, *Prosthetic Memory*, 31

64. Taylor, *Archive and the Repertoire*, 20.

65. Murray Smith, *Engaging Characters: Fiction, Emotion, and the Cinema* (Oxford: Clarendon Press, 1995), 82.

66. Although Leon's script calls for an actual image of the audience that changes nightly, the production was not able to accommodate these demands, instead using recordings of previous nights' audiences.

67. Lorène de Bonnay, "Précision dans le jeu des acteurs et chorégraphie millimétrée," *Lestroiscoups*, July 29, 2009, accessed December 1, 2015, http:// www.lestroiscoups.com/article-34874197.html.

68. Michael Bellon, "*Yo en el futuro* van Federico León: Drie generaties ikken," *brusselnieuws*, May 14, 2009, accessed December 1, 2015, http://www.brusselnieuws .be/nl/nieuws/yo-en-el-futuro-van-federico-leon-drie-generaties-ikken.

69. Barbara Rauchenberger, "Das Leben ist schön un die Zukunft war es auch," *Die Furche*, October 15, 2009, accessed December 1, 2015, http://www .steirischerherbst.at/2009/deutsch/presse/pressestimmen_details.php?oid=1078.

70. Ferál, "There Are at Least Three Americas," 57.

71. Andrés Gallina, "Intervenciones urbanas de Mariano Pensotti," *Karpa* 7 (Winter 2014): 21.

72. Andrea Pontoriero, "Vida liquida, teatro y narración en las propuestas escénicas de Mariano Pensotti," *Cuaderno 50* 15.4 (December 2014): 16.

73. Jeremy M. Barker, "UTR and COIL 2012: Mariano Pensotti on *El Pasado es un animal grotesco*," *Culturebot*, December 18, 2011, accessed February 27,

2013, http://www.culturebot.org/2011/12/11943/utr-coil-2012-mariano-pensotti -on-el-pasado-es-un-animal-grotesco/.

74. Program for Mariano Pensotti's *El pasado es un animal grotesco* at Teatro Sarmiento, Buenos Aires, Argentina, playbill, March 10, 2010 (Buenos Aires: Center for the Documentation of Theatre and Dance, Teatro San Martín).

75. Unless otherwise noted, all descriptions of staged action come from Mariano Pensotti, *El pasado es un animal grotesco*, directed by Mariano Pensotti, recorded March 10, 2010, Center for Documentation of Theatre and Dance, Teatro San Martín, Buenos Aires, DVD.

76. Rachel Saltz, "That Revolving Drama in Which All Are Actors," *New York Times*, January 10, 2012, accessed February 27, 2013, http://www.nytimes .com/2012/01/11/theater/reviews/el-pasado-es-un-animal-grotesco-at-the-public -theater.html.

77. Mariano Pensotti, *El pasado es un animal grotesco*, unpublished manuscript, 2010 (Buenos Aires: Center for the Documentation of Theatre and Dance, Teatro San Martín).

78. Audrey Jaffe, *Vanishing Points, Dickens, Narrative, and the Subjects of Omniscience* (Berkeley: University of California Press, 1991), 6.

79. Diego Benegas, "If There's No Justice: Trauma and Identity in Post-dictatorship Argentina," *Performance Research* 16.1 (Fall 2011): 20.

80. Barker, "UTR and COIL 2012."

81. James Wertsch, "The Narrative Organization of Collective Memory," *Ethos* 36.1 (March 2008): 121.

82. Jennifer Parker-Starbuck and Sarah Bay-Cheng, "Ecologies of the Festival. New York in 2012: COIL, Under the Radar, and American Realness," *Performance Research* 17.4 (August 2012): 142.

83. Pensotti, *El pasado es un animal grotesco*, 19.

84. Ibid, 21.

85. Ibid, 17.

86. Ibid, 24.

87. Ibid, 28.

88. Saltz, "That Revolving Drama."

89. Charles McNulty, "Theatre Review: *El pasado es un animal grotesco* at REDCAT," *Los Angeles Times*, February 24, 2012, accessed February 27, 2013, http://latimesblogs.latimes.com/culturemonster/2012/02/theater-review-the -past-is-a-grotesque-animal-at-redcat.html.

90. Véronique Hotte, "El pasado es un animal grotesco," *Théâtre du blog*, December 9, 2013, accessed December 28, 2013, http://theatredublog.unblog .fr/2013/12/09/.

4. Performing Public Memorialization of the Malvinas War

1. Throughout this chapter, I refer to the islands as the Malvinas rather than the Falklands, in keeping with the discourse of the Argentine government and its publics. In instances where individuals or plays use Falklands, I use their terminology.

2. David J. Keeling, "A Geopolitical Perspective on Argentina's Malvinas/ Falklands claims," *Global Discourse* 3.1 (August 2013): 159.

3. See Rosana Guber, *¿Por Qué Malvinas? De la causa nacionale a la guerra absurda* (Mexico City: Fondo de Cultura Económica, 2001) for a history of the Malvinas and its relationship to Argentina.

4. Luis Golger and Victor Ramos, "Guerra exilo y representación. Una entrevista con Beatriz Sarlo," *Lucero. Guerras fronteras y exilo* 15 (2005): 44.

5. See Guber, *¿Por Qué Malvinas?*; Federico Lorenz, *Las guerras por Malvinas* (Buenos Aires: Edhasa, 2006).

6. Constitution of the Argentine Nation, Article III, Section 1.

7. Klaus Dodds, "Stormy Waters: Britain, the Falkland Islands and UK-Argentine Relations," *International Affairs* 22.4 (December 2012): 686–87.

8. See Matthew C. Benwell and Klaus Dodds, "Argentine Territorial Nationalism Revisited: The Malvinas/Falklands Dispute and Geographies of Everyday Nationalism," *Political Geography* 30 (2011): 446; Klaus Dodds, "Consolidate! Britain, the Falkland Islands and Wider the South Atlantic/Antarctic," *Global Discourse* 3.1 (August 2013): 168.

9. James Billig, *Banal Nationalism* (London: Sage, 1995), 10.

10. Amelia Beatriz Garcia, "Textos escolares: La Malvinas y la Antártida para la 'Nueva Argentina' de Perón," *Antitesis* 2.4 (July 2009): 1034.

11. See Benwell and Dodds, "Argentine Territorial Nationalism Revisited"; Matthew C. Benwell, "From the Banal to the Blatant: Expressions of Nationalism in Secondary Schools in Argentina and the Falkland Islands," *Geoforum* 52 (2014): 51–60.

12. Hugo Vezzetti, *Sobre la violencia revolucionaria. Memorias y olvidos* (Buenos Aires: Siglo XXI, 2009), 37.

13. Benwell and Dodds, "Argentine Territorial Nationalism Revisited," 444.

14. See María Angélica Semilla Durán, "The Falklands War: Readings over Time," in *30 Years After: Issues and Representations of the Falklands War*, ed. Carine Berbéri and Monia O'Brien Castro (London: Ashgate, 2015), 58–76; Martín Kohan, Oscar Blanco, and Adriana Imperatore, "Transhumantes de neblina, no las hemos de encontrar. De cómo la literatura cuenta la guerra de Malvinas," *Espacios* 13 (1993–94): 82–86; Julieta Vitullo, *Islas imaginadas: La guerra de Malvinas en la literatura y en el cine* (Buenos Aires: Corregidor, 2012); Jorge Warley, *La guerra de Malvinas. Juan Forn, Rodrigo Fresán, Carlos Gamerro, Daniel Guebel, Raúl Vieytes* (Buenos Aires: Biblos, 2007).

15. Vitullo, *Islas imaginadas*, 7.

16. Jorge Dubatti, "Las Malvinas en el teatro argentino: Memoria en escena, del testimonio a la metáfora," *La revista del CCC* 14/15 (January–February 2012), accessed April 24, 2015, http://www.centrocultural.coop/revista/articulo/316/.

17. Ana Elena Puga, *Memory, Allegory, and Testimony in South American Theatre* (New York: Routledge, 2008), 15.

18. Guber, *¿Por que Malvinas?*, 31.

19. For more in-depth analysis of León's play, see Noe Montez, "Autobiographic Memory, Museums, and Objectivity in Federico León's *Museo Miguel Ángel Boezzio*," in *Public Theatres and Theatre Publics*, ed. Robert B. Shimko and Sara Freeman (Cambridge: Cambridge Scholars Press, 2012), 120–30; Brenda Werth, "A Malvinas Veteran Onstage: From Intimate Testimony to Public Memorialization," *South Central Review* 30.3 (Fall 2013): 83–100.

20. Carlos Pacheco, "El teatro se ocupa de la guerra por las Malvinas," *La Nación*, April 22, 2015, accessed April 23, 2015, http://www.lanacion.com.ar/1786404-sin-titulo; Ivana Soto, "Retórnicas sobre Malvinas: Parodias, realism y ideología," *Clarín*, June 14, 2012, accessed May 1, 2015, http://www.revistaenie.clarin.com/escenarios/teatro/Guerra-Malvinas-Teatro_0_718728356.html.

21. Vitullo, *Islas imaginadas*, 7.

22. National Education Law, Public Law 26,606, Argentine Statutes at Large, Title IV, Chapter 2, Article 92 (1996).

23. See Luis Ordaz, *Historia del teatro en el Río de la Plata* (Buenos Aires: Inteatro, 2010), for more information about this theatrical aesthetic.

24. Unless otherwise noted, all descriptions of staged action come from Julio Cardoso, *Islas de la memoria*, directed by Julio Cardoso, attended July 11, 2012, Teatro Cervantes, Buenos Aires.

25. Julio Cardoso, *Islas de la memoria*, unpublished manuscript, 2012, 1, personal collection.

26. Svetlana Boym, *The Future of Nostalgia* (New York: Basic, 2001), 13.

27. Cardoso, *Islas de la memoria*, 3.

28. Lorenz, *Las guerras por Malvinas*, 130.

29. Andrew Sofer, *The Stage Life of Props* (Ann Arbor: University of Michigan Press, 2003), 2.

30. Cardoso, *Islas de la memoria*, 9.

31. Hilda Cabrera, "Los argentinos tenemos heroes pero te los gambeteanos," *Página 12*, May 20, 2012, accessed April 12, 2015, http://www.pagina12.com.ar/diario/suplementos/espectaculos/10-25269-2012-05-20.html.

32. Paul Harvey Williams, *Memory Museums: The Rush to Commemorate* (London: Berg, 2007), 8.

33. Benwell, "From the Banal to the Blatant," 59.

34. Landsberg, *Prosthetic Memory*, 148.

35. Cardoso, *Islas de la memoria*, 13.

36. Robert L. Ivie, "Fighting Terror by Rite of Redemption and Reconciliation," *Rhetoric and Public Affairs* 10.2 (Summer 2007): 225.

37. Hugo Vezzetti, *Pasado y presente. Guerra, dictadura y sociedad en Argentina* (Buenos Aires: Siglo XXI, 2002).

38. Cristina Fernández de Kirchner, "Acto por el 30° aniversario de la guerra de Malvinas," political speech, Malvinas War Memorial, Tierra del Fuego, April 2, 2012.

39. Victoria M. Basham, "Telling Geopolitical Tales: Temporality, Rationality, and the 'Childish' in the Ongoing War for the Falklands/Malvinas Islands," *Critical Studies in Security* 3.1 (March 2015): 86.

40. Although it is beyond the scope of this book to fully engage in a discussion of childhood studies and the historical performances of childhood, for more detailed information about the history and scholarly trajectories of childhood studies, see Robin Bernstein, *Racial Innocence: Performing American Childhood and Race from Slavery to Civil Rights* (New York: New York University Press, 2011); Maija Holmer Nadesan, *Governing Childhood into the 21st Century: Biopolitical Technologies of Childhood Management and Education* (New York: Palgrave Macmillan, 2010).

41. Basham, "Telling Geopolitical Tales," 78.

42. Federico Lorenz, "How Does One Win a Lost War? Oral History and Political Memories," in *The Oxford Handbook of Oral History*, ed. Donald Ritchie (Oxford: Oxford University Press, 2010), 132.

43. Werth, "Malvinas Veteran Onstage," 85.

44. Unless otherwise noted, all descriptions of staged action come from Patricio Abadi, *Isla flotante*, directed by Patricio Abadi, attended May 31, 2015, Onírico Espacio de Arte, Buenos Aires.

45. Paola Boente, "La guerra de Malvinas se revive en los teatros porteños," *BAE Negocios*, March 31, 2015, accessed May 12, 2015, http://www.diariobae.com/notas/64705-la-guerra-de-malvinas-se-revive-en-los-teatros-portenos.html.

46. Patricio Abadi, *Isla flotante*, unpublished manuscript, 2015, 1, personal collection.

47. Julieta Vitullo, "Relatos de desertores en las ficciones de la guerra de Malvinas," *Hispamérica* 35.104 (August 2006): 31.

48. Jenny Edkins, *Trauma and the Memory of Politics* (Cambridge: Cambridge University Press, 2003), xv.

49. Abadi, *Isla flotante*, 15.

50. Victoria M. Basham and Nate Vaughn-Williams, "Gender, Race, and Border Security Practices: A Profane Reading of 'Muscular Liberalism,'" *British Journal of Political and International Relations* 15.4 (Winter 2013): 516.

51. Abadi, *Isla flotante*, 19.

52. Benwell and Dodds, "Argentine Territorial Nationalism Revisited," 447.

53. Marcos Novaro and Vicente Palermo, *La dictadura militar, 1976–1983: del golpe de estado a la restauración democrática* (Buenos Aires: Paídos, 2003), 467.

54. See Werth, "Malvinas Veteran Onstage," 83–84; Paola Ehrmantraut, "Aftermath of Violence: Coming to Terms with the Legacy of the Malvinas/Falklands War," *Arizona Journal of Hispanic Cultural Studies* 15 (2011): 98.

55. Vitullo, "Relatos de desertores," 32.

56. Rodolfo Fogwill, *Los pichiciegos* (Buenos Aires: De la Flor, 1983).

57. "Piedras dentro de la piedra, de Mariana Mazover," *Puesta en escena*, July 28, 2012, accessed August 1, 2012, http://www.puestaenescena.com.ar/teatro/761_piedras-dentro-de-la-piedra-de-mariana-mazover.php.

58. "En primera persona: Mariana Mazover—Piedras dentro de la piedra," *GEOteatral*, March 2012, accessed August 1, 2012, http://www.geoteatral.com.ar/nota/EnPrimeraPersona:MarianaMazover:PiedrasDentr.

59. Ibid.

60. Women could not join Argentina's air force until 2001 or the navy until 2002.

61. Soto, "Retórnicas sobre Malvinas."

62. Unless otherwise noted, all descriptions of staged action come from Mariana Mazover, *Piedras dentro de la piedra*, directed by Mariana Mazover, attended July 14, 2012, Teatro La Carpintería, Buenos Aires.

63. Mariana Mazover, *Piedras dentro de la piedra*, unpublished manuscript, 2012, personal collection.

64. Martín Kohan, "El fin de una épica," *Punto de Vista* 64 (1999): 8.

65. Ehrmantraut, "Aftermath of Violence," 100.

66. Beatriz Sarlo, "No olvidar la guerra: Sobre cine, literatura e historia," *Punto de vista* 49 (1994): 32; Vitullo, "Relatos de desertores," 32; Werth, "Malvinas Veteran Onstage," 86.

67. Martin Müller, "Reconstructing the Concept of Discourse for the Field of Critical Geopolitics: Towards Discourse as a Language and Practice," *Political Geography* 27 (2008): 333.

68. Basham, "Telling Geopolitical Tales," 78.

69. Dodds, "Stormy Waters," 683.

70. Fernández de Kirchner, "Acto por el 30° anniversario de la guerra de Malvinas."

71. Lorenz, "How Does One Win a Lost War?," 125.

72. Unless otherwise noted, all descriptions of staged action come from Lisandro Fiks, *1982 Obertura solemne*, directed by Lisandro Fiks and Diego Quiroz, attended June 17, 2012, Espacio Polonia, Buenos Aires.

73. Lisandro Fiks, *1982 Obertura solemna*, unpublished manuscript, 2012, personal collection, 3.

74. Lorenz, "How Does One Win a Lost War?," 130.

75. Ehrmantraut, "Aftermath of Violence," 104.

76. Fiks, *1982 Obertura solemne*, 5.

77. Rosana Guber, "The Malvinas Executions: (Im)Plausible Memories of a Clean War," *Latin American Perspectives* 35.5 (September 2008): 123–25.

78. Lorenz, "How Does One Win a Lost War?," 129.

79. Ehrmantraut, "Aftermath of Violence," 100.

80. Fiks, *1982 Obertura solemne*, 9.

81. Lorenz, "How Does One Win a Lost War?," 131; Guber "Los Veteranos truchos de Malvinas: La autenticidad como competencia metacomunicativa en las identidades de trabajo de campo," *Universitas humanistica* 63 (January–June 2007): 54.

82. Carol Martin, *Dramaturgy of the Real on the World Stage* (New York: Palgrave Macmillan, 2010), 18.

83. Soto, "Retórnicas sobre Malvinas."

Conclusion: The Next Stages of Theatrical Production, Postdictatorship Memory, and Transitional Justice

1. Francesca Lessa, "Justice without Borders: The Operation Condor Trial and Accountability for Transnational Crimes in South America," *International Journal of Transitional Justice* 9.3 (September 2015): 505.

2. Commisão Nacional da Verdade, "Relatorio Comissão Nacional da Verdade," December 10, 2014, accessed April 30, 2015, http://www.cnv.gov.br/.

3. "Para el 79% de la población, en la Argentina se vive al margen de la ley," *La Nación*, April 5, 2015, accessed May 28, 2015, http://www.lanacion.com.ar/1781730-para-el-79-de-la-poblacion-en-la-argentina-se-vive-al-margen-de-la-ley.

4. Socio-Economic Database for Latin America and the Caribbean, "Poverty Statistics," December 14, 2015, accessed December 14, 2015, http://sedlac.econo.unlp.edu.ar/eng/statistics-detalle.php?idE=34.

5. "No más venganza," *La Nación*, November 23, 2015, accessed November 23, 2015, http://www.lanacion.com.ar/1847930-no-mas-venganza.

6. Santiago del Carril, "Dictatorship Era Probes Hit by Cuts," *Buenos Aires Herald*, April 25, 2016, accessed April 25, 2016, http://buenosairesherald.com/article/213206/dictatorshipera-probes-hit-by-cuts.

7. Uki Goni, "Blaming the Victims: Dictatorship Is on the Rise in Argentina," *Guardian*, August 29, 2016, accessed August 29, 2016, https://www.theguardian.com/world/2016/aug/29/argentina-denial-dirty-war-genocide-mauricio-macri.

8. Héctor Schmucler, "Las exigencias de memoria," *Punto de vista* 23.68 (2000): 5.

9. Ricoeur, *Memory, History, and Forgetting*, 89.

10. Elizabeth Jelin, "Victims, Relatives and Citizens in Argentina: Whose Voice Is Legitimate Enough?" *Humanitarianism and Suffering: The Mobilization of Empathy*, ed. Richard A. Wilson and David D. Brown (New York: Cambridge University Press, 2009), 177.

11. Sosa, *Queering Acts of Mourning*, 156.

12. Horacio Verbitsky, "La Inquisición," *Página 12*, July 11, 2010, accessed May 28, 2015, http://www.pagina12.com.ar/diario/elpais/1-149246-2010-07-11.html.

13. Eduardo Chirinos, "El año que nací: Entrevista a Lola Arias," *Contratiempo*, December 16, 2013, accessed February 28, 2015, http://contratiempo .net/2013/12/el-ano-en-que-naci-entrevista-con-lola-arias/.

Bibliography

Abadi, Patricio. *Isla flotante*. Directed by Patricio Abadi. Buenos Aires: Onírico Espacio de Arte, attended May 31, 2015.

———. *Isla flotante*. Unpublished manuscript, 2015. Personal collection.

Agger, Inger, and Søren Buus Jensen. *Trauma and Healing under State Terrorism*. London: Zed Books, 1996.

Agüero, Felipe, and Eric Hershberg. "La Fuerzas Armadas y la memorias de la represión en el Cono Sur." In *Memorias militares sobre la represión en el Cono Sur*, edited by Eric Hershberg and Felipe Agüero, 1–34. Madrid: Siglo XXI, 2005.

Alternativa Teatral. Accessed January 31, 2016. http://www.alternativateatral.com/.

Andermann, Jens. *New Argentine Cinema*. London: I. B. Tauris, 2012.

———. "Showcasing Dictatorship: Memory and the Museum in Argentina and Chile." *Journal of Educational Media, Memory, and Society* 4.2 (September 2012): 69–93.

A'Ness, Francine Mary. "Resisting Amnesia: Yuyachkani, Performance, and the Postwar Reconstruction of Peru." *Theatre Journal* 56.3 (October 2004): 395–414.

Arditti, Rita. *Searching for Life: The Grandmothers of the Plaza de Mayo and the Disappeared Children of Argentina*. Berkeley: University of California Press, 1999.

Arias, Lola. *Mi vida después*. DVD. Directed by Lola Arias. Buenos Aires: Center for Documentation of Theatre and Dance, Teatro San Martín, recorded March 26, 2009.

———. *Mi vida después*. Unpublished manuscript, March 12, 2012. Personal collection.

Arreche, Araceli Mariel. "Teatro e Identidad—Violencia política y representación estética: Teatro x la Identidad, 2001–2010." *Stichomythia* 11–12 (2011): 109–17.

Asociación de Abuelas de la Plaza de Mayo. *La historia de Abuelas: 30 años de busqueda.* Buenos Aires: Ministerio de Relaciones Exteriores de Italia, 2007.

Barba, Eugenio. *Beyond the Floating Islands.* Translated by Judy Barba, Richard Fowler, Jerrold C. Rodesch, and Saul Shapiro. New York: PAJ Publications, 1986.

Barker, Jeremy M. "UTR and COIL 2012: Mariano Pensotti on *El Pasado es un animal grotesco.*" *Culturebot.* December 18, 2011, accessed February 27, 2013. http://www.culturebot.org/2011/12/11943/utr-coil-2012-mariano -pensotti-on-el-pasado-es-un-animal-grotesco/.

Basham, Victoria M. "Telling Geopolitical Tales: Temporality, Rationality, and the 'Childish' in the Ongoing War for the Falklands/Malvinas Islands." *Critical Studies in Security* 3.1 (March 2015): 77–89.

Basham, Victoria M., and Nate Vaughn-Williams. "Gender, Race, and Border Security Practices: A Profane Reading of 'Muscular Liberalism.'" *British Journal of Political and International Relations* 15.4 (Winter 2013): 509–27.

Bellon, Michael. "*Yo en el futuro* van Federico León: Drie generaties ikken." *brusselnieuws.* May 14, 2009, accessed December 1, 2015. http://www.brusselnieuws .be/nl/nieuws/yo-en-el-futuro-van-federico-leon-drie-generaties-ikken.

Benegas, Diego. "If There's No Justice: Trauma and Identity in Post-dictatorship Argentina." *Performance Research* 16.1 (Fall 2011): 20–30.

Benwell, Matthew C. "From the Banal to the Blatant: Expressions of Nationalism in Secondary Schools in Argentina and the Falkland Islands." *Geoforum* 52 (2014): 51–60.

Benwell, Matthew C., and Klaus Dodds. "Argentine Territorial Nationalism Revisited: The Malvinas/Falklands Dispute and Geographies of Everyday Nationalism." *Political Geography* 30 (2011): 441–49.

Bernini, Emilio. "Un estado (contemporáneo) del documental. Sobre algunos films argentines recientes." *Kilómetro* 111.5 (2004): 41–42.

Bernstein, A. E. "The Contributions of Marcel Proust to Psychoanalysis." *Journal of the American Academy of Psychoanalysis and Dynamic Psychology* 33.1 (March 2005): 137–48.

Bernstein, Robin. *Racial Innocence: Performing American Childhood and Race from Slavery to Civil Rights.* New York: New York University Press, 2011.

Bertuccio, Marcelo. *Señora, esposa, niña y joven desde lejos.* DVD. Directed by Cristian Drut. Personal collection, recorded February 1, 1998.

———. "Señora, esposa, niña y joven desde lejos." In *Teatro de la disintegración,* edited by Martín Rodriguez, 98–111. Buenos Aires: Eudeba, 1999.

Bianchedi, Elizabeth Tabak de, Marcelo Bianchedi, Marian Braun, et al. "La política de la memoria: El movimiento de derechos humanos y la construcción democrática en la Argentina." In *Restitución de niños, Abuelas de Plaza de Mayo,* edited by Elizabeth Tabak de Bianchedi, 217–41. Buenos Aires: Eudeba, 1997.

Bickford, Louise. "Human Rights Archives and Research on Historical Memory: Argentina, Chile, and Uruguay." *Latin American Research Review* 35.2 (Winter 2000): 160–82.

Billig, James. *Banal Nationalism.* London: Sage, 1995.

Boente, Paola. "La guerra de Malvinas se revive en los teatros porteños." *BAE Negocios.* March 31, 2015, accessed May 12, 2015. http://www.diariobae.com/notas/64705-la-guerra-de-malvinas-se-revive-en-los-teatros-portenos.html.

Bonner, Michelle D. "Defining Rights in Democratization: The Argentine Government and Human Rights Legislation, 1983–2003." *Latin American Politics and Society* 47.4 (Winter 2005): 55–76.

Bortnik, Aída. "Papá querido." In *Teatro Abierto 1981 21 Estrenos Argentinos,* vol. 2, edited by Miguel Angel Giella, 13–26. Buenos Aires: Corregidor, 1992.

Botta, Monica. "El derecho a la identidad y su correlato escénico en *A propósito de la duda,* de Patricia Zangaro." *Latin American Theatre Review* 45.2 (Fall 2010): 71–92.

Boyle, Catherine. "Text, Time, Process and History in Contemporary Chilean Theatre." *Theatre Research International* 26.2 (July 2001): 181–89.

Boym, Svetlana. *The Future of Nostalgia.* New York: Basic, 2001.

Brecht, Bertolt. *Brecht on Film and Radio.* Translated and edited by Marc Silberman. London: Methuen, 2001.

Brownell, Pamela. "El teatro antes del futuro: sobre *Mi vida después de Lola Arias.*" *Telondefondo* 10 (December 2009): 1–13.

Bruzzi, Stella. *The New Documentary.* New York: London, 2006.

Bystrom, Kerry. "The Public Private Sphere: Family Narrative and Democracy in Argentina and South Africa." *Social Dynamics* 36.1 (March 2010): 139–52.

Cabrera, Hilda. "Los argentinos tenemos heroes pero te los gambeteanos." *Página 12.* May 20, 2012, accessed April 12, 2015. http://www.pagina12.com.ar/diario/suplementos/espectaculos/10-25269-2012-05-20.html.

Campt, Tina M. *Other Germans: Black Germans and the Politics of Race, Gender, and Memory in the Third Reich.* Ann Arbor: University of Michigan Press, 2005.

Cano, Luis. *Los murmullos.* Buenos Aires: Editorial nueva generación, 2003.

———. *Los murmullos.* DVD. Directed by Emilio García Wehbi. Buenos Aires: Center for Documentation of Theatre and Dance, Teatro San Martín, recorded May 2, 2002.

Cardoso, Julio. *Islas de la memoria.* Directed by Julio Cardoso. Buenos Aires: Teatro Cervantes, attended July 11, 2012.

———. *Islas de la memoria.* Unpublished manuscript, 2012. Personal collection.

Cerrato, Laura. "Lo postmoderno en la literatura de habla inglesa." In *Doce vueltas a la literatura,* edited by Laura Cerrato, 158–69. Buenos Aires: Botella al mar, 1992.

Cerruti, Gabriela. "La historia de memoria. Entre la fetichización y el duelo." *Puentes* 1.3 (Fall 2001): 20–22.

Chernel, Lora. "Sophiensälle: Argentinien eingeladen, Arbieten die fehlenden Männer." *Wiener Zeitung*, June 6, 2000, 12.

Chirinos, Eduardo. "El año que nací: Entrevista a Lola Arias." *Contratiempo*. December 16, 2013, accessed February 28, 2015. http://contratiempo.net/2013/12/el-ano-en-que-naci-entrevista-con-lola-arias/.

Cohen, Matthew Isaac. "Puppetry and the Destruction of the Object." *Performance Research* 12.4 (2007): 123–31.

Cole, Catherine. *Performing South Africa's Truth Commission: Stages of Transition.* Bloomington: Indiana University Press, 1999.

Commisão Nacional da Verdade. "Relatorio Commisão Nacional da Verdade." December 10, 2014, accessed April 30, 2015. http://www.cnv.gov.br.

CONADEP (National Commission on the Disappearance of Persons). *Nunca Más.* Buenos Aires: Eudeba, 1984.

Cornago, Oscar. "Biodrama: Sobre el teatro de la vida y la vida del teatro." *Latin American Theatre Review* 39.1 (Fall 2005): 5–27.

Cossa, Roberto. *Nuestro fin de semana.* New York: Macmillan, 1966.

Costa, Ivana. "La palabra también es una desaparecida." *Clarín*. February 6, 1998, accessed June 22, 2014. http://edant.clarin.com/diario/1998/03/12/c-01401d.htm.

Crenzel, Emilio. "Between the Voices of the State and the Human Rights Movement: Never Again and the Memories of the Disappeared in Argentina." *Journal of Social History* 44.4 (Summer 2011): 1063–76.

Cruz, Alejandro. "El horror que navega en un recuerdo difuso." *La Nación.* February 6, 1998, accessed June 22, 2014. http://www2.lanacion.com.ar/nota.asp?nota_id=87227.

———. "Un espectáculo que no llega a conmover." *La Nación.* May 3, 2002, accessed June 1, 2014. http://www.lanacion.com.ar/393449-un-espectaculo-que-no-llega-a-conmover.

Daulte, Javier. *Martha Stutz.* Buenos Aires: Ediciones ultimo reino, 1997.

———. *Martha Stutz.* VHS. Directed by Diego Kogan. Buenos Aires: Center for Documentation of Theatre and Dance, Teatro San Martín, recorded May 23, 1997.

de Bonnay, Lorène. "Précision dans le jeu des acteurs et chorégraphie millimétrée." *Lestroiscoups.* July 29, 2009, accessed December 1, 2015. http://www.lestroiscoups.com/article-34874197.html.

del Carril, Santiago. "Dictatorship Era Probes Hit by Cuts." *Buenos Aires Herald.* April 25, 2016, accessed April 25, 2016. http://buenosairesherald.com/article/213206/dictatorshipera-probes-hit-by-cuts.

de los Ángeles Sanz, María. "Tras la senda de una identidad." *Teatro XXI* 11 (Fall 2000): 51–52.

Devesa, Patricia. "Aportes a la historia del teatro argentino: Teatro x la Identidad." In *El teatro de grupos, compañías y otras formaciones (1983–2002), Micropoéticas II*, edited by Jorge Dubatti, 390–412. Buenos Aires: Ediciones del Instituto Movilizador de Fondos Cooperativos, 2003.

Diaz, Silvina. "El teatro 'posmoderno' en Buenos Aires: Una repuesta a la globalización cultural." *Dramateatro Revista Digital* 6 (September–December 2005). Accessed October 21, 2014. http://dramateatro.fundacite.arg.gov.ve/ensayos/n_0016/silvina_diaz.htm.

"Diputados declaró 'politica del Estado' a los juicios por los crímines de lesa humanidad." *Página 12*. May 12, 2010, accessed May 22, 2015. http://www.pagina12.com.ar/diario/ultimas/20-145567-2010-05-12.html.

Diz, María Luisa. "Los modos de representación de la apropiación de menores y la restitución de la identidad durante el proceso de institucionalización de *Teatro x la identidad*." *Kamchatka* 3 (Fall 2014): 27–45.

Dodds, Klaus. "Consolidate! Britain, the Falkland Islands and Wider the South Atlantic/Antarctic." *Global Discourse* 3.1 (August 2013): 166–72.

———. "Stormy Waters: Britain, the Falkland Islands and UK-Argentine Relations." *International Affairs* 22.4 (December 2012): 683–700.

Donnelly, Pat. "Deconstructing the Bard: *Máquina Hamlet* Is a Dark, Prophetic Mix of Poetry and Politics." *Montreal Gazette*, May 28, 1999, D8.

Dubatti, Jorge. "El canon de multiplicidad." In *El teatro labertino: Ensayos sobre teatro argentino*, edited by Jorge Dubatti, 111–22. Buenos Aires: Atuel, 1999.

———. "El teatro argentino en la post-dictadura, 1983–2010: Época de oro, Destotalización, y Subjetividad." *Stichomythia* 11–12 (2011): 71–80.

———. "El teatro en la dictadura: A 30 años de Golpe militar." *Picadero* 16 (2006): 16—21.

———. "Las Malvinas en el teatro argentino: Memoria en escena, del testimonio a la metáfora." *La revista del CCC* 14/15. January–February 2012, accessed April 24, 2015. http://www.centrocultural.coop/revista/articulo/316/.

Dúran, María Angélica Semilla. "The Falklands War: Readings over Time." In *30 Years After: Issues and Representations of the Falklands War*, edited by Carine Berbéri and Monia O'Brien Castro, 58–76. London: Ashgate, 2015.

Edkins, Jenny. *Trauma and the Memory of Politics*. Cambridge: Cambridge University Press, 2003.

Ehrmantraut, Paola. "Aftermath of Violence: Coming to Terms with the Legacy of the Malvinas/Falklands War." *Arizona Journal of Hispanic Cultural Studies* 15 (2011): 95–106.

Elster, John. *Retribution and Reparation in the Transition to Democracy*. London: Cambridge University Press, 2006.

"En primera persona: Mariana Mazover—Piedras dentro de la piedra." *GEOteatral*. March 2012, accessed August 1, 2012. http://www.geoteatral.com.ar/nota/EnPrimeraPersona:MarianaMazover:PiedrasDentr.

Equipo Argentino de Anthropología Forense (EAAF). "Sección Especial—Derecho a la Verdad." In *Informe Anual 2002*. Buenos Aires: EAAF, 2002.

Estevez, Laia Quílez. "Autobiografía y ficción en el documental contemporáneo argentino." In *El cine argentino de hoy, Entre el arte y la política*, edited by Viviana Rangil, 71–85. Buenos Aires: Biblos, 2007.

Fanego, Daniel. "Las Abuelas nos abrieron el alma." *Página 12*. March 26, 2001, accessed May 12, 2015. http://www.pagina12.com.ar/2001/suple/Teatro/pag02.htm.

Feitlowitz, Marguerite. *A Lexicon of Terror*. New York: Oxford University Press, 2006.

Ferál, Josette. "There Are at Least Three Americas." In *The Intercultural Performance Reader*, edited by Patrice Pavis, 51–58. New York: Routledge, 1996.

Fernández de Kirchner, Cristina. "Acto por el 30° aniversario de la guerra de Malvinas." Political speech, Malvinas War Memorial, Tierra del Fuego, Argentina, April 2, 2012.

Fiks, Lisandro. *1982 Obertura solemne*. Directed by Lisandro Fiks and Diego Quiroz. Buenos Aires: Espacio Polonia, attended June 17, 2012.

———. *1982 Obertura solemne*. Unpublished manuscript, 2012. Personal collection.

Filc, Judith. *Entre el parentesco y la política: Familia y dictadura, 1976–1983*. Buenos Aires: Biblos, 1997.

Filippini, Leonardo. "Criminal Prosecution in the Search for Justice." In *Making Justice: Further Discussions on the Prosecution of Crimes against Humanity in Argentina*, edited by Centro de Estudios Legales y Sociales (CELS), 11–29. Buenos Aires: CELS, 2011.

Fletcher, Laurel E., and Harvey Weinstein. "Violence and Social Repair: Rethinking the Conditions of Justice to Reconciliation." *Human Rights Quarterly* 24 (2002): 573–639.

Fogwill, Rodolfo. *Los pichiciegos*. Buenos Aires: De la Flor, 1983.

Foucault, Michel. *Discipline and Punish: The Birth of the Prison*. Translated by Alan Sheridan. New York: Vintage Books, 1995.

Fuchs, Barbara. "Ventriloquist Theatre and the Omniscient Narrator: *Gatz* and *El pasado es un animal grotesco*." *Modern Drama* 57.2 (Summer 2014): 165–86.

Fuld, Roberto Gerardo. "Los imigrantes limítrofes ¿culpables de la desocupación en Argentina?" *Realidad Económica* 149 (1997): 7–28.

Gallina, Andrés. "Intervenciones urbanas de Mariano Pensotti." *Karpa* 7 (Winter 2014): 21–27.

Gandsman, Ari Edward. "Do You Know Who You Are? Radical Existential Doubt and Scientific Certainty in the Search for the Kidnapped Children of the Disappeared in Argentina." *Ethos* 37.4 (December 2009): 441–65.

———. "Retributive Justice, Public Intimacies, and the Micropolitics of the Restitution of Kidnapped Children of the Disappeared in Argentina." *International Journal of Transitional Justice* 6.3 (November 2012): 423–43.

Garcia, Amelia Beatriz. "Textos escolares: La Malvinas y la Antártida para la 'Nueva Argentina' de Perón." *Antitesis* 2.4 (July 2009): 1033–58.

Gatti, Gabriel. *El detenido-desaparecido.* Montevideo, Uruguay: Ediciones Trilce, 2008.

Giella, Miguel Angel. "Teatro Abierto: Fenómeno social-teatral argentino." *Latin American Theatre Review* 15.1 (Fall 1981): 89–93.

———. "Teatro Abierto 82: El comienzo de un sueño." *Latin American Theatre Review* 16.1 (Fall 1982): 67–69.

———. "Teatro Abierto 1984 y 1985." *Latin American Theatre Review* 18.1 (Fall 1984): 119–20.

———. *Teatro Abierto 1981.* Buenos Aires: Corregidor, 1992.

Gill, Lesley. *The School of the Americas: Military Training and Political Violence in the Americas.* Durham, NC: Duke University Press, 2004.

Golger, Luis, and Victor Ramos. "Guerra exilo y representación. Una entrevista con Beatriz Sarlo." *Lucero. Guerras fronteras y exilo* 15 (2005): 44.

Goni, Uki. "Blaming the Victims: Dictatorship Is on the Rise in Argentina." *Guardian.* August 29, 2016, accessed August 29, 2016. https://www.theguardian.com/world/2016/aug/29/argentina-denial-dirty-war-genocide-mauricio-macri.

Gonzáles-Bombal, Ines. *El diálogo politico: La transición que no fue.* Buenos Aires: Centro de Estudios de Estado y Sociedad, 1991.

Graham-Jones, Jean. *Evita Inevitably: Performing Argentina's Female Icons Before and After Eva Perón.* Ann Arbor: University of Michigan Press, 2014.

———. *Exorcising History: Argentine Theatre under Dictatorship.* Lewisburg, PA: Bucknell University Press, 2000.

———. "Rethinking Buenos Aires Theatre in the Wake of 2001 and Emerging Structures of Resistance and Resilience." *Theatre Journal* 66.1 (March 2014): 37–54.

Guber, Rosana. "Los Veteranos truchos de Malvinas: La autenticidad como competencia metacomunicativa en las identidades de trabajo de campo." *Universitas humanistica* 63 (January–June 2007): 49–68.

———. "The Malvinas Executions: (Im)Plausible Memories of a Clean War." *Latin American Perspectives* 35.5 (September 2008): 119–32.

———. *¿Por Qué Malvinas? De la causa nacionale a la guerra absurda.* Mexico City: Fondo de Cultura Económica, 2001.

Halbwachs, Maurice. *On Collective Memory*. Chicago: University of Chicago Press, 1992.

Hamber, Brandon, and Richard A. Wilson. "Symbolic Closure through Memory, Reparation, and Revenge in Post-Conflict Societies." In *The Role of Memory in Ethnic Conflict*, edited by Ed Cairns and Michéal D. Roe, 144–68. New York: Palgrave Macmillan, 2003.

Hayner, Priscilla. "Fifteen Truth Commissions, 1974–1994: A Comparative Study." *Human Rights Quarterly* 16.4 (November 1994): 597–655.

Hernández, Paola. "Biográfias escénicas: *Mi vida después* de Lola Arias." *Latin America Theatre Review* 45.1 (Fall 2011): 115–28.

———. *El teatro de Argentina y Chile. Globalización, resistencia y desencanto*. Buenos Aires: Corregidor, 2009.

———. "Memoria Incompletas: El espacio del escenario argentino de la posdictadura." *Symposium* 61.4 (Winter 2008): 266–77.

Hirsch, Marianne. *The Generation of Postmemory*. New York: Columbia University Press, 2008.

Hotte, Véronique. "El pasado es un animal grotesco." *Théâtre du blog*. December 9, 2013, accessed December 28, 2013. http://theatredublog.unblog.fr/2013/12/09/.

Hütter, Frido. "Die Tragödie der Verschwundenen." *Berliner Zeitung*, June 15, 2000, B5.

Huyssen, Andreas. *Present Pasts: Urban Palimpsests and the Politics of Memory*. Palo Alto, CA: Stanford University Press, 2003.

Inter-American Commission on Human Rights. "Report 21/00." *Case 12.059: Carmen Aguiar de Lapacó*. February 29, 2000.

Irazábal, Federico. "Manteniendo viva la memoria." *Cámara negra* (January 1998): 32.

Ivie, Robert L. "Fighting Terror by Rite of Redemption and Reconciliation." *Rhetoric and Public Affairs* 10.2 (Summer 2007): 221–48.

Jaffe, Audrey. *Vanishing Points, Dickens, Narrative, and the Subjects of Omniscience*. Berkeley: University of California Press, 1991.

Jelin, Elizabeth. *State Repression and the Labors of Memory*. Minneapolis: University of Minnesota Press, 2003.

———. "Victims, Relatives, and Citizens in Argentina: Whose Voice Is Legitimate Enough?" *Humanitarianism and Suffering: The Mobilization of Empathy*, edited by Richard A. Wilson and David D. Brown, 177–201. New York: Cambridge University Press, 2009.

Kaiser, Susana. "*Escraches*: Demonstrations, Communication, and Political Memory in Post-dictatorial Argentina." *Media, Culture, and Society* 24.4 (July 2002): 499–516.

——. "To Punish or Forgive? Young Citizens Attitudes of Impunity and Accountability in Contemporary Argentina." *Journal of Human Rights* 4.2 (2005): 171–96.

Kalb, Jonathan. *The Theatre of Heiner Müller*. London: Cambridge University Press, 1998.

Keeling, David J. "A Geopolitical Perspective on Argentina's Malvinas/Falklands Claims." *Global Discourse* 3.1 (August 2013): 158–65.

Kirchner, Néstor. "Address to the United Nations General Assembly." Political speech, New York, September 25, 2003.

Kohan, Martín. "El fin de una épica," *Punto de Vista* 64 (1999): 6–12.

Kohan, Martín, Oscar Blanco, and Adriana Imperatore. "Transhumantes de neblina, no las hemos de encontrar. De cómo la literatura cuenta la guerra de Malvinas." *Espacios* 13 (1993–94): 82–86.

Kollmann, Raúl. "La cultura de los derechos humanos." *Página 12*. July 8, 2012, accessed December 19, 2014. http://www.pagina12.com.ar/diario/elpais/1-198206-2012-07-08.html.

Landsberg, Alison. *Prosthetic Memory: The Transformation of American Remembrance in the Age of Mass Culture*. New York: Columbia University Press, 2004.

Lazzara, Michael. *Chile in Transition: The Poetics and Politics of Memory*. Gainesville: University of Florida Press, 2006.

——. "(Post-)Memory, Subjectivity, and the Performance of Failure in Recent Documentary Films." *Latin American Perspectives* 36.5 (September 2009): 147–57.

León, Federico. *Yo en el futuro*. DVD. Directed by Federico León. Buenos Aires: Center for Documentation of Theatre and Dance, Teatro San Martín, recorded August 15, 2009.

——. *Yo en el futuro*. Unpublished manuscript, 2009. Buenos Aires: Center for Documentation of Theatre and Dance, Teatro San Martín.

Lessa, Francesca. "Justice without Borders: The Operation Condor Trial and Accountability for Transnational Crimes in South America." *International Journal of Transitional Justice* 9.3 (September 2015): 494–506.

——. *Memory and Transitional Justice in Argentina and Uruguay*. New York: Palgrave Macmillan, 2013.

Levy-Daniel, Héctor. *El archivista*. DVD. Directed by Marcelo Mangone. Personal collection of Héctor Levy-Daniel, Buenos Aires, recorded April 2, 2001.

——. "El archivista." In *Teatroxlaidentidad*, edited by Hermina Petruzzi, 20–24. Buenos Aires: Colihue, 2009.

——. "Teatro. Sentido y política." *La Revista del CCC* 7. September 12, 2009, accessed May 15, 2015. http://www.centrocultural.coop/revista/articulo/138/teatro_sentido_y_politica.

Lewis, Megan. *Performing Whitely in the Postcolony: Afrikaners in South African Theatrical and Public Life.* Iowa City: University of Iowa Press, 2016.

Loka, Chara. "Lola Arias's *Mi vida después* at the Onassis Cultural Center in Athens." *City Box.* November 14, 2014, accessed November 23, 2015. http://cityboxathista.blogspot.com/2014/11/latin-america-mi-vida-despues-lola.html.

Lorenz, Federico. "How Does One Win a Lost War? Oral History and Political Memories." In *The Oxford Handbook of Oral History*, edited by Donald Ritchie, 124–41. Oxford: Oxford University Press, 2010.

———. *Las guerras por Malvinas.* Buenos Aires: Edhasa, 2006.

Lutz, Ellen. "Transitional Justice: Lessons Learned and the Road Ahead." In *Transitional Justice in the Twenty-First Century: Beyond Truth and Justice*, edited by Naomi Roht-Arriaza and Javier Marriezcurrena, 325–41. London: Cambridge University Press, 2006.

Lvovich, Daniel, and Jacqueline Bisquert. *La cambiate memoria de la dictadura. Discursos públicos, movimentos sociales y legitimidad demográcia.* Los Polverinos, Argentina: Universidad Nacional de General Sarmiento, 2008.

Magnarelli, Sharon. "The 1984 Theatre Season in Buenos Aires." *Latin American Theatre Review* 19.1 (Fall 1985): 83–90.

———. "Telling Stories: *Martha Stutz* by Javier Daulte." *Latin American Theatre Review* 35.1 (Fall 2001): 5–16.

Martin, Carol. "Bodies of Evidence." *TDR: The Drama Review* 50.3 (December 2006): 8–15.

———. *Dramaturgy of the Real on the World Stage.* New York: Palgrave Macmillan, 2010.

Maxwell, Richard. "Interview with Federico León." *Bomb Magazine* 123 (Spring 2013). Accessed January 14, 2015. http://bombmagazine.org/article/7095/federico-le-n.

Mazover, Mariana. *Piedras dentro de la piedra.* Directed by Mariana Mazover. Buenos Aires: Teatro La Carpintería, attended July 14, 2012.

———. *Piedras dentro de la piedra.* Unpublished manuscript, 2012. Personal collection.

McNulty, Charles. "Theatre Review: *El pasado es un animal grotesco* at REDCAT." *Los Angeles Times.* February 24, 2012, accessed February 27, 2013. http://latimesblogs.latimes.com/culturemonster/2012/02/theater-review-the-past-is-a-grotesque-animal-at-redcat.html.

Menem, Carlos. "Discurso de asunción del Presidente Carlos Saul Menem ante la Asemblea Legislatava al asumir como presidente de la nación." Political speech, Buenos Aires, Argentina, July 8, 1989.

Menendez, Mercedes. "Entrevista con Daniel Fanego: 'No hago tele porque no me llaman.'" *Tiempo Argentino.* September 8, 2010, accessed May 12, 2015. http://tiempo.infonews.com/nota/115249/no-hago-tele-porque-no-me-llaman.

Montez, Noe. "Autobiographic Memory, Museums, and Objectivity in Federico León's *Museo Miguel Ángel Boezzio.*" In *Public Theatres and Theatre Publics,* edited by Robert B. Shimko and Sara Freeman, 120–30. Cambridge: Cambridge Scholars Press, 2012.

Müller, Heiner. *Máquina Hamlet.* VHS. Directed by El Periférico de Objetos. Buenos Aires: Center for Documentation of Theatre and Dance, Teatro San Martín, Buenos Aires, recorded October 15, 1995.

———. *Máquina Hamlet.* Translated by Gabriella Massuh and Dieter Welke. Center for Documentation of Theatre and Dance, Teatro San Martín, Buenos Aires.

Müller, Martin. "Reconstructing the Concept of Discourse for the Field of Critical Geopolitics: Towards Discourse as a Language and Practice." *Political Geography* 27 (2008): 332–38.

Nadesan, Maija Holmer. *Governing Childhood into the 21st Century: Biopolitical Technologies of Childhood Management and Education.* New York: Palgrave Macmillan, 2010.

Nieto, Clara. *Master of War: Latin American and US Aggression from the Cuban Revolution through the Clinton Years.* New York: Seven Stories Press, 2001.

Nigh, Katherine. "Performing Trauma: 9/11, Hurricane Katrina, the Guerra Sucia." PhD diss., Arizona State University, 2011. UMI 2013.

"No más venganza." *La Nación.* November 23, 2015, accessed November 23, 2015. http://www.lanacion.com.ar/1847930-no-mas-venganza.

Novaro, Marcos, and Vicente Palermo. *La dictadura militar, 1976–1983: Del golpe de estado a la restauración democrática.* Buenos Aires: Paídos, 2003.

Ogas Puga, Grisby. "Teatroxlaidentidad: Un teatro busca en su identidad." *Latin American Theatre Review* 37.1 (Fall 2003): 141–53.

Olick, Jeffrey K., Vered Vinitzky-Serouissi, and Daniel Levy. Introduction to *The Collective Memory Reader,* 3–62. Oxford: Oxford University Press, 2011.

"Optimismo kelper por el triunfo de Macri y la derrota K." *Clarín.* July 23, 2015, accessed July 23, 2015. http://www.clarin.com/politica/Optimismo-kelper-triunfo-Macri-derrota_0_1472852924.html.

Ordaz, Luis. *Historia del teatro en el Río de la Plata.* Buenos Aires: Inteatro, 2010.

Pacheco, Carlos. "El teatro se ocupa de la guerra por las Malvinas." *La Nación.* April 22, 2015, accessed April 23, 2015. http://www.lanacion.com.ar/1786404-sin-titulo.

Page, Joanna. *Crisis and Capitalism in Contemporary Argentine Cinema.* Durham, NC: Duke University Press, 2009.

Page, Phillipa. *Politics and Performance in Post-dictatorship Argentine Film and Theatre.* Woodbridge: Tamesis, 2011.

"Para el 79% de la población, en la Argentina se vive al margen de la ley." *La Nación*. April 5, 2015, accessed May 28, 2015. http://www.lanacion.com.ar/1781730 -para-el-79-de-la-poblacion-en-la-argentina-se-vive-al-margen-de-la-ley.

Parker-Starbuck, Jennifer, and Sarah Bay-Cheng. "Ecologies of the Festival. New York in 2012: COIL, Under the Radar, and American Realness." *Performance Research* 17.4 (August 2012): 141–44.

Patraka, Vivian. *Spectacular Suffering: Theatre, Fascism, and the Holocaust*. Bloomington: Indiana University Press, 1999.

Pauchulo, Ana Laura. "Retelling the Stories of the Madres and Abuelas de Plaza de Mayo in Argentina." *Canadian Woman Studies* 27.1 (Fall 2009): 29–35.

Pauls, Alan. "Kidnapping Reality: An Interview with Vivi Tellas." Translated by Sarah J. Townsend. In *Dramaturgies of the Real on the World Stage*, edited by Carol Martin, 246–54. New York: Palgrave Macmillan, 2010.

Payne, Leigh. *Unsettling Accounts: Neither Truth nor Reconciliation in Confessions of State Violence*. Durham, NC: Duke University Press, 2009.

Peker, Luciana. "La deuda eternal." *Página 12*. May 10, 2013, accessed May 9, 2015. http://www.pagina12.com.ar/diario/suplementos/las12/13-8009-2013-05-10.html.

Pellettieri, Osvaldo, ed. *Historia del Teatro Argentino en Buenos Aires*. Vol. 5. Buenos Aires: Galerna, 2005.

———. *Teatro Argentino del 2000*. Buenos Aires: Galerna, 2000.

———. *Teatro Argentino y crisis, 2001–2003*. Buenos Aires: Eudeba, 2004.

Pensotti, Mariano. *El pasado es un animal grotesco*. DVD. Directed by Mariano Pensotti. Recorded March 10, 2010. Buenos Aires: Center for Documentation of Theatre and Dance, Teatro San Martín.

———. *El pasado es un animal grotesco*. Unpublished manuscript, 2010. Personal collection.

Perasso, Valerie. "Si la sangre fuera un mandato yo estaría condenada," *BBC Mundo*. March 25, 2010, accessed February 11, 2015. http://www.bbc.com/ mundo/lg/america_latina/2010/02/100126_mandamientos_honraras_padres _mz.shtml.

Perez, Mariana Eva. *Instrucciones para un coleccionista de mariposas*. In *Teatro x la Identidad*. DVD. Directed by Leonor Manso. Buenos Aires: Ministerio de Educación, Ciencia y Tecnología, 2004, recorded July 29, 2002.

———. "Instrucciones para un coleccionista de mariposas." *Kamchatka* 3 (Fall 2014): 5–9.

———. "Una carta a mi hermano." *Mensuario de las Madres de la Plaza de Mayo* 12 (June–July 2001): 7–9.

"Piedras dentro de la piedra, de Mariana Mazover." *Puesta en escena*. July 28, 2012, accessed August 1, 2012. http://www.puestaenescena.com.ar/teatro/761 _piedras-dentro-de-la-piedra-de-mariana-mazover.php.

Plas, Laura. "Et la mort, et l'humour et l'amour des pères." *Les Trois Coups*. December 19, 2011, accessed November 15, 2015. http://www.lestroiscoups .com/article-mi-vida-despues-de-lola-arias-critique-de-laura-plas-theatre -des-abbesses-a-paris-93339415.html.

Poggi, Damiana, and Virginia Jáuregui. *170 explosiones por segundo*. Directed by Andrés Binetti. Buenos Aires: El Portón de Sánchez, attended October 27, 2011.

———. *170 explosiones por segundo*. Unpublished manuscript, 2011. Personal collection.

Pontoriero, Andrea. "Vida liquida, teatro y narración en las propuestas escénicas de Mariano Pensotti." *Cuaderno 50* 15.4 (December 2014): 15–24.

Poore, Federico. "CFK Inaugurates Malvinas Museum." *Buenos Aires Herald*. June 11, 2014, accessed November 23, 2015. http://www.buenosairesherald .com/article/161783/cfk-inaugurates-malvinas-museum-.

Pozzoni, Maria, and Carla Sangrilli. "Algunas percepciones sobre el desencanto politico en la Argentina reciente." In *Memorias de la Argentina contemporánea, 1946–2002*, edited by Marcela Ferrari, Lila Ricci, and María Estella Spinelli, 183–202. Buenos Aires: Eudem, 2007.

Proaño-Gomez, Lola. "Posmodernidad y metáfora visual: *Máquina Hamlet*." *Gestos* 14.27 (April 1999): 75–83.

Program for Javier Daulte's *Martha Stutz* at the Teatro San Martín. Playbill, May 23, 1997. Buenos Aires: Center for Documentation of Theatre and Dance, Teatro San Martín.

Program for Mariano Pensotti's *El pasado es un animal grotesco* at the Teatro Sarmiento, Buenos Aires, Argentina. Playbill, March 10, 2010. Buenos Aires: Center for Documentation of Theatre and Dance, Teatro San Martín.

Puga, Ana Elena. "The Abstract Allegory of Griselda Gambaro's *Stripped* (El despojamiento)." *Theatre Journal* 56.3 (October 2004): 415–28.

———. *Memory, Allegory, and Testimony in South American Theatre*. New York: Routledge, 2008.

Radstone, Susannah. "Memory Studies: For and Against." *Memory Studies* 1 (January 2008): 31–39.

Rauchenberger, Barbara. "Das Leben ist schön un die Zukunft war es auch." *Die Furche*. October 15, 2009, accessed December 1, 2015. http://www .steirischerherbst.at/2009/deutsch/presse/pressestimmen_details.php?oid=1078.

Renov, Michael. *The Subject of Documentary*. Minneapolis: University of Minnesota Press, 2004.

Ricoeur, Paul. *Memory, History, and Forgetting*. Chicago: University of Chicago Press, 2004.

Robben, Antonius C. G. M. "State Terror in the Netherworld: Disappearance and Reburial in Argentina." In *Death Squad: The Anthropology of State Terror*, edited by Jeffrey A. Sluka, 91–113. Philadelphia: University of Pennsylvania Press, 2000.

Rodriguez, Alejandra, Leila Ocampo, and Mariana Milanesi. "Murmullos da ausencia." In *Teatro, cine, narrativa: Imagenes del nuevo siglo*, edited by Marta Lena Paz, 334–50. Buenos Aires: University of Buenos Aires Press, 2003.

Rodriguez, Martín. "La puesta en escena emergente y su futuro." In *Teatro Argentino del 2000*, edited by Osvaldo Pellettieri, 167–88. Buenos Aires: Galerna, 2000.

Roediger, Henry L., III, and James V. Wersch. "Creating a New Discipline of Memory Studies." *Memory Studies* 1 (January 2008): 9–22.

Roht-Arriza, Naomi. *Transitional Justice in the Age of Human Rights*. Philadelphia: University of Pennsylvania Press, 2006.

Rokem, Freddie. *Performing History: Theatrical Representations of the Past in Contemporary Theatre*. Iowa City: University of Iowa Press, 2000.

Roniger, Luis, and Mario Sznajder. "The Problem of Memory and Oblivion in Redemocratized Argentina and Uruguay." *History and Memory* 10.1 (Spring 1998): 133–69.

Rovit, Rebecca. *The Jewish Kulturbind Theatre Company in Nazi Berlin*. Iowa City: University of Iowa Press, 2013.

Sagaseta, Julia Elena. "*Los murmullos* de Luis Cano: Interrelación artística y compromiso." In *Teatro, cine, narrativa: Imagenes del nuevo siglo*, edited by Marta Lena Paz, 157–74. Buenos Aires: University of Buenos Aires Press, 2003.

Saltz, Rachel. "That Revolving Drama in Which All Are Actors." *New York Times*. January 10, 2012, accessed February 27, 2013. http://www.nytimes.com/2012/01/11/theater/reviews/el-pasado-es-un-animal-grotesco-at-the-public-theater.html.

Sánchez, María Teresa. "Intervención en la mesa el derecho a la identidad." In *Juventud e identidad: III Congreso Internacional*, 37–43. Buenos Aires: Abuelas de Plaza de Mayo, 1997.

Santner, Eric. *Stranded Objects: Mourning, Memory, and Film in Postwar Germany*. Ithaca, NY: Cornell University Press, 1993.

Sarlo, Beatriz. "No olvidar la guerra: Sobre cine, literatura e historia." *Punto de vista* 49 (1994): 32–34.

———. *Tiempo pasado: Cultura de la memoria y giro subjetivo*. Buenos Aires: Siglo XX, 2005.

Schmucler, Héctor. "Las exigencias de memoria." *Punto de vista* 23.68 (December 2000): 5–9.

Schneider, Michael. "Heiner Müllers 'Endspiele.'" *Literatur Konkret* 9.1 (Spring 1979): 31–37.

Shoemaker, Sydney. *Self-Knowledge and Self-Identity*. Ithaca, NY: Cornell University Press, 1963.

Sikkink, Kathryn, and Carrie Booth Walling. "The Impact of Human Rights Trials in Latin America." *Journal of Peace Research* 44.4 (July 2007): 427–45.

Skaar, Elin. *Judicial Independence and Human Rights in Latin America*. London: Palgrave Macmillan, 2011.

Small, Daniele Avila. "Actos físicos de la memoria, descripciones en la historia." *Questão de Crítica*. June 30, 2011, accessed November 22, 2015. http://www .questaodecritica.com.br/2011/06/actos-fisicos-de-la-memoria-reinscripciones -en-la-historia/.

Smith, Murray. *Engaging Characters: Fiction, Emotion, and the Cinema*. Oxford: Clarendon Press, 1995.

Socio-Economic Database for Latin America and the Caribbean. "Poverty Statistics." December 14, 2015, accessed December 14, 2015. http://sedlac.econo .unlp.edu.ar/eng/statistics-detalle.php?idE=34.

Sofer, Andrew. *The Stage Life of Props*. Ann Arbor: University of Michigan Press, 2003.

Sosa, Cecilia. *Queering Acts of Mourning in the Aftermath of Argentina's Dictatorship: The Performances of Blood*. London: Tamesis, 2014.

Soto, Ivana. "Retórnicas sobre Malvinas: parodias, realism y ideología." *Clarín*. June 14, 2012, accessed May 1, 2015. http://www.revistaenie.clarin.com/ escenarios/teatro/Guerra-Malvinas-Teatro_0_718728356.html.

Stern, Steve J. *Remembering Pinochet's Chile: On the Eve of London 1998*. Durham, NC: Duke University Press, 2008.

Strahler, Amy. "A Theatre of Dangerous Illusions: *Máquina Hamlet* at BAM." *Latin American Theatre Review* 34.2 (Spring 2001): 203–6.

Taussig, Michael. *Defacement: Public Secrecy and the Labor of the Negative*. Palo Alto: Stanford University Press, 1995.

Taylor, Diana. *The Archive and the Repertoire: Performing Cultural Memory in the Americas*. Durham, NC: Duke University Press, 2003.

———. *Disappearing Acts: Spectacles of Gender and Nationalism in Argentina's "Dirty War."* Durham, NC: Duke University Press, 1997.

———. "Transculturating Transculturation." *Performing Arts Journal* 13.2 (May 1991): 90–104.

———. "You Are Here: The DNA of Performance." *TDR: The Drama Review* 46.1 (Spring 2002): 149–69.

Tedesco, Laura. *Democracy in Argentina: Hope and Disillusion*. London: Frank Cass, 1999.

Todorov, Tzvetan. *The Morals of History*. Translated by Alyson Waters. Minneapolis: University of Minnesota Press, 1995.

Trastoy, Beatriz. "*Martha Stutz* de Javier Daulte: El teatro a través del espejo." In *Tradición, modernidad y posmodernidad*, edited by Osvaldo Pellettieri, 283–91. Buenos Aires: Galerna, 1999.

———. "Teatro Abierto 1981: Un fenómeno social y cultural." In *Historia del Teatro Argentino en Buenos Aires*, vol. 5, edited by Osvaldo Pellettieri, 104–11. Buenos Aires: Galerna, 2001.

———. *Teatro autobiográfico: Los unipersonales de los 80 y 90 en la escena argentina*. Buenos Aires: Nueva generación, 2002.

Vasquez, Claudio. "Lola Arias estrena versión chilena de obra sobre la dictadura argentina." *El Mercurio*. January 11, 2011, accessed November 23, 2015. http://www.bbc.com/mundo/lg/america_latina/2010/02/100126_mandamientos_honraras_padres_mz.shtml.

Verbitsky, Horacio. *El vuelo*. Buenos Aires: Planeta, 1995.

———. "La Inquisición." *Página 12*. July 11, 2010, accessed May 28, 2015. http://www.pagina12.com.ar/diario/elpais/1-149246-2010-07-11.html.

Verzero, Lorena. "La desmesura, o qué hacer con tanto pasado." *Teatro XXI* 15 (Spring 2002): 61.

Vezzetti, Hugo. *Pasado y presente. Guerra, dictadura y sociedad en Argentina*. Buenos Aires: Siglo XXI, 2002.

———. *Sobre la violencia revolutionaria. Memorias y olvidos*. Buenos Aires: Siglo XXI, 2009.

Vitullo, Julieta. *Islas imaginadas: La guerra de Malvinas en la literatura y en el cine*. Buenos Aires: Corregidor, 2012.

———. "Relatos de desertores en las ficciones de la guerra de Malvinas." *Hispámerica* 35.104 (August 2006): 29–38.

Walker, Marina. "Framing the Falklands/Malvinas War: National Interest in the *London Times*, *La Nación* (Argentina), and *El Murcurio* (Chile)." *Universum* 19.1 (Fall 2004): 198–219.

Walsh, Brian. "The Rest Is Violence: Müller Contra Shakespeare." *Performing Arts Journal* 23.3 (September 2001): 24–35.

Warley, Jorge. *La guerra de Malvinas. Juan Forn, Rodrigo Frésan, Carlos Gamerro, Daniel Guebel, Raúl Vieytes*. Buenos Aires: Biblos, 2007.

Weber, Bruce. "To Be or Not to Be Something." *New York Times*. October 20, 2000, accessed June 1, 2013. http://theater2.nytimes.com/mem/theater/treview.html?res=9905E3DE133EF933A15753C1A9669C8B63.

Werth, Brenda. "A Malvinas Veteran Onstage: From Intimate Testimony to Public Memorialization." *South Central Review* 30.3 (Fall 2013): 83–100.

———. "Performing the Family Portrait in Marcelo Bertuccio's *Señora, esposa, niña y joven desde lejos*." *Latin American Theatre Review* 40.2 (Spring 2007): 23–36.

———. *Theatre, Performance, and Memory Politics in Argentina*. New York: Palgrave Macmillan, 2010.

Wertsch, James. "The Narrative Organization of Collective Memory." *Ethos* 36.1 (March 2008): 120–35.

White, Hayden. *Metahistory: The Historical Imagination in Nineteenth-Century Europe*. Baltimore: Johns Hopkins University Press, 1973.

White-Nockleby, Anna. "Fragmentos del pasado: *Lo documental* en el teatro de una nueva generación." Paper presented at the IV Seminario Internacional Políticas de la Memoria, Buenos Aires, Argentina, September 28–October 1, 2011.

———. "Staging Recollections." *Drama in Argentina*. May 1, 2011, accessed September 12, 2012. https://dramainargentina.wordpress.com/.

Williams, Paul Harvey. *Memory Museums: The Rush to Commemorate*. London: Berg, 2007.

Yaccar, Mariela Daniela. "El pasado desde el presente." *Página 12*. September 6, 2010, accessed July 17, 2011. http://www.pagina12.com.ar/diario/suplementos/espectaculos/subnotas/19188-5279-2005-04-23.html.

Zangaro, Patricia. *A propósito de la duda*. DVD. Directed by Daniel Fanego. Buenos Aires: Archivo Digital, Centro Cultural Recoleta, recorded June 5, 2000.

———. "A propósito de la duda." In *Teatroxlaidentidad: Obras de teatro del Ciclo 2001*, edited by Hermina Petruzzi, 154–61. Buenos Aires: Eudeba, 2001.

Index

Italicized page numbers indicate figures.

NOE MONTEZ is an associate professor and the director of graduate studies in theatre and performance studies at Tufts University, where he teaches contemporary Latinx and Latin American theatre and performance studies. He has published scholarship in *Theatre Topics*, *Theatre History Studies*, *Texas Theatre Journal*, the *Journal of Religion and Theatre*, *Latin American Theatre Review*, and the collection *Public Theatres and Theatre Publics*.

Theater in the Americas

The goal of the series is to publish a wide range of scholarship on theater and performance, defining theater in its broadest terms and including subjects that encompass all of the Americas.

The series focuses on the performance and production of theater and theater artists and practitioners but welcomes studies of dramatic literature as well. Meant to be inclusive, the series invites studies of traditional, experimental, and ethnic forms of theater; celebrations, festivals, and rituals that perform culture; and acts of civil disobedience that are performative in nature. We publish studies of theater and performance activities of all cultural groups within the Americas, including biographies of individuals, histories of theater companies, studies of cultural traditions, and collections of plays.

Queries and Submissions
Scott Magelssen, Editor
magelss@uw.edu

Founder and Editor, Robert A. Schanke, 2000–2014